Philosophy and Linguistics

Philosophy and Linguistics

EDITED BY

Kumiko Murasugi
and Robert Stainton

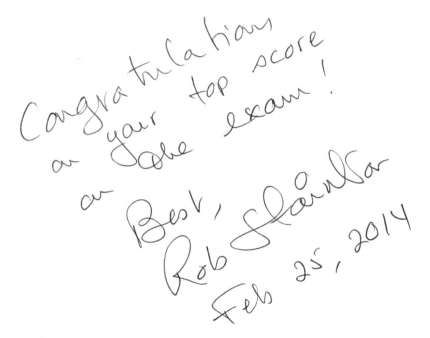

Congratulations on your top score on the exam!

Best,
Rob Stainton
Feb 25, 2014

Westview Press
A Member of the Perseus Books Group

Copyright © 1999 by Westview Press, A Member of the Perseus Books Group

Published in 1999 in the United States of America by Westview Press, 5500 Central Avenue, Boulder, Colorado 80301-2877, and in the United Kingdom by Westview Press, 12 Hid's Copse Road, Cumnor Hill, Oxford OX2 9JJ

A CIP catalog record for this book is available from the Library of Congress.
ISBN 0-8133-9085-0

The paper used in this publication meets the requirements of the American National Standard for Permanence of Paper for Printed Library Materials Z39.48-1984.

10   9   8   7   6   5   4   3   2   1

Contents

Contributors

Herman Cappelen
Philosophy Department
Vassar College

Susan Dwyer
United States Naval Academy
sue@philo.mcgill.ca

Reinaldo Elugardo
Department of Philosophy
The University of Oklahoma
relugard@interserv.com

James Higginbotham
Centre for Linguistics and Philology
University of Oxford
higgy@ermine.ox.ac.uk

Ernie Lepore
Center for Cognitive Science
Rutgers University
lepore@ruccs.rutgers.edu

Peter Ludlow
Department of Philosophy
State University of New York, Stony Brook
ludlow@well.com

Adèle Mercier
Department of Philosophy
Queen's University
merciera@post.queensu.ca

Stephen Neale
Department of Philosophy
University of California at Berkeley
neale@socrates.berkeley.edu

Paul M. Pietroski
Departments of Linguistics and Philosophy
University of Maryland at College Park
paul@philo.mcgill.ca

François Recanati
CREA, Paris
recanati@poly.polytechnique.fr

Robert J. Stainton
Philosophy Department
Carleton University
stainton@ccs.carleton.ca

Zoltán Gendler Szabó
The Sage School of Philosophy
Cornell University
zs15@cornell.edu

Acknowledgments

Our first thanks go to our editorial assistant, Derrick J. Lacelle, whose last-minute help has been invaluable. We are also grateful to Carleton University, which provided a special publication grant, and to the Social Sciences and Humanities Research Council of Canada for research awards to each of the editors. The authors deserve a special thank-you for their patience and understanding, as well as their very fine contributions.

Introduction

From Ordinary Use and
Regimentation to Systematic Theory

Zoltán Gendler Szabó

Every now and then philosophers fall in love with a particular science. The infatuation goes beyond intellectual curiosity and respect—there is the belief that this branch of scientific knowledge holds the key that would unlock the problems of metaphysics, epistemology or even ethics. So, philosophers engage in intensive scientific work, and they frequently reach remarkable results. But passionate love affairs often end in disillusionment. The scientific results are interesting on their own, their relevance to the philosophical questions remains clear, but ultimately they fail to solve or dissolve the problems philosophers were interested in in the first place.

Something like this seems to have happened to philosophical interest in linguistics in the last twenty years. In the 1960s and 1970s questions about the semantics of natural languages were of central concern to the vast majority of analytic philosophers. The work of Chomsky, Davidson, Grice, Donnellan, Kaplan, Kripke and Putnam was widely read by non-specialists. By now the enthusiasm has somewhat cooled down. After having been the center of attention, philosophers of language nowadays experience a modest degree of professional isolation. As Tyler Burge put it "many philosophers felt the philosophy of language had done its job—that the natural development of philosophical reasoning led into the philosophy of mind, or other adjacent areas" (1992: 28). Whether these philosophers were correct in their judgment is a hard question, but there is no doubt that they detected a certain impasse in the discussions of fundamental questions about linguistic meaning and structure.

The prominence of philosophy of language two decades ago was a consequence of the fact that it synthesized two major currents of thought within analytic philosophy: the philosophy of ordinary language and the philosophy of ideal language. Both of these proposed radical solutions to old problems through reflection on language. But while the main tool of analysis for ordinary language philosophers was a keen sense of the *proper use* of various expressions in everyday contexts, philosophers from the other camp were seeking formal tools to model the *machinery of scientific discourse.* To make their case convincing, philosophers in the first camp had to defend the relevance of linguistic intuitions to problems of philosophy, while philosophers in the second camp had to provide reasons for accepting the complicated formal rendering of ordinary locutions. As one reads Gilbert Ryle's arguments from features of our mental vocabulary to the debunking of the Cartesian conception of the mind, one might wonder whether the facts of usage Ryle is pointing at are superficial or deep characteristics of English and whether they have analogues in other natural languages. As one reads Quine's arguments that reference to numbers should be construed as shorthand for a complicated talk about sets, one might wonder whether this complication is an excessively high price for ontological perspicuity and whether such a regimentation captures everything that matters about the language of arithmetic. Language was crucial in both currents of analytic philosophy, but it was not entirely clear how such a crucial role was to be justified.

Russell's theory of definite descriptions provides a useful illustration of the ambiguities of philosophical appeals to language. The central claim of Russell's theory was that "denoting phrases [and among them definite descriptions] never have any meaning in themselves, but that every proposition in whose verbal expression they occur has a meaning" (1905: 43). Sentences containing definite descriptions express general propositions which have no constituents corresponding to the descriptions themselves. If one says 'The author of Waverley was Scotch,' one does not say anything about Sir Walter Scott, one is merely stating the general truth that one and only one person wrote Waverley and whoever wrote Waverley was Scotch.

On the face of it, this seems to be a theory about the semantics of the definite article. Russell himself, however, frequently emphasized that his analysis is not intended to capture the nuances of English.[1] His reservations could be developed in two different directions. On one reading, Russell reports something about a particular use—call it 'uniquely referring use'—of the English article 'the'. The Russellian claim is then about what speakers do when they use descriptions in this way: *prima facie,* they seem to indicate particular objects, but in fact they are making general assertions. This is how Strawson and most of the ordinary language tradition understood Russell.[2] On another reading, Russell proposes a certain method for the regimentation of natural language. On this interpretation, the Russellian claim is simply that descriptions can, for certain theoretical purposes, be replaced by quantificational devices. This is how Quine and most of the ideal language tradition understood Russell.[3]

By the early 1960s debates about descriptions—as well as related debates about conditionals, the existential import of quantification, identity statements and modality—revealed that there is no clear and broadly shared conception of how linguistic analysis is supposed to work. To improve the situation two things were necessary: a theory about what is essential and what is accidental about human languages, and another theory about how the essential features of human languages relate to the minds of language users and to the world they are talking about. The outcome of the intense research in the 60s and 70s in these areas was mixed. Despite substantial progress and a vague consensus about some of the basic elements of these theories, it became obvious that answering such fundamental questions about language is extremely difficult. In fact, it seemed easier to address questions about Cartesian souls and numbers directly—without the intervention of the analysis of our talk of minds and numbers—than to try to justify the importance of linguistic analysis.

Losing popularity is always hard, but in the case of philosophy of language it also had its benefits. Freed from the responsibility of ultimately answering all philosophical questions, philosophers of language were free to confess an interest in language *per se*. This happened at the same time when—due largely to the work of Noam Chomsky—theoretical linguistics took an interesting turn. It became possible to raise some of the traditional problems about reference, meaning and use as issues about the conceptual foundations of that science. Linguistics also generated a number of new theoretical concepts—anaphoric link, binding, discourse referent, empty category, genericity, incorporation, scalar implicature, thematic role, and type shifting to mention a few—that are of philosophical interest.

The three main branches of linguistics that are of special philosophical significance—syntax, semantics and pragmatics—operate today within the broad frameworks laid by philosophically minded linguists and linguistically minded philosophers. Syntactic theories come and go, but they all try to capture within a formal system the most striking features of what Chomsky called the "creative aspect of language use" (1980: 76–77). Although many object to innatism, it remains popular to think of grammar as an internalized system of rules and principles that enables the speaker to parse and generate a potentially infinite number of complex expressions. Semanticists disagree about what the meaningfulness of various expressions consists in, but there is practical unanimity that at least one important role of a theory of meaning is the assignment of truth-conditions to the syntactically well-formed sentences of natural languages. Despite stark differences between the desert landscapes of Davidsoneans and the intensional jungle of Montagoveans, there is common ground within semantics concerning how such an assignment should be construed. This is to a large extent a consequence of a rough agreement about the limits of semantics. Grice's theory of conversational implicature provided an example of how pragmatic elements within the full information content of an utterance are separable from the semantic contribution of the expressions used. Although the details are controversial and open questions abound, the general idea of how to divide meaning into semantic and pragmatic constituents is broadly accepted.

Perhaps the most exciting thing about recent philosophy of language is its openness towards genuine linguistic problems. There was a time when philosophers could write about semantics with no regard to what linguists would say about the expressions they were considering. They had the excuse that questions about exactly how natural languages manage to express what they do had not yet been investigated in formal detail. When raising questions about the truth-conditions of a certain type of sentence, they could simply suggest a formula in *Logish*[4] (a mixture of first-order logical symbolism and simplified English), replace the original sentence with it and discuss this 'translation' instead. Philosophers of language these days are required to call their translations 'logical forms'. The shift is not merely terminological. Philosophers today are supposed to think of these formulae as—perhaps somewhat simplified—representations of the real syntactic and semantic complexity of natural language sentences, and they are supposed to show—or at least indicate—how these formulae are derivable from acceptable rules and principles of syntax and semantics.

The fate of Russell's theory can again be used to illustrate the reorientation of philosophy of language in recent years. Most contemporary philosophers of language tend to bracket Russell's reservations about the subtleties of 'the' and take his theory of description to be directly about the interpretation of natural language sentences. According to this line, definite descriptions can be *identified* with a certain type of quantificational device. What the Russellian quantificational form of a sentence containing a definite description yields is neither a characterization of a use of the sentence (as Strawson and with him the ordinary language philosophers maintained), nor a useful proxy for the sentence (as Quine and the ideal language tradition have argued), but a perspicuous presentation of its exact truth-conditions.[5] Some semanticists go even further. They argue that for the Russellian account to be acceptable, it is not enough that all sentences containing singular definite descriptions have Russellian truth-conditions. The quantifier postulated by the Russellian must have syntactic reality: it must appear on the level of the logical form. Its presence there must be syntactically testable; it must be subject to the usual syntactic operations that quantifier phrases can undergo.[6]

Understanding Russell in this way puts new burdens on a Russellian. How does the Russellian analysis fare when one considers sentences with multiple quantifiers, modal operators, propositional attitude verbs? Can one expand the Russellian account to cover plural descriptions, generic descriptions or descriptions containing mass nouns? What is the relationship between definite descriptions and anaphoric pronouns that can often replace them within complex sentences? Such problems would not exist for either Strawson or Quine. Strawson could argue that the definite article is not employed in a singularly referring manner in most of these complicated cases, so the Russellian theory narrowly construed says nothing about the truth-conditions of uses of such sentences. Quine could argue that there is no obvious need for incorporating all of this complexity into the regimented language of science. The very point of philosophical analysis for him is the elimination of some of the more obscure features of ordinary language. But if one is interested in assigning truth-conditions to English sentences, one cannot bypass the complications. Their presence is a fact of language to be accounted for by the semanticist.

Should we think of the current linguistic focus of much of philosophy of language as a sign of 'naturalizing' another branch of traditional philosophy? Some do.[7] But it is not obvious that the new interest in logical form—a concern for harmonizing one's views on reference, meaning and use with the results of linguistics—will yield *solutions* to most philosophical problems about the nature of language. After all, as linguistics matures, linguists increasingly turn their backs on the foundational issues of their discipline. If they defer to philosophers who in turn defer to linguists in these matters, we can hardly expect progress. One might hope, more modestly but perhaps still in harmony with some version of naturalism, that the results of linguistics will sharpen our understanding of the old problems and that they will provide new and interesting *constraints* on philosophical reflection on them.

* * *

This volume presents the reader with a variety of papers which exemplify the current reorientation of philosophy of language. At the core are questions of logical form: a joint linguistic and philosophical investigation into the syntax and semantics of various natural language constructions. The papers by Higginbotham and Neale are concerned with the logical form of perceptual reports and plural definite descriptions, respectively. The project of uncovering logical form is supplemented by philosophical reflection on the limits of semantics and on the methodology of linguistic research. The former are represented here by a paper by Mercier on the problem of naming and a paper by Recanati on how to accommodate context-dependence within semantics. The latter are represented by a paper by Dwyer's paper on a possible application of Chomsky's innatism in moral psychology and a paper by Ludlow on how to evaluate simplicity-claims in linguistics.

The last section of the volume contains a case study. In the first article, Cappelen and LePore offer a paratactic analysis of sentences containing mixed quotation, like 'Alice said that life is "difficult" to understand.' Their account is an elegant combination of slightly modified versions of the Davidsonean semantics for direct and indirect quotation. Since—as the authors argue—the rivals of the paratactic account have no straightforward way of achieving a similar theoretical unity, the paper can be seen as a new argument for a Davidsonean semantics for propositional attitudes. The replies by Elugardo, Pietroski and Stainton contain detailed criticism of the proposal and alternatives for the syntax, semantics and pragmatics of mixed quotation.

The exchange about mixed quotation illustrates two of the most striking features of many contemporary debates in philosophy of language. First, the focus is a specific linguistic phenomenon, but the analysis is used in support of general theses about the interpretation of natural languages. Second, argument and criticism are sensitive to detailed linguistic considerations. The discussion about Cappelen and LePore's proposal brings together questions about logical form, the limits of semantics and methodology, thereby exemplifying the current interplay between philosophy and linguistics.

Notes

1. In "On Denoting," Russell expressed some reservations about the uniqueness implications of the definite article: "Now *the,* when it is strictly used, involves uniqueness; we do, it is true, speak of '*the* son of So-and-so' even when So-and-so has several sons, but it would be more correct to say '*a* son of So-and-so'. Thus for our purposes we take *the* as involving uniqueness" (1905: 44). Later, he expressed his attitude towards ordinary language rather unequivocally thus: "I . . . am persuaded that common speech is full of vagueness and inaccuracy, and that any attempt to be precise and accurate requires modification of common speech both as regards vocabulary and as regards syntax" (1957: 123).

2. See Strawson (1950). Strawson (1950: 151) criticized Russell for not providing "a correct account of the use" of definite descriptions.

3. Quine regards Russell's theory primarily "as a means of getting on in science without use of any real equivalent of the vernacular 'the'" (1953: 151). Russell himself embraced Quine's reading of his theory.

4. The term is, I believe, due to Richard Jeffrey.

5. According to Neale (1990), the theory "can be seen as a contribution to a purely semantical project, that of constructing an empirically adequate theory of meaning for natural language" (p. 6).

6. The principle that underlies this demand is that semantic rules interpret only structure given by syntax. See Larson and Segal (1995: 78–79).

7. See, for example, the Preface to Ludlow (1997).

References

Burge, T. 1992. "Philosophy of Language and Mind: 1950–1990." *Philosophical Review* 100: 3–52.

Chomsky, N. 1980. *Rules and Representations.* New York: Columbia University Press.

Larson, R. and G. Segal. 1995. *Knowledge of Meaning.* Cambridge, MA: MIT Press.

Ludlow, P. 1997. "Preface." *Reading in the Philosophy of Language.* Cambridge, MA: MIT Press: xiii–xvii.

Neale, S. 1990. *Descriptions.* Cambridge, MA: MIT Press.

Quine, W. V. O. 1953. "Mr. Strawson on Logical Theory." *Mind* 62. Reprinted in *The Ways of Paradox.* Cambridge, MA: Harvard University Press: 137–157.

Russell, B. 1905. "On Denoting." *Mind* 14. Reprinted in *Logic and Knowledge,* edited by R. C. Marsh. London: Unwin Hyman: 39–56.

Russell, B. 1957. "Mr. Strawson on Referring." *Mind,* 66. Reprinted in *Essays in Analysis.* London: Unwin Hyman: 120–126.

Strawson, P. 1950. "On Referring." *Mind,* 59. Reprinted in *Essays on Bertrand Russell,* edited by E. D. Klemke. Chicago: University of Illinois Press: 147–172.

PART ONE

Philosophy, Syntax, and Semantics

1

Perceptual Reports Revisited

James Higginbotham

1. Introduction

In Higginbotham (1983), an article prompted by several important observations and a theoretical proposal due to Barwise (1981), I considered a
number of issues in the syntax and semantics of perceptual reports with so-
called "naked infinitive" (NI) complements in English, exemplified by (1):

(1) John sees Mary enter.

Since publishing that article I have learned, partly on my own and partly
owing to the kind offices of others, of work on the subject that overlapped
with some of my views. In addition, there have been several further papers
and published articles on the subject of perceptual reports, some of them
directly critical of my proposal, or Barwise's, or both. In this article I will
consider antecedents to Barwise's article and mine, and the subsequent
critical literature. Naturally, my own reflections on the subject have contin-
ued over the years, and I will also explain here where these have led me.

After a brief general discussion in section 2 following, I will consider in
turn a number of the syntactic and semantic points about NI complements
that have came under recent discussion. Sections 3–10 are intended to
serve as a critical guide to some of the major issues in an area where the
last word has surely not been said.

2. General Discussion

Barwise (1981) pointed out that none of the standard semantic theories allowed embedded sentences to have the peculiar combination of semantic
properties of NI complements. These properties might be summed up in
the statement that (i) perceptual reports are both factive and *almost exten-*

sional, in that they permit substitutivity of singular terms, and (with some exceptions to be discussed below) fail to exhibit the ambiguities of scope normally associated with clausal arguments, but (ii) conspicuously fail to permit substitution *salva veritate* of predicates, and, as a striking corollary, fail to permit the interchange of logical equivalents. How could a construction that is almost extensional fail to be fully extensional? And how could a non-extensional construction show the substitutivity properties and uniqueness of scope that NI complements show? If NI complements are clausal arguments, neither the Fregean perspective nor any of the variants of possible-worlds semantics seems equipped to answer these questions.

Barwise was led to propose (2) as giving, under appropriate interpretation of its key terms, the truth conditions of (1):

(2) [∃s] (John sees *s* & *s* supports the truth of 'Mary enter')

The thing John sees, if (1) is true, is a (visual) *scene*. Scenes may be represented as partial models, mentioning some but generally not all objects, and some of the properties they have and relations they stand in. What it is for a scene to support the truth of a sentence is a matter for definition, from which the semantic properties of NI complements should follow. But then the theory of scenes and situations, a piece of substantive metaphysics, must be combined with standard semantic methods if the properties of language are to be theoretically described.

In Higginbotham (1983), I responded to Barwise's points by sketching what I called the *individual events account* of NI complements. On this account, the assumption that NI complements are clausal arguments is abandoned. Instead, it is proposed that the NI constituent, the expression 'Mary enter' of (1), has the semantics of an indefinite description of events, whose quantifiable place, following Davidson, is supposed to be provided by a hidden open position within the predicate. I will follow my subsequent practice and call this the *E-position* of the predicate. On the individual events account, (1) can be rendered more explicitly as in (3):

(3) [∃e: enter(Mary,e)] John sees *e*

Crucial to my account was the proposal that the *clause* 'Mary enter' is not a constituent of (3) at all. Nor is the subject-predicate combination 'Mary enter' an argument of anything. Hence, far from being mysterious from the point of view of the most important general accounts of non-extensional embedded contexts, NI complements are orthogonal to the questions these accounts raise, since they are not embedded at all.

I argued also that the properties that Barwise had discerned as peculiar to NI complements followed from the individual events account, and I gave several extensions that were said to favor it. These arguments will figure in the discussion in later sections of this paper. Besides these several points, however, there are also questions of philosophy and of general semantic orientation. Among recent critical discussions, ter Meulen and Bouma (1986), Neale (1988), and Barwise (1989) seem to me to have missed some of the philosophical points at issue, and in the case of the latter two to have misconstrued the conception of semantics with which I was working.

Neale (1988) makes rather heavy weather of the question of the relations of the English syntax to interpretation. In the interest of clarification, let me state the propositions (i)–(iii) to which that account is committed.

(i) The syntactic structure at the linguistic level LF of (1) is (4):

(4) $[_S[\text{Mary enter}]_i \, [_S \text{John sees } t_i]]$

(ii) The matrix '$[_S \text{John sees } t_i]$' of (4) is an open sentence in one free variable t_i and its truth conditions are as in (5):

(5) If a is an assignment of values to free variables (traces), then a satisfies '$[_S\text{John sees } t_i]$' iff $[\exists e] \, [\text{sees}(\text{John},a(t_i),e]$

(iii) The prefix '$[\text{Mary enter}]_i$' of (4) is interpreted as an existential quantifier binding t_i, whose restriction is to assignments to t_i satisfying 'Mary enter'; these are assignments a such that

$\text{enter}(\text{Mary},a(t_i))$

From (i)–(iii) taken together it follows that (1) is true iff (6):

(6) $[\exists e': \text{enter}(\text{Mary},e')] \, [\exists e] \, \text{sees}(\text{John},e',e)$

These points may clear up any obscurity that was responsible for Neale's assertion that the semantic import of my suggestion was vague, and still more his statement that "if event quantification is general [as in (6) above] then the syntactic, logical, and interpretive character of NI clauses is quite superfluous" (1988: 317). Event quantification *is* general, in Davidson's sense: each simple sentence contains an implicit existential quantification over events. But what was said to be peculiar to NI complements was not that they contained quantification over events, but that they themselves *were* existential quantifications. The objection confuses the two.

Barwise's brief comments (1989: 3–4) construe my view correctly as intending semantics proper, and not just conditions on syntactic structures. However, Barwise contrasts the "Davidsonian program of truth-conditional semantics, with a heavy reliance on logical form" with his work "within the model-theoretic tradition, which is quite different." Distinctive of the latter tradition, according to Barwise, is the view that "valid entailments are valid not in virtue of form, but in virtue of content." In Barwise's opinion, "Higginbotham and I start from such different starting points that it really is hard to make contact in a useful way."

Barwise's statement is complex, and subject to interpretation. But there is one remark at least that seems to be a misconstrual. This is the remark that investigations into logical form are committed to the thesis that what Barwise calls "valid entailments" are valid in virtue of "form" rather than "content." There is a tradition of calling implications "formally valid" when their correctness follows from logic alone; but that should not be taken to imply that it is anything other than the content of the logical words that makes them valid. Anyway, the individual events account of the semantic properties of sentences with NI complements does not rely upon a form-content distinction.

I close this section with a brief discussion of an early published treatment of NI complements that sticks within the possible worlds framework, the article Niiniluoto (1982) (this article was not known to me at the time I wrote). Citing Barwise, Niiniluoto acknowledges that the NI complements are not covered by an account in terms of sentence-embedding with a possible-worlds semantics, and he proposes one that invokes what he calls individual events and also retains the idea that all clausal complements to perception verbs are clausal arguments of those verbs. In the case of (1), Niiniluoto would give (7):

(7) $(\exists e)$ e consists of Mary's entering & John sees $[(\exists e') \ e' = e]^1$

The idea is that, although there is always a clausal complement to verbs of perception, the complement is not the NI complement itself, but the supplied constituent 'something is identical to the event e'.

An apparent difficulty with Niiniluoto's view is that, just because it interprets the NI complements on a par with complements of other types, and takes both, following Hintikka, on the model of the propositional attitudes, it may not allow the genuinely non-epistemic use of the NI complements. Perhaps, whenever an agent sees an event e she sees also *that* there is an event identical to e. At least this might be so if events have to register in thought to be truly seen (by the person, not her eyes), and if they actually have to be singled out in thought. If so, what applies to events would apply to other objects. It is at least plausible that if I see a box b, then I see that something is identical to b. To the extent that such implications hold, Niiniluoto would have located in (7) a necessary condition for the truth of a perceptual report with an NI complement. But it seems very doubtful that (7) is also a sufficient condition for the truth of such a report, at least as intuitively understood. First, it seems to fail to sufficiency for the case of seeing ordinary objects. For example, if I look at the reverse of a coin x, it seems that I see that something is identical to the obverse y of x; but I do not see y. For the case of perceptual reports with NI complements, similar examples seem to me compelling: if I see by looking around the empty room that John left, then I see that there is something identical with his leaving; but I do not see him leave.

But we cannot in view of these examples conclude that Niiniluoto's interpretation is not faithful to the semantics of NI complements. For there are at least two degrees of freedom in the theory. In the case of the coin, it might be responded that I do not have a visual impression of y, and so cannot be said to see that there is something identical to it. The requirement that I have a visual impression might be built into the definition of truth. In the case of seeing that John left, there might also be a scope distinction, between seeing that there is something identical to John's leaving, and his leaving being a thing x such that one sees that there is something identical to x. However, it does appear that, if the individual events account of NI complements can be sustained, then Niiniluoto's further apparatus is redundant.

3. The Role of E

The individual events account of perceptual reports makes essential use of Davidson's view that ordinary predicates, or some of them anyway, contain an extra argument-place for events. This hypothesis of an E-position has played a role in issues of the semantics of modification and adverbial quantification, and other places. The hypothesis fits into a rather general framework for looking at the problems of linguistic semantics. The most significant feature of that framework is the thesis that the only ways of combining constituents, apart from that of predicate and individual argument, are given by the quantifiers and truth functions. Arguments of higher type then go by the board, and combinations that have been taken on the model of functions of higher type call for other devices to play the role of semantic glue. The major such device is the extra argument place provided by the E-position. In such a manner does ontology—the individual events over which the E-position ranges—become the measure of the conceptual complexity of a language limited in its combinatorial resources.

Some recent work on structures of quantification, inspired by David Lewis's original discussion in Lewis (1975), has emphasized the role of frequency adverbials as quantifiers over events. Suppose we assume that in sentences like (8) we have quantification as in (9) (where B is some background condition, such as John's travels to work):

(8) John rarely walks to work.
(9) [Rare *e:* $B(e)$] [walk to work(John,e)]

Since the adverb *rarely* binds the E-position, and since the E-position of an NI complement is taken up by existential quantification, we expect restrictions on the use of such adverbs in NI complements, although not in finite clauses. Indeed these are found, thus providing some evidence in favor of taking (10) as in (11), and the individual events account more generally:

(10) ??I saw John rarely walk to work.
(11) I saw that John rarely walked to work.

Similarly, Mittwoch (1990: 110) notes that the only interpretation of (12) represents (using my terminology) quantification over occasions of perception, not occasions of leaving:

(12) I saw Mary leave twice.

That frequency adverbials, at least when they are taken to quantify over events rather than times, cannot be construed within NI complements follows if we suppose that existential quantification is given directly with the complement, so that there is no free E-position to be bound by the quantificational adverb whose office is to bind it.

But why can't the frequency adverbial simply *replace* the existential quantification (as it does in fact in (8), if the interpretation shown in (9) is correct)? If it did, that would give (8) the interpretation shown in (13):

(13) [Rare *e:* walk to work(John,e)] I saw *e*

A possible explanation for this fact is that the adverb *rarely* (unlike the adjectival form, *rare*) is not permitted to occur, as it would have to do in (13), with an *explicit* restriction on *e*. Thus we cannot have (14) in the meaning, "Rare among the things John does with a fork is eat," or more formally (15):

(14) John rarely eats with a fork.
(15) [Rare *e:* with a fork(e)] eats(John,e)

In my 1983 article I noted, following earlier published discussion, especially by James Gee, that there was a restriction on NI complements to perception verbs, that they, or the situations over which they ranged, be somehow active or transient, rather than stative or permanent. I considered it possible that statives were denied an E-position, and so considered that the oddity of (16) and the like reflected the absence of a place to serve as the argument of 'see', and correlatively as the range of the indefinite description:

(16) I saw John be in the room.

Conjectures of this type have been advanced recently in connection with the interpretation of absolutives and related constructions, as in Kratzer (1995).[2] Thus consider the contrast between (17) and (18):

(17) With food in their bellies, cats are sleepy.
(18) With eyes in their heads, cats are sleepy.

The latter is odd, and we can see from examples that the reason is that having eyes in its head is not a property that comes and goes in cats. The examples reinforce the natural suggestion that absolutives express the thought that some situations (e.g., a cat's having been fed) are correlated with others (e.g., that cat's being sleepy). But if the absolutive clause of (18) lacks an E-position, then no such correlation could be expressed. Hence its oddity, or so the account might run.

The intuitions about the examples are not to be denied (any more than the intuitions about (16)), but I now believe that the account suggested by Kratzer for (18), and by me for (16) is mistaken in principle; for further discussion, see Higginbotham and Ramchand (1996). If we continue to suppose that there is an E-position in all grammatical predicates, then the absence of statives from NI complements is not a matter of the absence of an appropriate argument; we are still left with the task of explaining its basis. I return to this question in section 9 below.

4. Connectives

Among the grammatical conjunctions of English (including both "coordinating" and "subordinating" conjunctions) only truth-functional conjunction 'and' and disjunction 'or' (and the 'nor' of 'neither . . . nor') occur with NI complements. As Barwise observed, (19) implies (20), but not conversely, and (21) and (22) are equivalent:

(19) John sees Bill dance and Mary sing.
(20) John sees Bill dance and he sees Mary sing.
(21) John sees Bill dance or Mary sing.
(22) John sees Bill dance or John sees Mary sing.

If equivalences like the last pair are the norm, then nothing special needs to be said about them. For the failure of (20) to imply (19), I had conjectured that conjunction might work so as to sum events, so that (on one interpretation) (19) has it that John saw a complex event, whose parts included Bill dancing and Mary singing, so that (20) is implied; but since one might see each event without seeing their sum, (20) did not imply (19).[3]

I now think that the notion of summation wrongly suggests a mereological account of (19). Another way to proceed is by strict analogy with plural NPs, which do not refer to sums. I will adopt, without rehearsing the background here, the view of the role of plurals taken in Schein (1986) and Higginbotham and Schein (1989). The central idea is that an argument of a head contributes to interpretation a statement about what objects were stand in the appropriate thematic relation to events of the type indicated by the head. A singular argument A contributes the statement that the reference of A stands in that relation, and a plural argument B contributes the statement that each of the various things to which it refers stands in that relation. Thus if the relation is Q, then the argument 'Bill' contributes the statement

$$\Theta(\text{Bill},e)$$

and the argument 'Bill and Mary' contributes

$$\Theta(\text{Bill},e) \ \& \ \Theta(\text{Mary},e)$$

Pairs such as (23)–(24) have the same relations of implication as (19)–(20):

(23) John saw Bill and Mary
(24) John saw Bill and John saw Mary

If Θ_1 and Θ_2 are the thematic relations of the external and internal arguments, respectively, of the verb 'see' to events of seeing, then (24) will have the truth conditions in (25):

(25) $(\exists e) [\text{see}(e) \ \& \ \Theta_1(\text{John},e) \ \&$
      $(\forall x) (\Theta_2(x,e) \leftrightarrow x=\text{Bill})] \ \&$
      $(\exists e') [\text{see}(e') \ \& \ \Theta_1(\text{John},e') \ \&$
      $(\forall y) (\Theta_2(y,e') \leftrightarrow y=\text{Mary})]$

These are also the truth conditions of the interpretation of (23) according to which it is a reduced conjunction of sentences. For the other interpretation of (23) Schein's account of the contribution of plural arguments gives (26):

(26) $(\exists e) [\text{see}(e) \ \& \ \Theta_1(\text{John},e) \ \&$
      $(\forall x) (\Theta_2(x,e) \leftrightarrow x=\text{Bill or } x=\text{Mary})]$

that is, there was a seeing by John such that the things seen in it were exactly Bill and Mary. On this view of (23), and assuming that the event of seeing is appropriately divisible into subevents, it implies (24). The converse fails in any case, since there may be no single event of seeing that involves in the role of Θ_2 both Bill and Mary.

If we apply the above account of plurals to the pair (19)–(20), we obtain the right relations of implication. The conjoined complement in (19) is a conjunction of indefinite descriptions rather than singular terms, and so should be parallel to (27):

(27) John saw a man and a woman.

The latter is as in (28), and so (19), not understood as a conjunction reduction, comes out as in (29):

(28) $[\exists x, y: \text{man}(x) \,\&\, \text{woman}(y)] \,(\exists e)\, [\text{see}(e) \,\&\, \Theta_1(\text{John}, e) \,\&\,$
  $(\forall z)\, (\Theta_2(z, e) \leftrightarrow z = x \text{ or } z = y)]$

(29) $[\exists e_1, e_2: \text{dance}(\text{Bill}, e_1) \,\&\, \text{sing}(\text{Mary}, e_2)] \,(\exists e)\, [\text{see}(e) \,\&\,$
  $\Theta_1(\text{John}, e) \,\&\, (\forall e')$
  $(\Theta_2(e', e) \leftrightarrow e' = e_1 \text{ or } e' = e_2)]$

Simply put, then, (19) has it that there was an event of seeing by John that involves in the role Θ_2 John's dancing and Mary's singing, and nothing else. The result is in harmony with the individual events account, and requires no otherwise extraneous metaphysical intrusion. Notice that to secure the result we had to expose fully the E-position in the main verb 'see', as well as in the complement verbs.

5. Scopes of Quantifiers

Barwise observed that perceptual reports with NI complements do not display the usual ambiguities of scope associated with embedded clauses. I assumed Barwise's generalization as a datum, and tried to account for it. But it has since been observed (by Vlach (1983)) that to the extent that the datum fails Barwise's approach faces difficulties, and also (by Asher and Bonevac (1985b)) that it is not so easy to secure it to the extent that it does hold within the general framework that Barwise assumes. Finally, although the version of my own piece circulated at MIT was more expansive on the question of quantifier scopes, I have since become aware that I did not say nearly enough about the subject, or penetrate it with sufficient depth. In this section, I will consider Asher and Bonevac's discussion, then Vlach's, and finally, guided in part by the above discussion of plurals, append some remarks on how the individual events account might go.

Asher and Bonevac (1985b) have endeavored to carry out a precise formulation of Barwise's notion '*s* supports the truth of Φ' that would actually have the intended consequences for the semantic properties of perceptual reports. I consider an example representative of the problems they observe. The extensionality of NI complements brings existential generalization with it, so that (1), together with the premise that Mary is a woman, implies (30):

(30) John sees a woman enter.

On the individual events account, the implication is trivial. On Barwise's view, however, there are complications. It may be that no scene John saw represented Mary as a woman, or contained the information that she was a woman; all may have left the question open. Hence, the implication of (30) fails.[4] To secure the implication, they propose that the restriction on a quantifier be evaluated only for maximal expansions of the contextual situations with respect to which the predicate quantifier is evaluated. It thus becomes sufficient for the truth of (30) that John have seen something enter that was, in point of fact, a woman.

There is a simpler path to the same conclusion, namely: require all overt quantifiers to be construed outside the existential quantification '($\exists s$)' associated with NI complements. In that case, whether an object satisfies their restrictions is not dependent on what descriptions of objects happen to be available in the contextual situation, and we arrive at truth conditions for (30) that makes it an obvious consequence of (1) and the empirical premise that Mary is a woman. This simpler path could have been taken for all the examples that Asher and Bonevac give in their paper.

I may be in disagreement with Asher and Bonevac about their diagnosis of the problem of existential generalization. They appear to hold that, although as a matter of fact quantifier-restrictions are evaluated with respect to a maximal expansion of the situation, things could have been otherwise; that is, that there could have been a locution that shared the factivity of (1), but for which existential generalization failed. That would happen if the initial setting (or resource situation, to use the technical term) was indeterminate in certain respects. Furthermore, they refer (on p. 216 and elsewhere) to individuals in scenes as being "vague," and so characterize the familiar fact that we might see something without seeing "what it is." But more important is their apparent view that there could be a non-epistemic use of 'see' and the other perception verbs that disallowed existential generalization, and the several other logical implications that follow as a matter of course if the quantifiers of NI complements take obligatory wide scope. On the individual events account, such a use is impossible.

In Vlach's view, one construes the NI form of a declarative (present-tense) sentence Φ as a predicate of events of the type that Φ classifies, or TE[Φ] in his terminology. There is an existential quantification, so that (1) may be paraphrased by (31):

(31) ($\exists e$) [John sees e & TE['Mary enter'](e)]

The account goes thus partway toward the individual events account. It is less worked out in that it does not endorse a view of how TE[Φ] is obtained, given Φ, and correspondingly does not have as many semantic consequences.

One of Vlach's objections to Barwise is that the sense in which conjunctions of perceptual reports do not imply the report of their conjunction, as in (19)–(20), repeated below, is unobtainable in the setting of "Scenes and Other Situations," or in other formulations of situation semantics:

(19) John sees Bill dance and Mary sing.
(20) John sees Bill dance and he sees Mary sing.

The reason, according to Vlach, that (20) may be construed as not implying (19) is that the latter may report John as having seen a single event that is a "combination of events," and there may be no such combination for certain pairs of events (just as, in Vlach's view, there may be no physical object that is a combination of certain other physical objects).

As may be inferred from the discussion of the last section, I disagree with Vlach's analysis here. The conjunction 'and' produces simple plurals, not combinations of events. Just as any two NPs can be conjoined so can any two NI complements. The conjunctions produce perceptual reports that, however unlikely to be true, cannot be ruled out on metaphysical grounds. Vlach's objects that the recursive rule that suggests itself for conjunctions of NI complements as in (32) is too general, in that we would find cases where the right-hand side was true and the left-hand side false:

(32) s supports the truth of (Φ & Γ) iff s supports Φ and s
      supports Γ

But this conclusion need not be accepted.

Vlach observes that Barwise's scheme is incapable of distinguishing the interpretations differing in the scope of 'everyone' in sentences like (33):

(33) John saw everyone leave.

Vlach's interpretation, or mine, easily distinguishes the case of John's having seen, for each person x, the event of x's leaving from the case of his having seen the single event of everyone's leaving, where the latter does not require that each departure constitute a part of the event seen. To Barwise's view as originally presented, however, the objection is powerful. Barwise would assign (33) the truth conditions of (34):

(34) [∃s] John sees *s* & *s* supports the truth of 'everyone leave'

What else could it be for a situation to "support the truth of" the mentioned clause besides its supporting the truth of '*x* leave' for every value of '*x*'? But if *s* has the latter property, then (35) follows, and (35) gives the truth conditions of (36), which were agreed to be distinct from those of (33):

(35) [∀x] [∃s] John sees *s* & *s* supports the truth of '*x* leave'
(36) Every person is an *x* such that John saw *x* leave

To answer Vlach's objection, one might adopt the view that there are intrinsically general situations, or types of situations. If so, then a visual scene might support the truth of 'everyone leave' by containing this general fact directly. Could it then support the truth of 'someone leave' without supporting the truth of '*x* leave' for any person as value of '*x*'? If so, that would be unfortunate, for we do not find cases where the scope of an existential quantifier potentially matters in a perceptual report; for instance, (37) does not have two meanings:

(37) John saw some woman leave.

I shall leave the question here, observing only that the ambiguities seem, on the individual events account, to arise just where they ought to.

In examples like (33), we may have the interpretation indicated in (38), where the quantifier 'everyone' takes narrow scope:

(38) [∃e: (∀x) leave(x,e)] John saw *e*

To see more closely what (38) means, observe that if we use the breakdown of a verb into a conjunction of a predicate of events and thematic relations between events and their participants, as carried out in connection with the discussion of plurals above, then the restriction in (38) is (39):

(39) leave(e) & (∀x) Θ(x,e)

What then becomes of Barwise's generalization? It seems to me that its importance is not impugned, particularly since there are a number of apparent potential ambiguities that do not seem to arise in NI complements. For example, there is nothing in principle semantically wrong about taking (40) as equivalent to (33) with narrow scope for 'everyone':

(40) John saw each person leave.

That this does not happen presumably follows from a fact about the meaning of the word 'each', namely its propensity for wide scope.

6. Anaphora

Davidson, as far back as his original article on the subject, had used the existence of apparent anaphoric reference in sentences like (41) as a consideration in favor of what I am calling the E-position.

(41) John buttered the toast. He did it in the bathroom.

The pronoun is naturally taken to refer to the event of buttering the toast. Hence it is plausible that reference to the thing John did is carried somehow in the first sentence, this reference supplying an antecedent for the anaphor. But if we suppose an E-position, such reference is almost a matter of course, and cross-reference to what John did is nearly as much a matter of course as cross-reference to a thing given by an ordinary indefinite description.

Neale (1988) calls attention to a point about pronominal anaphora that seems to have been first noticed in Geis (1975), who observed that we cannot back-refer to events as given in the manner of (41) with plural pronominals:

(42) ??John buttered the toast and cleaned the fish. He did them in the bathroom.

Perception verbs and causatives show the same anomaly:

(43) ??John saw Mary cry and Bill dance. Did you see *them?*
(45) John helped Mary pack. Nobody else helped with *it.*

(44) ??John helped Mary pack and Bill drive. Nobody else helped with *them.*

The anomaly raises interesting linguistic questions, but no semantic problems. For we can see by examples that the failure of cross-reference is a property of plural pronominals 'they' and 'them', and not a property of anaphoric elements in general. Both Neale and I judge that anaphora is possible in (46) but impossible in (47), which displays the pronominal. Likewise, cross-reference is acceptable in (48) and (49):

(46) John saw May dance and Bill faint, but you didn't see either.
(47) *John saw Mary dance and Bill faint, but you didn't see either of *them*.
(48) John saw Mary cry and Bill dance. Did you see *those things?*
(49) John buttered the toast and cleaned the fish. He did *both things* in the bathroom.

In general, plural pronominals may not have clausal antecedents:

(50) John told me Mary was happy, but I didn't believe *it*.
(51) John told me Mary was happy and Bill was sick, but I didn't believe either of *those propositions*.
(52) *John told me Mary was happy and Bill was sick, but I didn't believe *them*/either of *them*. (that Mary was happy or that Bill was sick)
(53) John told me two dubious things, but I didn't believe *them*/either of *them*.

As the acceptability of (51) shows, the ungrammaticality of (52) is not owing to any failure of clausal reference; and as the acceptability of (53) shows, it is not due to the nature of that reference (propositions).

7. Negation

Neale's contribution contains a substantive discussion of the interpretation of sentences containing negated NI complements. On the view that I defended, there would be, potentially, three possible interpretations for a sentence such as (54), namely (55)–(57):

(54) John saw Mary not cry.
(55) $\neg[\exists e\colon \text{cry}(\text{Mary},e)]$ John saw e
(56) $[\exists e\colon \neg(\text{cry}(\text{Mary},e))]$ John saw e
(57) $[\exists e\colon \text{cry}(\text{Mary},e)]\ \neg(\text{John saw }e)$

Of these, (57) is not available as an interpretation of (54), presumably because negation cannot escape the scope of the S-Structure predicate, here 'cry', with which it occurs. But (55) is also unavailable, since that amounts to

John did not see Mary cry

We are then left with (56), whose meaning is

John saw some event that was not a cry by Mary

which fails intuitively to be either necessary or sufficient for (54). It is not sufficient, since (55) will be true if John saw anything at all other than a cry by Mary, and not necessary, since (54) might sum up all John saw on some occasion. The conclusion, then, is that negation has no clausal scope at all in (54).[5]

It might seem that Barwise's account of NI complements is to be preferred for examples like (54), since it is possible to distinguish situations in his sense, coming as they do with clusters of objects, properties, and relations, more finely than situations in the sense of Davidson. Take a situation, for instance, in which Mary laughs. On the individual events account, reference to that event can be made by saying it was an episode of laughter, and to the extent that such episodes cannot co-occur with crying, it follows that it was not an episode of crying. Suppose that some cases in which I see Mary laugh are cases in which I see her not cry, and others are not. How is the difference between these to be registered? On Barwise's account, the difference between the situations that I see is that some contain merely Mary's episode of laughter, or, in the terminology of Barwise and Ferry (1983), are represented as in (58):

(58) <laugh,Mary>, yes

while others are represented as in (59):

(59) <laugh,Mary>, yes
      <cry,Mary>, no

The situations I see when I see Mary not cry are of the latter kind.

There are cases in which assertions of (54) and the like would be warranted. They include those in which one sees Mary refrain from crying, and other, weaker cases in which she might merely have been expected to cry, but did not.[6] But we do not report ourselves as having seen Mary not cry in any and all circumstances in which we saw her engaged in some activity incompatible with her crying. Barwise's account, as presented by Neale, construes the cases in which we would not say we saw Mary not cry as cases in which the scene was as in (58), and the others are as in (59). It thus reaps a technical advantage, but one that is ultimately no advantage at all. What we wanted to know was *which* situations that we saw were of type (58), and which were of type (59); but for this purpose the formal distinction is no help. On the individual events account, the question of what we see when we see Mary not cry arose within the semantics; there was no rich conception of situations to pin the question onto. But Barwise's account, in taking situations as the realization of universals, merely trades the semantic problem for a problem of metaphysics, about which there is silence.[7]

8. Extensionality and Causation

One can gather some support for the individual events account of perceptual reports from a comparison of their verbs with the single other class of verbs that permits NI complements, namely the verbs of causation, 'make', 'let', 'help', and 'have' (in the sense of "I'll have John bring the car").

The causatives show much in common with the verbs of perception. For example, the referential transparency of the contexts 'make ___', 'let___', and the others, when the blanks are filled by an NI complement clause, is supported in simple cases. But a difference between contexts of perception and contexts of causation that is of import with respect to the individual events account is that the latter but not the former freely allow quantifiers within the NI complement to have narrow scope. In both agent-causation and event-causation with 'make', for instance, we can understand indefinite descriptions, such as 'a book' in (60) and (61) as having narrow scope:

(60) John made Mary read a book.
(61) The foul weather made Mary read a book instead of venturing outside.

(i.e., we can understand an assertion of (60) as putting out of order the question, "Which book did John make Mary read?"). Now, the possibility of different understandings of (60) is a serious matter, because the individual events account will give first of all (62):

(62) $[\exists e: \text{read}(\text{Mary,a book},e)]$ John made e

whose interpretation is fixed up to logical equivalence, since whether 'a book' ultimately gets wide or narrow scope does not matter here. If there is an event e of reading a book, b say, that John made happen, then he made happen the event of reading b, and so, according to the individual events account, there is a book, namely b, that John made Mary read, contrary to the observation that the question which book John made Mary read can be out of order.

Putative counterexamples to referential transparency are cut to the same mold as the problem of the scope of indefinite descriptions, in the sense that an agent or situation may make something happen with respect to a thing *x* where it just chanced to be *x* and not something else that was involved in what the agent did, or what the situation brought about. Suppose that the desire to appear well-dressed made John put on a fine shirt, and he happened to choose the yellow one rather than the white one. His desire to appear well-dressed made him put on the shirt he's wearing, a yellow shirt. But did his desire to be well-dressed make him put on his yellow shirt? My desire to read something in Italian doesn't make me pick up *1912+1* rather than *Il Fuoco,* even if it is *1912+1* that I pick up; some more particular circumstance must have made that happen.

Putting these observations together, it appears that the contrast between NI complements and tensed or infinitival complements for causatives is not as sharp as would be expected. The important discussion in Ritter and Rosen (1990) further underscores this point.

9. Tense and Aspect

In this section I return to the question of the status of (16), repeated here:

(16) I saw John be in the room.

A natural thought is that its anomaly is correlated with the absence of an E-position in statives; and this was my conjecture in Higginbotham (1983). As I observed in section 3 above, this conjecture sits oddly with the explanation I suggested for the difference between (63) and (64), namely that the state of being tall is, and the state of being drunk is not, a temporary or transient state of its possessor:

(63) I saw John tall.
(64) I saw John drunk.

for how can temporariness or transience change the logical character of a predicate?

Notice furthermore that if adverbs of quantification quantify over events, then the appearance of such adverbs with statives shows that they to must contain an E-position, as in (65):

(65) John is rarely drunk.

Many similar examples show that there are principled arguments for endowing every predicative head with an E-position, inasmuch as productive semantic processes understood as involving this position in the case of ordinary action verbs apply outside action verbs as well. See further Higginbotham and Ramchand (1996).

Neale (1988) suggested that sentences like (66) are acceptable in certain contexts (e.g., a high-stakes poker game); but his example, far from being an objection, abets a pragmatic explanation of the phenomenon:

(66) I saw John own a house.

A more serious problem is that of what I will call the *true statives,* exemplified by (67):

(67) I saw John know that p

I conjecture that (67) is deviant, period. Even if John has a stone in his forehead that glows just when it would be true of him to say that he knows that $p,$ one cannot see the state he is in when he knows it. Consider a circumstance in which it would be appropriate to assert (68):

(68) I saw the farmer hope for rain.

I think that (68) can be asserted only if one saw the farmer *do* something (gaze skyward, with gestures). But the state of hoping for rain is not tied to any particular manifestation of the farmer's hope, a sign that the assertion is not literal. The conclusion is that (67) and (68), taken literally, are in the nature of category mistakes. Mental states that do not require any particular behavioral manifestation are intrinsically imperceptible. Note that the conclusion allows for an E-position in predicates denoting mental states, and so does not conflict with the generalization of the E-position to all ordinary predicates.

'There'-insertion sentences are resistant to occurrence as NI complements (with the exception of examples due to Gee, as discussed below):

(69) I saw there be a man in the room.

In these cases, the restriction to temporariness or transience is insufficient, since (64) contrasts strongly with (70):

(70) I saw there be a man drunk.

A better explanation for the deviance of (70) comes from an observation due to Williams (1984), who points out that, unlike the auxiliary verb 'be' the main verb 'be' imputes agency. Gee's examples, such as (71), gain in acceptability just because the modal context invites an interpretation in which agents are in control:

(71) I wouldn't like to see there be so many mistakes next time.

Compare (72):

(72) *I didn't like to see there be so many mistakes last time.

10. Other Syntactic Issues

In (1983) I attributed the absence of passive from NI complements to perception verbs, as in the ungrammatical (73) below, to a violation of binding theory that would result if in (1) the subject of the complement were raised to the sentential subject under passive morphology and the complement, with the trace of NP-movement, were raised by QR to a higher position, as in (74):

(73) *Mary was seen enter
(74) $[t_i \text{ enter}]_j$ $[\text{Mary}_i \text{ was seen } t_j]$

In (74), the antecedent 'Mary$_i$' does not c-command its trace, producing a syntactic violation at LF. This conjecture brought with it some problems even in English, and a wider set of issues if other languages are considered.

In English, there is first of all the problem that passive is permitted in complements supported by progressive '-ing', as in (75):

(75) Mary was seen entering.

But these complements have almost the same semantic properties as the NI complements, so that if they too underwent QR there would be a violation of binding theory at LF for (75) as well as (74). I had conjectured that the progressive predicate might represent an adjunct clause, as in (76), with the meaning, "I saw Mary while she was entering":

(76) I saw Mary$_i$ [PRO$_i$ entering]

Kroch, Heycock, and Santorini (1986) suggest an argument against applying QR as in (74), based on data from VP-deletion. I elaborate on their suggestion in a way that I think makes the argument even stronger. VP-deletion is supported in (77), with 'each man' taking wide scope:

(77) John saw each man leave, but Bill didn't Ø

Moreover, sentences like (78) show the classical restrictions on interpretation that VP-deletion induces:

(78) Somebody saw each man leave, but Bill didn't Ø

The first clause of (78) is ambiguous by itself, but in the context is disambiguated, with the universal 'each man' being incapable of wider scope than the subject. The usual explanation of such restrictions is that, since the substitution of the antecedent of the deleted VP Ø at LF must produce a closed sentence, the quantifier 'each man' must not be allowed to escape that VP. But that explanation implies that (77) can be taken with the quantifier confined to the VP, and so with the NI complement, which then contains the variable it binds, confined to the VP as well. Then the complement need not raise outside the VP, and nothing from binding theory or the Θ-criterion prevents the passive (73).

Guasti (1989) offers an explanation of the absence of passive that turns on visibility conditions for Θ-marking. On her view, the verb 'see' of (1) can Θ-mark the NI complement only by assigning Case to it, and since the passive morphology absorbs Case such assignment, and therefore the Θ-marking on which it depends, is unavailable in (73). But sentences comparable to the forbidden English passive are grammatical, for instance in Italian, for the NI complements of both perceptual reports and causatives. For such languages, Guasti suggests, in part following Manzini (1983), that there is complex verb formation (which Guasti calls *incorporation*). Supposing that this is correct, I will close by remarking on the semantics of incorporation, and the way that it may fit into the theory as a whole.

Incorporation is one method of executing *reanalysis,* or the redescription of a phrase marker. In the context of trace theory and head-to-head movement, it takes a specific form, namely the fusion of a lower head with a higher one, leaving a trace in the position of the lower. In the case of (1), we may simplify the description of the output of incorporation to (79):

(79) John [[sees-enter] Mary *t*]

For the semantics of incorporation, we must distinguish two cases. In the first case, the trace is semantically inert, and we have really created a compound verb 'sees-enter' which, like other verbs, must discharge its thematic roles in an appropriate manner. This semantics is perhaps realized in the case of lexical causatives. In the second case, the trace is semantically active, and retains all of the thematic properties of its antecedent. In particular, in (79) it retains the two argument positions of the antecedent 'enter', Θ-marks the object 'Mary', and together with it forms a constituent at LF which is interpreted as an existential quantification. Thus the trace is a second-order anaphor, whose antecedent is a verb. Indeed, the case is exactly comparable to a raising construction, and hence of no particular semantic interest.

The first case, where 'sees-enter' is truly a compound verb, assigning thematic roles to the arguments 'John' and 'Mary', is of theoretical interest, not because there is any problem in giving a mechanism (assuming the semantics of the unincorporated form) that will produce for the incorporated form the same meaning as the original, but rather because the mechanism that does this can be taken to be of a very restricted kind, far more restricted than those standardly available for instance in Montague grammar, or any semantic formalism that employs the theory of types.

Our mechanism will have for its inputs the verbs 'see' and 'enter', with their particular thematic properties, and will have for its output the verb 'see-enter', whose properties depend upon those of the input. In the terminology of my (1985), the inputs are

see, [+V,-N], <1,2,E>
enter, [+V,-N], <3,E'>

The information within the angled brackets shows the places of the predicate, and of course its E-position.[8] The output is arrived at by (i) identifying position 2 of 'see' with the E-position of 'enter', and (ii) taking the existential closure of the resulting compound with respect to that position. The result is a verb whose thematic structure is

see-enter, [+V,-N], <1,2,E>

The operation is perhaps clearer if we use for expository purposes free variables instead of thematic positions. The inputs are

$see(x,y,e)$
$enter(z,e')$

and the output is

$(\exists e')\ see\text{-}enter(x,e',z,e)$

which abbreviates

$(\exists e')\ see(x,e',e)\ \&\ enter(z,e)$

For simple sentences such as (1), when the compound verb Θ-marks the arguments 'John' and 'Mary', and, finally, the free e in 'see' is discharged through existential closure, we will have (80):

(80) $(\exists e)\ (\exists e')\ (see(John,e',e)\ \&\ enter(Mary,e))$

which is a logical equivalent to the truth conditions given by the individual events account.[9]

Notes

1. I have taken inessential liberties with Niiniluoto's notation. The verb 'sees' in this example is also not factive, and might better be read 'seems to see'.

2. This article was circulated as Kratzer (1988), and represents the author's view at that time.

3. Van der Does (1990) raises these issues very clearly.

4. More precisely, if we understand scenes as (representable by) sets of true atomic sentences and negations of atomic sentences, then John's visual scene may contain 'enter(Mary)' without containing 'woman(Mary)' or anything else to that effect, and so without supporting the truth of '(x) (woman(x) & enter(x))'.

5. Mittwoch (1990) is rather disparaging of the data here, observing that spontaneous examples of negated NI complements are vanishingly rare.

6. See also van der Does (1990) and Mittwoch (1990).

7. van der Does (1990) develops a system with both an internal and an external negation for cases like (54).

8. Obviously, more information is needed. I am not proposing that the above representations figure in some linguistic level, only that, as I have interpreted them, they contain information necessary to the syntax and the semantics of the item in question.

9. This article is based upon a draft growing out of the Gargano Conference on Perception and Language, sponsored by the University of Milan in 1991. I am grateful to the organizers, and indebted in several places to the discussion that took place there.

References

Asher, N. and D. Bonevac. 1985a. "Situations and Events." *Philosophical Studies* 47: 57–77.

Asher, N. and D. Bovevac. 1985b. "How Extensional is Extensional Perception?" *Linguistics and Philosophy* 8: 203–228.

Barwise, J. 1981. "Scenes and Other Situations." *The Journal of Philosophy* 18: 369–397. Reprinted in Barwise (1989): 5–36, with an appendix, "Reply to Lakoff."

Barwise, J. 1989. *The Situation in Logic.* CSLI Lecture Notes, no. 17. Center for the Study of Language and Information, Stanford University.

Barwise, J. and J. Ferry. 1983. *Situations and Attitudes.* Cambridge, Massachusetts: MIT Press. A Bradford Book.

Does, J. van der. 1990. "A Generalized Quantifier Logic for Naked Infinitives." Institute for Language, Logic, and Information, University of Amsterdam.

Geis, M. 1975. "Two Theories of Action Sentences." *Ohio State University Occasional Papers in Linguistics.*

Guasti, M. 1988. "Romance Infinitive Complements of Perception Verbs." ms., University of Geneva.

Higginbotham, J. 1983. "The Logic of Perceptual Reports: An Extensional Alternative to Situation Semantics." *The Journal of Philosophy* 80: 100–127.

———. 1985. "On Semantics." *Linguistic Inquiry* 16: 547–593. Reprinted in *New Directions in Semantics*, edited by E. Lepore. London: Academic Press, 1987.

Higginbotham, J. and B. Schein. 1989. "Plurals." *NELS XIX Proceedings*. GLSA, University of Massachusetts, Amherst.

Higginbotham, J. and G. Ramchand. 1996. "The Stage-Level/Individual-level Distinction and the Mapping Hypothesis." *Oxford University Working Papers in Linguistics, Philology and Phonetics 2*.

Kratzer, A. 1995. "Stage-Level and Individual-Level Predicates." In *The Generic Book*, edited by G. Carlson et al. Chicago: The University of Chicago Press.

Kroch, A., E. Heycock and M. Santorini. 1986. "Bare Infinitives and External Arguments." ms., University of Pennsylvania.

Lewis, D. 1975. "Adverbs of Quantification." In *External Semantics of Natural Language*, edited by E. Keenan. Cambridge: Cambridge University Press: 3–15. Reprinted in *Philosophical Papers I*. Oxford: Oxford University Press.

Manzini, M-R. 1983. *Restructuring and Reanalysis*. Unpublished doctoral dissertation, MIT, Cambridge, Massachusetts.

Meulen, A. ter and G. Bouma. 1986. *Research on the Semantics of Natural Language and Visual Situations: The Semantics of Perception Reports*. Report for the Fraunhofer Institut für Arbeitswissenschaft und Orginasation Stuttgart, Stuttgart, FRG.

Mittwoch, A. 1990. "On the Distribution of Bare Infinitive Complements in English." *Journal of Linguistics* 26: 103–131.

Muskens, R. 1989. *Meaning and Partiality*. Doctoral dissertation, University of Amsterdam.

Neale, S. 1988. "Events and 'Logical Form'." *Linguistics and Philosophy* 11: 303–321.

Niiniluoto, I. 1982. "Remarks on the Logic of Perception." In *Acta Philosophica Fennica 35: Intensional Logic: Theory and Applications*, edited by I. Niiniluoto and E. Saarinen: 116–129.

Ritter, E. and S. Rosen, S. 1990. "Causative Have." ms. Université du Québec à Montréal.

Schein, B. 1986. *Event Logic and the Interpretation of Plurals*. Unpublished doctoral dissertation, MIT, Cambridge, Massachusetts.

Vlach, F. 1983. "On Situation Semantics for Perception." *Synthese* 54: 129–152.

Williams, E. 1984. "'There'-Insertion." *Linguistic Inquiry* 15: 131–153.

2

Coloring and Composition

*Stephen Neale**

" . . . it may well happen that we have more simple propositions than sentences."

—Gottlob Frege

§1. Introduction

In one form or another, the idea that an utterance of a basic (nondeviant) declarative sentence has a truth condition (and truth-value) and the idea that

---

*The work on singular terms in this paper was first presented in November 1986 at CNRS, Paris and University College London, and in January 1987 at Stanford University. The broader work on levels of speech acts and multiple propositions was prepared for a colloquium of the Czech Institute of Philosophy held at Karlovy Vary in September 1993 (abstract in *From the Logical Point of View* 1 (1993), pp. 55–56) and a symposium at CREA, Ecole Polytechnique, held in October 1993. Audiences at Cumberland Lodge, Grinell College, Iowa State University, the University of Iowa, Konstanz University, Kings College London, Lund University, McGill University, the University of Maribor, the University of Maryland, M.I.T., Ohio State University, Oslo University, Simon Fraser University, Stockholm University, and Tromsø University have shown me just how much more work there is to do on this topic. In order that the work might finally see the light of day (albeit in compressed form), many excellent points and suggestions had to be ignored; I hope this causes no offense. I thank Liz Camp for insightful comments and help in preparing manuscript for publication. The central theme of the essay—that an utterance may express more than one proposition—is hardly without precedent. It manifests itself with varying degrees of explicitness, in work by Frege (1892), Grice (1989), Karttunen and Peters (1979), Perry (1993), Searle (1975), Stalnaker (1978), and Strawson (1952). Where singular terms are concerned some of my analyses end up close to notational variants of those given by Perry.

such an utterance expresses a single true-or-false proposition has dominated philosophical discussions of meaning in this century. Refinements aside, such ideas are not so much substantive theses as part of a background against which particular theories of meaning are evaluated. There are good reasons for looking at what happens if such assumptions are dropped, not least of which are phenomena (noted by Frege, Strawson, and Grice) that threaten at least the completeness of classical theories of meaning, which associate with an utterance of a simple sentence a truth-condition, a Russellian proposition, or a Fregean thought. A framework within which utterances express *sequences* of propositions may provide much of what is needed to account for the relevant phenomena, a better overall picture of the way language works, and an enticingly uniform perspective on semantic problems raised by sentence connectives, sentence modifiers, proper names, demonstratives, descriptions, apposition, and verbs used to report psychological states.

I do not care for theories that multiply propositions by appealing to propositions "presupposed" or to pairs of Fregean and Russellian propositions, for theories that show no respect for a distinction between *semantics* and *pragmatics*—where the former is the study of propositions whose *general form and character* is determined by word meaning and syntax—or for theories that blithely abandon general principles of composition and semantic innocence. And so, I would like to sketch a package based on four interconnected ideas: (i) the meaning of an individual word is a *sequence of instructions* for generating a *sequence of propositions* (in conjunction with compositional instructions (syntax) and elements of context); (ii) utterances themselves are not bearers of truth or falsity; (iii) judgments of truth, falsity, commitment, and conflict are shaped, in part, by the weights attached to individual propositions that occur in sequences expressed by utterances, weights that may be set (and reset) by contextual considerations; (iv) Fregean senses are superfluous; propositions might as well be Russellian (Mont Blanc and all its snow fields will do as well as any mode of presentation). A rigorous semantics for the expressions used to motivate the multiple proposition framework will have to await another occasion.

I shall do some scene-setting and motivational spadework for this package with examples of what Frege calls *coloring* and Grice calls *conventional implicature.* My primary interest is not in the history of such examples but in how we might piece together elements of the work of Frege, Grice, and others, and thereby extricate ourselves from what appears to me to be a semantic straitjacket. I begin with Frege only to abandon him completely in mid-stream.

§2. Frege: Sense, Reference, Coloring, Composition

Frege (1892) distinguishes between the *reference* (*Bedeutung*) and *sense* (*Sinn*) of an expression; but in some intuitive sense of our word 'meaning', it appears to be Frege's view that sameness of meaning is guaranteed by neither sameness of reference nor sameness of sense. The referent of a singular term is its bearer, its sense a "mode of presentation" of the bearer. The referent of a sentence (a type of singular term) is its truth-value, its sense a thought/proposition (*Gedanke*). The names 'Hesperus' and 'Phosphorus' have the same reference but differ in sense; by contrast, the sentence connectives 'and' and 'but' not only have the same reference—a particular truth-function—they also have the same sense: they differ only in *coloring (Färbung)*. Unfortunately, Frege does not say very much about coloring; but what he does say suggests that it is a general property: every word has it, and such things as word order and intonation patterns may also contribute to the coloring of a phrase or sentence. Consider the following:

(1) Alfred has still not arrived
(2) Alfred has not arrived yet
(3) Alfred has not arrived.

According to Frege, someone who utters (1) or (2) "actually says" that Alfred has not arrived "and at the same time hints—but only hints—that Alfred's arrival is expected" (1914, p. 23). The hints supplied by 'still' or 'yet', as used in (1) and (2), make no difference to reference: if Alfred is not expected (1) and (2) are still true as long as Alfred has not arrived. Furthermore, 'still' and 'yet' make no difference to *sense:* (1)–(3) express the same thought. Indeed, Frege's view may well be that although 'still' and 'yet' have coloring, they have *no sense:*

> 'although' . . . has no sense and does not change the sense of the clause [to which it is attached] but only illuminates it in a peculiar fashion. (*Footnote:* Similarly in the case of 'but' and 'yet'). (1892, p. 73)

The point Frege is making in the footnote is taken up in his later paper "Thoughts":

> [t]he way that 'but' differs from 'and' is that we use it to intimate that what follows it contrasts with what was to be expected from what preceded it. Such conversational suggestions make no difference to the thought. . . . Thus the content of a sentence often goes beyond the thought expressed by it. (1914, pp. 39–40)

On Frege's account, then, (4)–(6) have the same sense and differ only in coloring:

(4) Alfred is poor and he is honest

(5) Alfred is poor but he is honest
(6) Although he is poor, Alfred is honest.

Active-passive pairs are also said to share a sense; similarly certain pairs of common nouns, for example 'horse' and 'steed'.

Two expressions that differ in coloring serve only to conjure up different ideas or mental images (*Vorstellungen*), which on Frege's account are subjective entities. Dummett (1980, pp. 85–6) shows decisively that Frege's positive position on coloring is untenable, so I will spend no time on it. For Frege's *logical* purposes, the phenomenon was merely a nuisance that could be ignored; but anyone interested in providing a semantic theory for a natural language will, at some point, be forced to say something about the contributions made by the sorts of words Frege pushed aside to the meanings of sentences that contain them.

I want briefly to look at what Frege says about compositionality before saying more about coloring. A declarative sentence, for Frege, refers to a truth-value—Truth or Falsity—and has as its sense a "thought" (*Gedanke*). (Whether truth-values are objects is of no importance to present concerns.) Church (1943), Gödel (1944), and others have claimed to see in Frege's work at least the glimmer of an argument to the effect that there is no viable alternative to the view that if sentences refer, then there is a unique entity to which every true sentence refers and a unique and distinct entity to which every false sentence refers. Russell (1918) and others have found something repugnant in at least the idea that every true sentence stands for the same thing. According to Russell, a true sentence stands for a *fact,* and there are meant to be many distinct facts. In a similar vein, many philosophers view sentences, whether true or false, as standing for *propositions,* and there are meant to be many more than two propositions.

It is unclear whether Frege (1892, pp. 62–5) provides anything that should be viewed as a deductive argument for the thesis that the reference of a sentence is a truth-value; but he does juggle a number of interconnected logical and epistemological points in ways that make the thesis attractive, or at least palatable. The formal arguments that Church and Gödel produce cannot be found in Frege's work; but it is not difficult to see Frege's influence on these arguments, largely through the *Principle of Composition:* the reference of an expression is determined by the references of its parts and their syntax (*mutatis mutandis* for sense).

The referent of a singular term is its bearer, that of a sentence its truth-value. The syntax and references of other major categories are functions of those of singular terms and sentences. Suppose, for the moment, that we have just singular terms, one-place sentence connectives (e.g., 'it-is-not-the-case-that'), two-place sentence connectives (e.g., 'and' and 'but'), and intransitive verbs (e.g., 'smile').

Syntax. The notation of categorial grammar serves well here, where S is the category *sentence* and N the category *singular term*. A one-place sentence connective is of the syntactic category S/S (a device that combines with a sentence to form another sentence); a two-place connective is of the category S/(S,S) (a device that combines with a pair of sentences to form a sentence); an intransitive verb is of the category S/N (a device that combines with a singular term to form a sentence).

Reference. Sentence connectives refer to truth-functions: a one-place connective refers to a function from sentence referents to sentence referents, i.e., a function from truth-values to truth-values: $V \rightarrow V$; a two-place connective such as 'and' or 'but' refers to a function from pairs of sentences referents to sentence referents, i.e., a function of the form $<V,V> \rightarrow V$; an intransitive verb (effectively a one-place predicate) refers to a function from singular term referents to sentence referents, i.e., a function from objects to truth-values: $O \rightarrow V$.

Matters get slightly more interesting when transitive verbs are added. In logic, it is common to treat transitive verbs as two-place predicates. On such an account a transitive verb is of the category S/(N,N) and refers to a function from ordered pairs of objects to truth-values: $<O,O> \rightarrow V$. But linguistic theory will have none of this: it treats a transitive verb and its direct object as a sentence constituent (a verb phrase), i.e., as an expression of the category S/N. On such an account, a transitive verb is of the category (S/N)/N and refers to a function from objects to functions from objects to truth-values: $O \rightarrow (O \rightarrow V)$.

Excitement begins once sentential verbs (e.g., 'believe' and 'say') are thrown into the pot: Frege's Principle of Composition *seems* to be threatened. A sentential verb appears to be of the category (S/N)/S—an expression that combines with a sentence to form a verb phrase—and should therefore refer to a function from truth-values to functions from objects to truth-values: $V \rightarrow (O \rightarrow V)$. But this seems wrong. 'Plato' and 'Aristocles' refer to the same man, so (7) and (8) have the same truth-value:

(7) Aristocles is wealthy
(8) Plato is wealthy.

But (9) and (10) need not have the same truth-value:

(9) Socrates believes Aristocles is wealthy
(10) Socrates believes Plato is wealthy.

This looks like a problem for Frege because (10) appears to differ from (9) only in the replacement of parts with the same reference (viz. sentences (7) and (8), which have the same truth value).

But the way Frege proceeds, the Principle of Composition remains intact. There is an important disanalogy between transitive verbs and sentential verbs. The verb 'like' takes as its complement the sort of expression that refers to an object;[1] this comports with the intuitive idea that things liked are objects. The verb 'believe' takes a sentence as its complement (on Frege's account), and a sentence is the sort of expression that refers to a truth-value. This would seem to lead to the thoroughly *counterintuitive* idea that things believed are truth-values. Frege wanted to capture the idea that things believed are *thoughts,* i.e., the sorts of things that are the *senses* rather than the references of sentences. And so he reaches the position that a sentence subordinate to a verb like 'believe' has as its reference, in such a linguistic environment, its customary sense (i.e., the sense it would have if it were unembedded). And since (7) and (8) do not have the same sense—they contain parts that differ in sense, viz. 'Aristocles' and 'Plato'—substituting one for the other as the complement of 'believe' need not preserve reference (truth-value) of the whole, i.e., (9) and (10) can differ in truth-value.[2] In short, the Principle of Composition still holds good, but a *second,* antecedently plausibly, principle has now been rejected. It might be thought reasonable to assume that the reference of an unambiguous expression does not depend on the surrounding linguistic environment. This assumption is often called the *Principle of Semantic Innocence* after a famous remark of Davidson's:

> Since Frege, philosophers have become hardened to the idea that content sentences in talk about propositional attitudes may strangely refer to such entities as intensions, propositions, sentences, utterances, and inscriptions. . . . If we could but recover our pre-Fregean semantic innocence, I think it would be plainly incredible that the words "the earth moves," uttered after the words "Galileo said that," mean anything different, or refer to anything else, than is their wont when they come in other environments. No doubt their role in *oratio obliqua* is some sense special; but that is another story. Language is the instrument it is because the same expression, with semantic features (meaning) unchanged, can serve countless purposes. (1984, p. 108)

Frege has abandoned Semantic Innocence and thereby saved the Principle of Composition. In this he was followed by (e.g.) Church; but the price has seemed exorbitant, and many able philosophers have attempted to construct semantic theories that respect both Semantic Innocence and the Principle of Composition.

A third principle that has loomed large in recent semantic investigations is the *Principle of Direct Reference* (DR). In connection with a singular term *a,* this principle holds that the referent of *a* is the only thing associated with it that is relevant to determining the proposition expressed by an utterance of a sentence containing *a,* and so the only thing associated with *a* that is relevant to determining the truth-value of an utterance of a sentence containing *a.* From the fact that Frege accepts the Principle of Composition in connection with sense as well as reference, it follows that he rejects the Principle of Direct Reference: the *sense* of the unembedded sentence 'Plato is wealthy' serves as its *reference* when embedded in (e.g.) 'Socrates thinks that Plato is wealthy', and this sense depends upon the customary sense of 'Plato'. So Frege and Church propose theories that are

(11) +Composition
      –Semantic Innocence
      –Direct Reference.[3]

Non-Fregeans have discussed the extent to which it possible, and desirable, to construct semantic theories that respect two or three of these principles; for example, some of those of a Russellian leaning have suggested that taking the reference of a sentence to be a structured proposition (rather than a truth-value) is a first step towards the construction of such a theory. I propose to shelve traditional worries about Semantic Innocence and Direct Reference until we have thought more about the relationship between utterances and the propositions they are thought to express (whether of a Fregean or a Russellian nature); but I want to push on with the Principle of Composition for a moment by returning to the matter of *why* sentences should refer to truth-values on Frege's account. This will give us a better handle on Frege's notion of thought identity and open up the way to a final rejection of the idea that linguistic expressions have Fregean senses.

Since reference is subject to the Principle of Composition, the reference of a sentence, says Frege,

> ... must remain unchanged when a part of the sentence is replaced by an expression with the same reference. ... What feature except the truth-value can be found that belongs to ... sentences quite generally and remains unchanged by substitutions of the kind just mentioned? (1892, pp. 64–5)

This passage appears to admit of two interpretations. On one, Frege appears to be suggesting that if the reference of a sentence can be altered only by replacing one of its parts *x* by an expression that does not have the same reference as *x,* then, all true sentences have the same reference, and similarly all false ones. On the other interpretation, he appears to be suggesting that, given the same condition, the reference of a sentence must be a truth-value because the truth-value of a sentence is the only *semantically relevant entity* associated with a sentence that survives all substitutions of coreferential expressions. Perhaps the latter reading is supported by the fact that in the next paragraph Frege gives us the following conditional:

> If now the truth-value of a sentence is its reference, then on the one hand all true sentences have the same reference and so, on the other hand, do all false sentences. (1892, p. 65)

Let us assume, with Frege, that sentences *do* refer and see if we might find ourselves pointed in the direction of the idea that truth-values serve as their references by other features of Frege's theory. On Frege's account, two singular terms, e.g., 'Hesperus' and 'Phosphorus', might agree in reference yet differ in sense, a fact that he exploits in explaining various semantic puzzles. On the assumption that the Principle of Composition applies to both reference and sense, two sentences agreeing in reference could still differ in sense. However, on the Fregean assumption that sense determines reference (that reference is a function of sense) two sentences cannot agree in sense yet differ in reference.

Question: What does it take for two sentences to agree in sense, to express the same thought? In a letter to Edmund Husserl written on October 30 and November 1, 1906, Frege says that

> In logic one must decide to regard equipollent propositions as differing only according to form. After the assertoric force with which they have been uttered is subtracted, equipollent propositions have something in common in their content, and this is what I call the thought they express. This alone is of concern to logic. The rest I call the coloring and the illumination of the thought. (p. 67)

This naturally leads one to ask for a precise characterization of equipollence, for the criterion of identity of thought that Frege has in mind when he declares that (1)–(3) have the same sense and that (4)–(6) have the same sense. The clearest statement of Frege's view on this matter comes in another letter to Husserl, written on December 9, 1906 in response to two letters (now lost) that Husserl had written in response to the letter quoted from above. Frege appears to suggest the following criterion for identifying thoughts: for any two sentences A and B, if (i) '$A \bullet \neg B$' and '$\neg A \bullet B$' can *both* be shown to be contradictions using only "purely logical laws" (and without relying on knowledge of the truth-value of either sentence), and (ii) neither A nor B contains a logically "self-evident" sentence as a part, then A and B have the same sense.[4] *Modulo* the prohibition on "self-evident" subsentences, Frege seems to be fairly close to making the suggestion that sentences which are "logically equivalent"—at least syntactically speaking—have the same sense (and hence the same reference). So given the Principle of Composition, we find ourselves heading in the direction of idea that in nonoblique contexts (a) *coreferring singular terms* may be substituted for one another without altering the reference of the whole and (b) *logically equivalent sentences* may be substituted for one another without altering the reference of the whole. If this were established, it would not, of course, establish that there are only two possible references for a sentence; rather it would scream out for an argument from the premiss that the substitution of neither coreferring singular terms nor logically equivalent sentences can affect the reference of a sentence, to the conclusion that there are just two possible references for a sentence. It is just this sort of argument that Church and Gödel present (although there is no evidence to suggest either was moved by the discussion in Frege's letter to Husserl). From the soundness of such arguments it would still not follow that the possible references of a sentence are Truth and Falsity: any two distinct things would do, for example the numbers 0 and 1. However, truth-values would have an obvious appeal, if only for the reason that an adequate Principle of Composition would very likely dictate that a sentence lacks a reference if one of its parts lacks a reference, and taking truth-values to be the references of sentences squares nicely with the (almost) pretheoretic idea that a sentence lacks a *truth-value* if one of its parts lacks a reference. (Frege scouts other considerations, but they do not bear on any of the points I wish to make here.)

It is now a commonplace of philosophy that we must distinguish between what a sentence means and what a particular dated utterance of that sentence expresses. The distinction seems obvious once we notice the role of context-sensitive expressions such as 'I', 'this', 'present', 'now', and so on. I take it we would not be much moved by the claim that the existence of such expressions undermines principles of Semantic Innocence and Composition. As far as the former is concerned, the claim would involve confusing *context* and *environment,* i.e., the context of an utterance of an expression ϕ and the linguistic, structural environment in which ϕ occurs. With regard to the latter, it is hard to see how the claim might be defended without the presentation of a set of rather odd strictures on compositional semantic theories. The linguistic meaning of 'I am here now' is determined by, and only by, the meanings of the lexical items of which it is composed and the syntactic structure that here holds them together. In theory, what a particular dated utterance of the sentence expresses can be determined by following a set of instructions associated with the individual lexical items and projecting the results in accordance with instructions associated with the syntax (the notion of sentence meaning will thus drop out as epiphenomenal).

What makes 'I', 'here', and 'now' relatively easy is that straightforward linguistic rules can be assigned to them (e.g., an utterance of 'I' refers to the person producing it). But words like 'next', 'previous', and 'contemporary' seem to require instructions with broader possibilities, as do third person pronouns, which may or not be anaphoric on other noun phrases. Matters become more complex when we turn to, for example, the possessive marker. When I use the description 'Tom's horse' the precise relation I have in mind between Tom and a particular horse—the horse he owns, the horse he is riding, the horse he has backed in the Cheltenham Gold Cup . . .—does not appear to be fixed by a linguistic rule associated with the possessive, but rather by contextual factors. Examples due to Searle (1975), Sperber and Wilson (1986), Carston (1988), force more or less the same issue. Searle asks us to compare 'I have cut the cake', 'I have cut my fingernails', and 'I have cut the grass', (with a knife, nail clippers, or a lawnmower?); Sperber and Wilson ask us to compare 'I have had breakfast' and 'I have been to Tibet' (different temporal domains are needed for proper understanding); Carston asks us to compare cases in which 'and' delivers logical conjunction and something stronger (e.g., temporal or causal connection). The morals that are very rightly drawn from such examples are (i) that linguistic meaning radically underdetermines the proposition expressed, and (ii) that the same sorts of principles that play a role in theories of pragmatic implications (such as Grice's conversational implicatures or Sperber and Wilson's contextual implications) and nonliteral meaning ought to have an equally important role in theories that purport to characterize the proposition, or propositions straightforwardly expressed by an utterance. To the best of my knowledge, no one has presented a good reason to think that these facts threaten Composition or Semantic Innocence.

§3. Truth, Sense, and Contrast

For Frege's logical purposes, unlike the distinction between sense and reference, the distinction between sense and coloring could be ignored. But a number of facts conspire to make coloring, whatever it is, more semantically interesting than one might initially suppose.

(i) As Strawson (1952) and Grice (1961, 1989) observe, there are many rather ordinary words—some of which are of philosophical utility—that give rise to the problems associated with coloring: 'therefore', 'consequently', 'so', 'since', 'still', 'yet', 'even', 'although', 'but', 'moreover', 'furthermore', 'besides', 'indeed', 'nevertheless', 'unfortunately', 'arguably', and one of philosophers' favorites: 'obviously'. Arguably, the purported two-place connectives in this list make the same contribution to truth conditions as 'and'; and the unary connectives make no contribution to truth-conditional content at all (rather like multiplying a number by 1).[5] It would seem, then, that an adequate semantic theory for English should include something to supplement a theory of (e.g.) truth conditions. Furthermore, even a theory of Fregean senses must be supplemented by this something. A semantic theory that fails to account for coloring fails to treat a host of common sentence connectives. It will not do to say that coloring is a "merely pragmatic" phenomenon: it concerns *the meanings of individual words.* Anyone who antecedently delimits semantics to individual specifications of truth-conditional content or even to individual specifications of Fregean senses is guilty of an *ad hoc* dismissal of a range of semantic data (perhaps on the grounds that his or her theory cannot accommodate it).

(ii) It has been argued by Strawson (1952) and others that there are grounds for doubting that the semantics assigned to the truth-functional connectives '&', 'v', and '⊃' can be used to characterize the semantics of the English connectives 'and', 'or', and 'if . . . then' in an unadorned way. Grice has shown that the problems are not, perhaps, quite as severe as Strawson once supposed; but there are problems nonetheless. If we can better explicate the workings of 'but', although', 'so', 'therefore' and so on, we might find ourselves with a better perspective on the semantics of 'and', 'or', and 'if . . . then'.

(iii) The existence of coloring poses a problem for Griceans interested in providing an analysis of the philosophically important notion of *what is said* (i.e., an analysis of the form "by uttering *x*, *U* said that *p* iff . . .") in terms of what is *meant* (i.e., by means of a locution of the form "by uttering *x, U* meant that *p*"). Grice himself was painfully aware of the difficulty this created for his own program, but gave only hints as to how he might be tempted to address it, hints that I shall take up later.

(iv) Neo-Russellians about propositions have suggested individuating propositions in virtue of the objects and properties that are their components; and these entities are simply those that are supplied by a theory of *reference.* Since 'ϕ and ψ' and 'ϕ but ψ' do not differ in reference, neither do 'and' and 'but'. They refer to the same function from pairs of truth-values to truth-values.

(v) Neo-Fregeans about propositions have suggested individuating propositions in virtue of the entities supplied by a theory of *sense.* Since 'ϕ and ψ' and 'ϕ but ψ' do not differ in sense (for Frege, at least), this puts further pressure on the Neo-Fregeans to say something about the relationship between lexical items and senses.

(vi) As Frege observes, the case of the connectives 'and' and 'but' seems to have something interesting in common with cases involving pairs of general terms with the same sense (e.g., 'horse' and 'steed'; 'physician' and 'doctor'). Pairs of words one of whose members has pejorative connotations provide further examples (e.g., 'German' and 'Kraut').

By shifting the initial stage of our investigations from singular terms to sentence connectives, we might end up shedding new light on the substitution puzzles Frege brought to our attention and on other problems involving singular terms.

Let us return to the sentence connective 'but'. In some very ordinary and intuitive sense, the following sentences differ in meaning:

(1) She is poor but she is honest
(2) She is poor and she is honest.

As Frege would put it, (1) and (2) differ in coloring despite agreeing in sense (and reference). Since 'but' and 'and' are perfectly good words of English, the contributions they make to the meanings of sentences containing them ought to be characterized by a compositional semantics for English. We are concerned with the meanings of *individual words,* so it simply will not do to say that this is a matter for pragmatics and hence of no concern to semantics. Such a position is as irresponsible as the position that the problems raised by the substitution of coreferring singular terms in propositional attitude contexts are of concern only to the theory of sense, or only to pragmatics. Singular terms and sentence connectives are perfectly respectable citizens of the linguistic world; they have conventional meanings and contribute to the meanings of sentences containing them. So the question arises how, precisely, are we to characterize the difference between 'and' and 'but' within a semantic theory.

Suppose we put the following question to those who would construe a theory of meaning for a language as a recursively structured truth theory for that language: What form should an appropriate truth-theoretic axiom for 'but' take? Suppose (3) is an appropriate truth-theoretic axiom for 'and':

(3) s satisfies 'ϕ and ψ' iff s satisfies ϕ and s satisfies ψ

where 's' ranges over sequences and 'ϕ' and 'ψ' range over formulae (initially placed quantifiers $(\forall s)(\forall \phi)(\forall \psi)$ will be assumed throughout).

How do we obtain an appropriate axiom for 'but'? Do we simply replace the object-language occurrence of 'and' on the left-hand side of this biconditional by 'but'? Or must we also replace the metalanguage occurrence on the right-hand side? (The same question can be asked about an axiom for 'although', assuming that 'although ϕ, ψ' has the same truth conditions as 'ϕ and ψ'.)

An answer to this question is often suggested by those wish to view truth theories through Fregean eyes. McDowell (1977) distinguishes between the reference and the sense of an expression and suggests that the distinction can do some work in a truth theory capable of serving as a theory of meaning. According to McDowell, although (4) is an appropriate axiom for 'Hesperus', (5) is not:

(4) Ref('Hesperus', s) = Hesperus
(5) Ref('Hesperus', s) = Phosphorus.

Since 'Hesperus' and 'Phosphorus' are names of the same object, (4) and (5) are both true. But according to McDowell, there is an important difference.

> The role played by [an axiom for a name], in the derivation of assignments of truth conditions to sentences in which the name occurs, would *display* [my italics, SN] the contribution made by that name to those truth conditions. . . . such a clause, considered as having what it says fixed by its location in a theory which yields acceptable content-specifications, gives—or more strictly, in that context as good as gives—the sense of the name. (p. 143)

The problem with (5), as McDowell sees it, is that although it gets the referent of 'Hesperus' right, unlike (4) it cannot find a place in a theory of truth that is to serve as a theory of sense, at least not if it is supposed to be a theory, knowledge of which would suffice for understanding the language. McDowell concludes that

> [w]hat we have here is a glimpse of the way in which, by requiring the theory's consequences to help us to make sense of speakers of the language, we force ourselves to select among the multiplicity of true theories of truth.

(4) "displays" the *sense* of 'Hesperus'; (5) does not.

I think McDowell is onto *something* here; but as it stands his suggestion cannot be generalized beyond the case of coreferential names to (e.g.) coreferential predicates or coreferential sentence connectives. The suggestion that (6) is an appropriate axiom for 'but' because it displays the sense of the word in a way that (7) does not is of no value:

(6) *s* satisfies 'φ but ψ' iff *s* satisfies φ but *s* satisfies ψ
(7) *s* satisfies 'φ but ψ' iff *s* satisfies φ and *s* satisfies ψ.

Like the names 'Hesperus' and 'Phosphorus', the connectives 'and' and 'but' are coreferential (they refer to the same truth-function). Thus sentences 'φ and ψ' and 'φ but ψ' are coreferential. But according to Frege they also express the same thought, i.e., they have the same sense. So the right-hand sides of the axioms given in (6) and (7) share a sense (unlike the axioms given in (4) and (5)). And since the 'iff' of the truth-theoretic axioms McDowell is examining is truth-functional, neither (6) nor (7) *displays* the sense of 'but' any better than the other. (Moreover, on Frege's account, the difference in coloring between 'and' and 'but' serves only to conjure up different *Vorstellungen,* which on his account are subjective entities.) All of this suggests there is little to be gained by slimming down the range of acceptable truth theories by appealing to Fregean senses. However, I suspect that proper names have a semantic quality that justifies something very like McDowell's suggestion that (4) is a better axiom than (5), and I shall say something about this later.

§4. Frege: Complex Sentences and Multiple Thoughts

In the second half of "On Sense and Reference" Frege examines a variety of complex sentences in connection with the Principle of Compositionality, which entails that "the truth-value of a sentence containing another sentence as a part must remain unchanged when the part is replaced by another sentence having the same truth-value" (1892, p. 65). We have seen already how Frege accounts for apparent exceptions involving sentences subordinate to sentential verbs like 'say', hear', and 'thinks': the subordinate sentence refers to a thought (its customary sense) rather than a truth-value (its customary reference). Thus Frege abandons Semantic Innocence.

Frege's analyses of other complex sentences have received less attention. This is regrettable as they contain deep insights, foreshadow a number of contributions of more recent vintage, and contain the germ of an idea that I think can be exploited to great effect, the idea that a simple sentence may express more than one thought. As a way of clarifying what is at stake and softening up the terrain, consider the following:

(1) Napoleon, who recognized the danger to his right flank, personally led his guards against the enemy position.

According to Frege, this sentence expresses two thoughts (in certain contexts):

(2) Napoleon personally led his guards against the enemy position
(3) Napoleon recognized the danger to his right flank.[6]

There are two points worthy of note here. First, on this account the subordinate clause, like the main clause, expresses a complete thought and refers to a truth-value (its customary reference), making it quite different from a clause subordinate to a sentential verb. Second, Frege seems to think that if two thoughts are expressed they must stand to one another as conjuncts of a conjunction, witness his remark that someone asserting (1) says something false if either (2) or (3) is false. But this is not the only way one might proceed here; one might hold that (1) expresses a *sequence* (of two) thoughts, i.e., the one expressed by (2) as in some sense a "primary thought" with the one expressed by (3) piggy-backing via the injection of a subordinate clause into a preexisting sentence. On such an account, the falsity of only one of (2) and (3) would render an utterance of (1) partly true and partly false: a sequence of thoughts is not the right sort of thing to be true or false *simpliciter,* but it is the sort of thing to *contain* things that are true or false. There might not seem to be any sort of serious issue here as far as (1) is concerned; but there are, I think, constructions in which the contrast between conjunctions and sequences is more significant.

At one point Frege briefly examines the idea that in some contexts the analysis of (1) just presented may be inadequate, that a *third* thought is in the air. Sometimes a subordinate clause does not have a "simple sense":

> Almost always, it seems, we connect with the main thoughts expressed by us subsidiary thoughts which, although not expressed, are associated with our words, in accordance with psychological laws, by the hearer. And since the subsidiary thought appears to be connected with our words on its own account, almost like the main thought itself, we want it also to be expressed. The sense of the sentence is thereby enriched and it may well happen that we have more simple thoughts than clauses. In many cases the sentence must be understood in this way, in others it may be doubtful whether the subsidiary thought belongs to the sense of the sentence or only accompanies it. (1892, p. 75)

There is much here that seems to presage important work by Grice (1961, 1989) on *implicature* and Sperber and Wilson (1986) on *explicature.* As far as example (1) is concerned, Frege's point is that it is at least arguable that in some contexts it expresses not only the thoughts expressed by (2) and (3), but also the thought that "the knowledge of the danger was the reason [Napoleon] led the guards against the enemy position" (1892, p. 75). Frege is inclined to think that the third thought is "just lightly suggested" rather than expressed. Suppose Napoleon's decision to lead the guards against the enemy position had been made before he recognized the danger to his right flank. Frege's intuition is that this would be insufficient to render (1) false and so he concludes that the third thought is not expressed by the sentence. "The alternative" he goes on, "would make for a complicated situation: We would have more simple thoughts than clauses." (1892, p. 75). It is just this sort of complication that forms the basis of the semantic framework I want to construct; however, I am inclined to agree with Frege that in this particular case the "complication" is unnecessary: the thoughts expressed by (2) and (3) exhaust the sense of (1).

Among the devices of subordination that Frege discusses are those used to introduce talk about causes or explanations ('because', 'since', 'as'), those used to talk about temporal order ('after', 'before'), and those used to talk counterfactually. It will suffice to mention just one of these:

(4) Because ice is less dense than water, it floats on water.

Frege begins by saying that (4) appears to express three thoughts, those expressed by the following:

(5) Ice is less dense than water
(6) If anything is less dense than water, it floats on water
(7) Ice floats on water.

He then says that "[t]he third thought, however, need not be explicitly introduced, since it is contained in the remaining two" (1892, p. 76). The idea here seems to be that since (7) is *derivable* from (5) and (6) using logical laws alone, it is enough to say that (4) expresses the thoughts expressed by (5) and (6). He concludes that the subordinate clause 'because ice is less dense than water' expresses the thought expressed by (5) "as well as part of" the thought expressed by (6). And this is meant to explain the non-truth-functional nature of (4):

> This is how it comes to pass that our subsidiary clause cannot be simply replaced by another of equal truth-value; for this would alter our second thought and thereby might well alter its truth-value. (1892, p. 77)

There is potential and actual confusion here. The occurrence of the pronoun 'it' in (4) does not seem to be essential to Frege's point; so let us replace 'it' by 'ice' and avoid distracting issues about cross-clausal anaphora. One component of Frege's proposal seems to be the idea that the main clause 'ice floats on water' does not *in this construction* express a complete thought, the argument for this being that the thought one might be tempted to see it expressing—the one expressed by (7)—is already contained in two other thoughts the entire sentence expresses, viz. those expressed by (5) and (6). A second component is the idea that the subordinate clause expresses a simple thought—the one expressed by (5). The final component is the idea that the subordinate clause and the main clause *together* express a second thought—the one expressed by (6). So we see Frege hanging onto the Principle of Compositionality by giving up Semantic Innocence again. *In this linguistic environment* the clause subordinated is not restricted to expressing a single thought (its customary sense) for "the sense of a part of the subordinate clause may likewise be a component of another thought" (1892, p. 78). Thus Frege concludes that

> It follows with sufficient probability from the foregoing that the cases where a subordinate clause is not replaceable by another of the same truth-value

cannot be brought in disproof of our view that a truth-value is the meaning of
a sentence that has a thought as its sense. (1892, p. 78)

It appears to be Frege's view, then, that whenever there is a threat to the
claim that the reference of a sentence is a truth-value it will come from a
sentence involving subordination and that in such cases either (i) the subordinate sentence refers to its customary sense (as in the case of a sentence
subordinated to a sentential verb), or (ii) the subordinate sentence refers
to its customary reference (i.e., a truth-value) "but is not restricted to so
doing, in as much as its sense includes one thought and part of another"
(1892, p. 77).

There is much more that could be said about Frege's discussion of subordination, which has not attracted as much attention as it deserves. It is
the idea of sentences expressing more than one thought that I find appealing, and I want to use it (i) to provide an account of coloring, (ii) to under-
cut the need for Fregean senses, (iii) to deal with some residual puzzles
about sentence connectives, and (iv) to approach problems about substitution, identity, and the contingent *a priori*. Moreover, I wish to accomplish
this while holding on to both Semantic Innocence and the Principle of
Composition. The remainder of this paper is a series of steps in the direction I take to be most fruitful. As I move away from Frege, I shall switch
from talk about *thoughts* to talk about *propositions,* leaving it open, for the
time being, whether such entities should be viewed as Fregean thoughts or
as Russellian complexes (of objects and properties).

§5. Strawson: Logical Particles and Stylistic Variants

The idea that expressions of natural language have an exact semantics that
can be captured using the devices of classical logic was attacked compre-
hensively by Strawson (1950, 1952), whose first target was Russell's (1905)
Theory of Descriptions. It is a part of the meaning of 'the *F*', Strawson originally claimed, that such an expression is used correctly only if there is an
F. If this condition is not satisfied—if the "presupposition" that there is an
F is false, as he later put it—a use of e.g., 'the *F* is *G*' cannot be considered
to express a proposition that is either true or false. (My wording here is
supposed to be neutral between (a) a proposition is expressed but it is neither true nor false, and (b) no proposition is expressed at all. Strawson is
not consistent on this matter.) So we must reject the view, perhaps borrowed from classical logic, that every use of an indicative sentence involves
the expression of a truth or a falsehood, says Strawson. In particular, we
must reject Russell's Theory of Descriptions, according to which the proposition expressed by a sentence of the form 'the *F* is *G*' is the general proposition that there is exactly one *F* and every *F* is *G*.

According to Strawson, someone uttering a sentence of the form '*p* or *q*' will standardly be taken to imply that he has non–truth-functional grounds for the assertion, i.e., he will standardly be taken to imply that he does not know which of *p* and *q* is true. Impressed by this observation, Strawson concludes that an utterance of '*p* or *q*' in which this condition is not satisfied involves a misuse of language. It is, in some sense, *part of the meaning* of '*p* or *q*', that such a locution is used correctly only if the speaker does not know that *p* is true and does not know that *q* is true. If this condition is not satisfied, the utterance is defective (on its strongest interpretation, the utterance cannot be taken to express a truth). So it would be a mistake to suppose that the meaning of the English word 'or' is given by the semantics of the logical particle 'v'; the semantics of 'v' is *stipulated* by the logician to be truth-functional, but the semantics of the word 'or' is determined by actual linguistic practice (use), which does not square with the logician's truth-functional analysis. (Similar points are made in connection with utterances of the form 'ϕ and ψ', where the speaker is taken to imply that the event described by ϕ *preceded* the event described by ψ, or even that the former *caused* the latter.)

Strawson also has a few things to say about expressions for which logicians have not attempted to provide formal analyses. From a logical point of view, says Strawson, 'provided that', 'given that', and 'under the condition that' are "mere stylistic variants" of 'if'; while 'also' and 'in addition' are stylistic variants of 'and'. But Strawson claims that 'but', 'although', and 'nevertheless' are *not* mere stylistic variants of 'and', and that the implications they engender fall outside the logician's net:

> Their use implies at least that there is some element of contrast between the conjoined statements or attributes; and, sometimes, that the conjunction is unusual or surprising. But this kind of implication, though it must not be neglected when we are discussing the meanings of words, is not readily expressible in terms of an entailment- or inconsistency-rule. (1952, p. 48)

Strawson does not mention Frege, but he implicitly concurs that whatever 'but', 'although', and 'nevertheless' contribute to sentences, it is not something that can be captured in terms of logical implication. But what exactly is Strawson's positive position? He says that,

> If a man said 'although she is kind, she is gentle', we should be surprised and think that he had made some kind of mistake of language (perhaps that he didn't know what 'kind' meant); but we should not say that he was being inconsistent or that he had contradicted himself. (1952, p. 48)

This passage reveals Strawson's own particular ordinary language approach to meaning. The speaker's mistake in the example is insufficient to render the utterance false or without truth-value. So the linguistic transgression must pertain to some speech act other than the assertions that the speaker is making (viz. that she is kind and that she is gentle). It is an explicit version of this idea that Grice (1961, 1989) proposes.

§6. Grice: Higher-order Speech Acts

Grice's work contains scattered discussions of coloring (but no reference to the brief remarks made by Frege and Strawson). "The vital clue" for dealing with the phenomenon, Grice suggests, is " . . . that speakers may be at one and the same time engaged in performing speech acts at different but related levels." (1989, p. 362). It is this idea that shapes the framework I want to explore.

Notoriously, Grice disagrees with Strawson about the semantics of the English words 'and', 'or', 'if', 'every', 'a', and 'the': the formal devices capture the essence of their meanings. The implications that Strawson latched onto, Grice suggests, although very common, are *not* determined by linguistic conventions governing the use of 'or' and 'and'; they are *conversational implicatures,* context-dependent, pragmatic implications that do not contribute to what the speaker *says* (in Grice's technical sense), which is to say they do not impinge upon the *truth-conditions* of utterances containing them. (Both what is said and what is conversationally implicated should be regarded as propositional in nature). That these non-truth-functional implications attaching to utterances containing 'and', 'or', and 'if . . . then' are conversational implicatures is meant to be borne out by (i) the fact that they can be canceled without fear of linguistic transgression (e.g., without fear of contradiction), (ii) the fact that the presence and content of such an implication can be explained by appeal to Grice's Cooperative Principle and maxims of conversation (themselves explained by a philosophical psychology), and (iii) the "fact" that the same implication would arise in a language for which the semantics of 'and' and 'or' are given explicitly by the truth-tables for '&' and 'v'.[7] (Similar points are meant to hold in connection with 'if', 'every', 'a', and 'the'.)

For Grice, such implications are different in kind from those attaching to utterances of sentences containing words like 'but', 'yet', 'although', 'whereas', 'so', 'therefore', 'moreover', and 'furthermore'. The latter class Grice calls *conventional* implicatures: they are determined, at least in part, by the linguistic conventions governing the uses of the words in questions. In short, unlike conversational implicatures, conventional implicatures have a genuinely semantic dimension. They do not bear on what speakers *say* (on the truth conditions of utterances), says Grice; but they are not (mere) *conversational* implicatures because they are not cancelable without linguistic transgression and depend for their existence not just upon

facts about context and rational interaction (as embodied in the Cooperative Principle and maxims) but also upon the presence of *those very words
themselves,* used with their conventional meanings, rather than words that
are equivalent in respect of their contributions to the truth-conditions of
utterances. As Grice puts it, what is implicated in such cases is implicated
(at least in part) *by virtue of the words used.*

A speaker's selection of 'but' over 'and' contributes in some way to the
generation of an implicature. This, in fact, forms the basis of Grice's proposal for distinguishing between conversational and conventional implicature: conversational implicatures are *non-detachable* in the following
sense: if one uses an expression φ and thereby conversationally implicates
that ψ, one will not be able find an alternative expression $φ'$ with which
one could have used and thereby said (e.g., stated) exactly what one actually said by uttering φ, that does not itself give rise to the same implicature.[8] In the case of 'but', says Grice, there are good grounds for suspect-
ing that the implicature in question is detachable, since in place of (1) one
could use (2),

(1) She is poor but she is honest
(2) She is poor and she is honest

and be saying the same thing; yet the implication of contrast between honesty and poverty (or her poverty and her honesty) would be lacking. In
short, we are meant to regard the implicature in question as somehow connected to a difference in meaning between 'and' and 'but'.[9]

A conventional implicature is not a *presupposition,* as originally characterized by Strawson (1952, p. 175) and adopted by others: *A* is a presupposition of *B,* just in case the truth or falsity of *B* requires the truth of *A.* (If
the truth of *B* requires the truth of *A,* but the falsity of *B* does not, *A* is an
entailment of *B*). Put another way, if *B* presupposes *A, B* lacks a truth value
if *A* is false. In the case of an utterance of (1), says Grice,

> . . . even if the implied proposition were false, i.e., if there were no reason in
> the world to contrast poverty with honesty either in general or in her case, the
> original statement could still be false; it would be false for example if she were
> rich and dishonest. One might perhaps be less comfortable about assenting to
> its truth if the implied contrast did not in fact obtain; but the possibility of fal-
> sity is enough for the immediate purpose. (1961, p. 127)

So the implication in question is not a presupposition, at least not on the
standard semantic conception of that notion.[10]

Grice proposes to handle conventional implicatures by supposing them
to stem from uses of conventional devices signaling the performance of

"higher-order" ("noncentral") speech acts parasitic upon the perfor-mance of "ground-floor" ("central") speech acts. The basic idea can be brought to life with one of Grice's examples, worth quoting in close to its entirety:

> If a man says "My brother-in-law lives on a peak in Darien; his great aunt, on the other hand, was a nurse in World War I," his hearer might well be some-what baffled; and if it should turn out on further inquiry that the speaker had in mind no contrast of any sort between his bother-in-law's residential location and the one time activities of his great aunt, one would be inclined to say that a condition conventionally signified by the presence of the phrase "on the other hand" was not in fact realized and so that the speaker had done violence to the conventional meaning of, indeed had misused, the phrase "on the other hand." But the nonrealization of this condition would also be regarded as in-sufficient to falsify the speaker's statement. . . .
>
> One part of what the . . . speaker is doing is making what might be called *ground-floor* statements about the brother-in-law and the great aunt, but at the same time he is performing these speech-acts he is also performing a higher-order speech-act of commenting in a certain way on the lower-order speech-acts. He is *contrasting* in some way the performance of some of these lower-order speech acts with others, and he signals his performance of this higher-order speech-act in his use of the embedded enclitic phrase, "on the other hand." The truth or falsity . . . of his words is determined by the relation of his ground-floor speech-acts to the world; consequently, while a certain kind of misperformance of the higher-order speech-act may constitute a semantic offense, it will not touch the truth-value . . . of the speaker's words. (1989, pp. 361–2)

Several questions are left open by these remarks. What constitutes a ground floor speech act? Are higher-order speech acts propositional in na-ture? Are higher-order speech acts meant to be comments on the contents of lower-order acts or on the acts themselves? How does a theory of higher-order speech acts work when simple sentences are embedded within larger sentences such as conjunctions, conditionals, and attitude re-ports? Will such a theory satisfy Principles of Composition and Semantic Innocence?

Within Grice's framework, there appear to be three types of ground floor ("central") speech act (acts of *saying* in his favored sense): *stating* that *p, asking* whether *p,* and (roughly) *enjoining* someone to make it the case that *p*. Presumably there is meant to be a broad range of higher-order ("noncentral") speech acts; Grice explicitly mentions *contrasting* (signaled by expressions such as 'on the other hand', 'but', 'yet, 'although', 'whereas', and 'despite the fact that'), *explaining* (signaled by expressions such as 'therefore', 'so', 'hence', 'thus', 'consequently', and 'as a result'), and *adding* (signaled by expressions such as 'furthermore', 'moreover', and 'additionally').

When Grice talks of conventional implicatures, he talks of them as if they are propositional in content, and hence candidates for truth or falsity. (At the same time the falsity of a conventional implicature is insufficient to render the utterance to which it attaches false.) Since conventional implicatures are meant to be analyzable in terms of higher-order speech acts, it is clear that such acts will have propositional contents on his account.

When he says that the speaker is performing a higher-order speech-act of "commenting in a certain way on the lower-order speech-acts" Grice seems to be leaving it open that the speaker could be commenting on the propositional contents of those speech acts or on the acts themselves. But his remark about "*contrasting* in some way the *performance* [my italics, SN] of some of these lower-order speech acts with others" suggests it is the acts themselves (perhaps the term "higher-order" speech act carries such an implication too).[11]

Getting two more of Grice's examples on the table, one involving *explaining* and another involving *contrasting,* will help to sharpen what is at issue here and lead the way into the framework I think we should explore. Grice claims that implications attaching to the use of 'therefore' in utterances of (3) and (4) are conventional implicatures analyzable as the products of higher-order speech acts of *explaining:*

(3) Bill is a philosopher; he is, therefore, brave
(4) Bill is a philosopher, therefore he is brave.[12]

According to Grice, someone who sincerely and nonironically utters (3) *says* that Bill is a philosopher, *says* that Bill is brave, but does *not* say that Bill's being brave follows from his being a philosopher. "The semantic function of the word 'therefore'," he claims, "is to enable a speaker to *indicate,* though not to *say,* that a certain consequence holds" (1989, p. 121). The falsity of the proposition that Bill's being brave follows from his being a philosopher is not sufficient, according to Grice, to render an utterance of (3) false; so it is (merely) a conventional implicature.

Some share Grice's intuition on this matter, others do not: according to McCawley (1993) the falsity of the connecting proposition renders an utterance of (3) false.[13] I am inclined to think that neither party has the full story here and that the divergent intuitions need to be explained rather than argued for. Indeed, I take the fact that intuitions differ to be important semantic data. According to the position that attracts me, Grice is right in thinking that an utterance of (3) is not equivalent to an utterance of the *conjunction* of (5)–(7) but wrong in thinking that the falsity of (7) cannot be sufficient to render and utterance of (3) false:

(5) Bill is a philosopher
(6) Bill is brave
(7) Bill's being brave follows from his being a philosopher.

Let us now move away from Grice's own terminology to talk of *propositions expressed*. (For present purposes, I shall not distinguish the locutions "*U*'s utterance of *X* expressed the proposition that *p*," "by his utterance of *X*, *U* expressed the proposition that *p*" and "relative to *U*'s utterance of it, *X* expressed the proposition that *p*." In a more serious exposition these would need to be separated. I will sometimes use the outrageous shorthand "*X* expresses the proposition that *p*.") For the moment, I want to appear agnostic about the nature of propositions; it will suffice to say that they have truth conditions. The leading idea here is that an utterance of (3) expresses a *sequence* (rather than a conjunction) of the three propositions expressed individually by (5)-(7), the expression of the third proposition in the sequence being parasitic upon the expression of the other two. The semantics of 'therefore' encodes the instructions that a first and a second proposition are to be seen as standing in some sort of consequence relation, the precise nature of which is no doubt determined contextually just as the precise relation between Tom and a particular horse is determined contextually when the noun phrase 'Tom's horse' is used. (To put matters back into Grice's language for a moment, although the *presence* and *shape* of a conventional implicature are signaled conventionally, the precise contents of at least some of those that are conceived as higher-order acts of *explaining*—those signaled by the presence of (e.g.) 'therefore', 'so', hence', etc.—may have to be worked out in much the same way that the contents of *conversational* implicatures are worked out, viz. by appeals to context and pragmatic principles such as those embodied in Grice's Cooperative Principle and maxims. This should occasion no surprise: it has been noted already that aspects of *what is said* (the content of a ground-floor speech act) must often be worked out in this way;[14] so there is nothing odd about those propositions serving as the contents of conventional implicatures having contextually determined dimensions.)

Intuitions about the truth-value of an utterance are a function of the perceived truth-values of the particular propositions that make it into the sequence of propositions expressed by that utterance. In situations in which the three propositions expressed by (5)–(7) are judged true, an utterance of (3) will be judged true; in situations in which the three propositions are judged false, the utterance will be judged false. If (5) and (6) are judged true, in many situations an utterance of (3) will be judged true even if (7) is judged false; but in certain circumstances it may be judged false because the alleged connection between being a philosopher and being brave, or the (contextually determined) nature of the connection, might be of such importance to the particular conversational context. I am inclined to think that Grice and McCawley had different sorts of contexts in mind and that this explains their conflicting intuitions. The following preliminary generalization suggests itself: an utterance is judged true (false) if and only if some contextually weighted number of the propositions it expresses are judged true (false).

Let us return now to 'but' and 'although'. On Grice's account, by uttering 'She is poor but she is honest' or 'although she is poor, she is honest', the speaker is performing *three* speech acts: he is *saying* that she is poor, *saying* that she is honest, and *contrasting* the two things he has said. (On the account I am attempting to motivate, the utterance expresses three propositions.) But what exactly does the higher-order act of *contrasting* involve? A cursory look at common examples indicates that it is not something that can be wrapped up succinctly. Dummett seems to be on the right track when he says, in his discussion of Frege's account of coloring, that

> [t]he word 'but' is used to hint that there is some contrast, relevant to the context, between the two halves of the sentence: no more can be said, in general, about what sort of contrast is hinted at. It is the indefiniteness of the contrast, and the vagueness of the notion of relevance, that resolve the mystery of the distinction between asserting and suggesting: while we should regard a man's use of 'but' as inappropriate if he was unable to mention a contrast we considered relevant, or genuine, examples of this kind can furnish no foundation for the view that we can assign any *definite* condition for the appropriateness rather than the truth of a statement. (1980, p. 86)

It is common to suppose that someone using 'but' or 'although' is always indicating, or suggesting, that he thinks the truth of one or other of the pair of sentences in the construction is surprising, unexpected, or remarkable given the truth of the other. But even this is too rigid: if someone were to claim that all poor people were dishonest, it would be perfectly acceptable to counter with the sentence 'Martha is poor but she is honest' thereby indicating one's refusal, or at least reluctance, to accept the other's claim of contrast. And sentences such as 'Volvos are safe but Porsches are fast', 'Porsches are fast but John won't get a speeding ticket', 'I prefer tea but my wife prefers coffee', 'Jones is tall but Smith is (even) taller' create further problems for too rigid an account of the contents of higher-order speech acts associated with uses of 'but'. (We see very clearly here that even though the *presence* and *shape* of a conventional implicature are signaled conventionally, the precise *contents* of those that are conceived as higher-order acts of *contrasting* may have to be worked out in much the same way that the contents of conversational implicatures are worked out, viz. by appeals to context and pragmatic principles.)[15]

In view of the position that is emerging, it is tempting at this point to revisit a controversial case of what Grice views as *conversational* implicature. According to the ambiguity theorist, 'and' has at least three distinct meanings—logical, temporal, and causal—exemplified in 'Bill is English and Joan is Welsh', 'Bill took off his boots and he got into bed', and 'the president entered the room and everyone stood up'. Grice, by contrast, views the temporal and causal implications attaching to utterances of these sentences as only conversational implicatures. Many people find that the aesthetic appeal of Grice's view is offset by a problem it seems to encounter in connection with the Principle of Composition. It is at least arguable that when a sentence of the form 'ϕ and ψ' is embedded in a larger sentence—e.g., when it serves as the antecedent or consequent of a conditional—the truth-value of the larger sentence might be sensitive to the temporal or causal implication that Grice sees as only conversational. Uncontroversial examples are, perhaps, not easy to find, but the following might help Grice's opponent. Let A and B be children, and let C be one of their parents. Now consider utterances of the following sentences:

(8) If B yells and A hits B, then C will punish A and B
(9) If A hits B and B yells, C will punish A and B.

It is arguable that (8) and (9) can differ in truth value. E.g., if C thinks that A should not be punished for a yelling induced by being hit, couldn't (9) be false even if (8) were true? If so, there would appear to be a problem for Grice. If something pertaining to the order of the proceedings described in the antecedents of (8) and (9) is only conversationally implicated, how is it possible for (8) and (9) to diverge in truth value? It looks as though Grice will have to say that a conversational implicature of the antecedent of a conditional somehow gets into the truth conditions of the conditional as a whole. And the unacceptability of this might suggest that Grice will have to concede that at least some occurrences of 'and' have a genuinely temporal (or causal) component.

Carston (1988) has come up with a story about 'and' that neither succumbs to the tentacles of the ambiguity theorist nor generates the compositional problem the official Gricean story faces. The meaning of 'and' is given by logical conjunction, but a hearer seeking a relevant interpretation will often construe the contents of the conjuncts as (e.g.) temporally sequenced or causally related. And if, for example, a temporally sequenced understanding of a subutterance of 'ϕ and ψ' is retrieved, it will be this (stronger) conjunction that forms the content of the antecedent of the full utterance 'if ϕ and ψ then χ.

Karttunen and Peters (1979) and Levinson (1983) point out that many more expressions than those discussed by Grice appear to generate conventional implicatures, e.g., 'even', 'still', 'yet', 'anyway', 'however', 'nevertheless', 'in fact', and 'besides'. (Levinson also argues that the 'tu'/'vous' distinction in French and a range of honorifics in, for example, Japanese, Korean, and Tamil are associated with conventional implicatures.) Frege, as we saw earlier, took (10) and (11) to have the same sense:

(10) Alfred has not arrived yet
(11) Alfred has not arrived.

On Grice's account, what someone says by uttering these sentences is the same (that Alfred has not arrived), but by uttering (11) he is also indicating or suggesting that someone (perhaps the speaker) expects Alfred to arrive (again, this is too narrow). In the framework I am trying to motivate, the content of the suggestion is a *second proposition expressed,* parasitic upon the ground-floor proposition (that Alfred has not arrived). The difference is, perhaps, not very interesting in many cases (including this one), but it may make for the construction of a more systematic compositional semantics overall.

Compare the following:

(12) Alfred cashed a check today
(13) Alfred managed to cash a check today
(14) Alfred succeeded in cashing a check today.

Someone who utters any of these says the same thing on Grice's view. But by uttering (13) or (14) the speaker performs a higher-order speech act of indicating that Alfred's cashing of a check today was something of a challenge, or less of a challenge than someone might have thought, or that there was some risk of failure (again, the precise content of this *conventionally signaled* implication may be determined contextually). On the view I am exploring, the speaker has again expressed two propositions, one parasitic on the other, something a compositional semantics needs to explain.

The phenomena noted by Frege, Grice, and others are, I think, quite natural once we take into account the nature of communication. We do not seek to transmit information only about the world; communication may also involve the transmission of information about our attitudes and emotions; thus we convey information using expressions such as 'It is raining' and also sentences such as 'Damn, it's raining', 'I think it's raining', and 'Damn, I think it's raining'. That is, in many cases we use simple sentences to express a single proposition and we use modifications of those sentences to express the original proposition (or its "negation," as in 'Alfred failed to cash a check today' and 'Alfred tried unsuccessfully to cash a check today') together with a second (third, . . .) proposition. I turn now to the idea that sequences of propositions expressed are not restricted to Fregean-Gricean examples of coloring, which may constitute only the tip of a semantic iceberg.[16]

§7. Multiple Propositions and Noun Phrases

In the vein in which we have been proceeding, let us suppose that an utterance of a sentence expresses an initial (ground floor) proposition that plays a part in the characterization of a second (third, . . .) proposition expressed by the same utterance in a *parasitic* or *dependent way,* a fact ultimately attributable to semantic features of lexical items. We need, I believe, to distinguish quite generally between ground-floor speech acts and those speech acts built upon the ground-floor, which may or may not be commentaries on the ground-floor speech act, and which may or may not carry the primary conversational burden.

There appear to be two types of meaningful noun phrase in natural language, *referring expressions* and *restricted quantifiers.* The former are used as the subjects of sentences, utterances of which express singular (object-dependent) propositions, the latter as the subjects of sentences, utterances of which express general (object-independent) propositions. Let us look briefly at those NPs that occur in the singular.

(i) The class of *singular referring expressions* (singular terms) contains proper names ('Hesperus', 'Plato', and so on) as well as the simple (i.e., semantically unstructured) indexicals 'I' and 'you', the simple demonstratives 'this' and 'that', and the pronouns 'he' and 'she' (when used either as demonstratives or as anaphors that inherit their references from other singular referring expressions). For a moment, let us assume, following Kripke and Kaplan, that these expressions all refer rigidly. To be sure, the context-sensitive nature of (e.g.) the indexicals means that the semantic axioms governing these expressions will have a degree of complexity not encountered in the simplest formal languages; but let us put this aside as only an engineering fact.

(ii) The class of grammatically singular *quantificational noun phrases* is usually taken to consist in semantically structured phrases of the form 'DET *F*' where *F* is a simple or complex nominal expression ('man', 'tall man', 'man who lives in London', etc.) and DET is a quantificational determiner such as 'some', 'every', 'a', 'one', 'no', or 'neither'. Assuming that a quantificational noun phrase 'DET *F*' acts as a restricted quantifier '[DET *x: Fx*]', Tarskian axioms of the following form are thought to suffice as far as truth-conditional content is concerned:

(1) '[DET $x_{k:}$ ϕ] ψ' is satisfied by a sequence s iff DET sequence satisfying ϕ and differing from s at most in the k-th place also satisfies ψ.

Now what are we to say about the various types of grammatically singular noun phrases not yet covered, e.g., those of the form 'the F' (definite descriptions) and 'that F' (demonstrative descriptions) occurring as the subjects of the following sentences?

(2) The mayor is a Republican
(3) That man is a Republican.

And what are we to say about the truth conditions of complex sentences such as the following, which involve apposition?

(4) The current mayor, Albert Smith, is a Republican
(5) Albert Smith, the current mayor, is a Republican.

Suppose, for the moment, we go along with Russell in (a) rejecting the idea that definite descriptions are singular terms and (b) analyzing utterances of sentences with descriptions as their subjects as quantificational (that is, as expressing general propositions). In restricted quantifier notation, Russell's quantificational semantics for definite descriptions is straightforwardly encoded thus (an instance of (1) above):

(6) '[the $x_{k:}$ ϕ] ψ' is satisfied by a sequence s iff the sequence satisfying ϕ and differing from s at most in the k-th position also satisfies ψ.

(The right hand side of (6) is to be understood in a Russellian spirit, i.e., as equivalent to "there is exactly one sequence satisfying ϕ and differing from s at most in the k-th position and every such sequence also satisfies ψ.")

How might we then treat examples like (4) and (5)? It might seem natural to follow Frege's approach to nonrestrictive relative clauses here: after all an appositive could be viewed (semantically) as a truncated restrictive relative. In a footnote to *Descriptions*, I tentatively followed Frege in suggesting that one might view utterances of such sentences as expressing *conjunctions*, an utterance of (4) expressing the conjunction of (7) and (8):

(7) The current mayor is a Republican
(8) The current mayor is Albert Smith.

In the present context, there is, I believe a better idea. Suppose that the current mayor is a Republican but not Albert Smith. What do we want to say about the truth-value of an utterance of (4) in such circumstances? We don't feel inclined to say that it is true and we don't feel inclined to say that it is false. Why is this?

Under the influence of Strawson (1950), many philosophers, when presented with examples for which they are reluctant to render a judgment, have a tendency to start talking about presuppositions. But this cannot be correct here: If the current mayor is not a Republican and not Albert Smith, an utterance of (4) would be straightforwardly false. I would like to suggest that the reluctance to render a clear judgment in the previous case might stem from the fact that the question is ill-formed. The idea that an *utterance* has a truth-value is only as robust as the idea that an utterance of a sentence expresses a single proposition. Suppose we drop this assumption, and allow that an utterance may express *one or more* propositions. On such an account, utterances themselves do not have truth-values; *the propositions they express do.* An utterance of (4) expresses not a conjunction but *two distinct propositions,* (7) and (8). We can now account for the reluctance to render a judgment as to the truth or falsity of an utterance of (4) when the current mayor is a Republican but is not Albert Smith: one proposition is true, the other false. In certain circumstances, it might even be the case that one proposition carries more conversational weight than the other, and a *judgment* as to the truth or falsity of the utterance—for certainly utterances are *judged* true or false—will reflect this fact. It is not difficult to engineer scenarios in which the speaker is primarily seeking to convey the information that the current mayor is a Republican to one audience and the information that the current mayor is Albert Smith, or the information that Albert Smith is a Republican, to another (many cases of dramatic irony exploit this possibility). It is not implausible to suppose that ordinary judgments as to truth or falsity might not be swayed by such considerations.[17]

§8. Demonstrative Descriptions

A few years ago, I flirted with the idea that every meaningful noun phrase in natural language is either (i) a semantically unstructured, rigid, referring expression or (ii) a semantically structured, restricted quantifier. I pushed this thesis as much on aesthetic and methodological grounds as anything else, and it turned out to be surprisingly more resilient than I had initially supposed. I pointed out that the most glaring problem for the thesis was posed by phrases of the form 'that *F*', which seem to be both referential and structured. At bottom, my problem with such phrases was an acute version of a general problem stemming from the fact that such expressions seem to function a bit like demonstratives and a bit like (Russellian) definite descriptions. The matter of demonstrative descriptions has received a good deal of attention of late but it is safe to say that no one seems entirely sure how to provide an adequate treatment of demonstrative descriptions, and in the light of the way we have been proceeding, I would like to explore the idea that they function in two ways at once (which is why I prefer the label "demonstrative description" to the label "complex demonstrative").

Consider an utterance by me of the following sentence, accompanied by the demonstration of a person:

(1) That man drinking water has written on descriptions.

If the person I am demonstrating is Keith Donnellan and he is drinking water, my utterance should be judged *true*. If the person I am demonstrating is Keith Richards and he is drinking water, then it should be judged *false*. But what if it is Donnellan and he is drinking a Martini? Or Richards and he is drinking a martini? Judgments in such cases are far from robust, and it seems to me that *this fact ought to be part of the data of semantics, not something upon which semantic theory should deliver a precise ruling.* If a demonstrative description is viewed as either (i) straightforwardly referential or (ii) straightforwardly descriptive, the data seem to be out of reach. Let us consider the case where it is Donnellan and he is drinking a martini.

(i) If an utterance of a demonstrative description gets its referent by demonstration or by demonstrative intention (rather than by description), then on a traditional single-proposition theory my utterance of (1) ought to be straightforwardly true. But this doesn't seem like a completely natural thing to say.

(ii) Now suppose we take the other line: demonstrative descriptions are genuinely quantificational and descriptive. Kaplan (1989) has argued that the simple demonstrative pronoun 'that' is not equivalent to the definite description 'the thing I am indicating' (assume that the indexical 'I' is a rigid referring expression). However, he points out that the competent user of a demonstrative must grasp its "character," which can be thought of as a rule for determining its reference on a particular occasion of use. So it looks as though, unlike in the case of a proper name, in the case of a demonstrative there may be some privileged description or other that is associated with the expression (on the assumption that its character can be described). So although there are counterfactual considerations that might preclude treating 'that' as simply equivalent to the ordinary definite description 'the thing I am indicating', it is not wholly unreasonable to suppose that something like this description captures its character. And so it might be thought possible to view demonstratives as equivalent to (or as having their references fixed by) Russellian descriptions (hence quantifiers) whose predicates all occur within the scope of 'actual'. For example (again, on the assumption that 'I' is a rigid referring expression), it might be thought possible to analyze a demonstrative description 'that F' in terms of a definite description such as 'the actual F I am indicating' (leaving it open whether it is desirable to go on and analyze 'I' as 'the actual speaker', in a way that avoids obvious circularity).

One way of implementing such an idea would be to view 'this' and 'that' as quantificational determiners on a par with 'every', 'no' and 'the' (assuming, for the moment, that this is Russellian), etc. (If simple demonstratives are deemed to fall within the domain of the theory, then perhaps they will be treated as demonstrative descriptions composed of the determiner and a semantically general and phonetically null complement). One special stipulation might seem to be required however: although the insertion of the 'actual' into a description effectively eliminates a certain type of scope ambiguity in modal contexts, for some speakers it has no analogous impact on other nonextensional contexts (unless, of course, the adjective is assigned the semantics of a fancy *actuality* operator of the sort that is employed by some intensional logicians). For example, the English string (2) is said by some to be ambiguous between *de re* and *de dicto* readings, naturally captured by allowing the description to have either large or small scope as in (3) and (4) respectively:

(2) John thinks: the actual man I am indicating is a fool
(3) [the x_1: actually (man x_1 & I am indicating x_1)]
    John thinks: x_1 is a fool
(4) John thinks:
    [the x_1: actually (man x_1 & I am indicating x_1)] x_1 is a fool.

But nobody understands (5) as ambiguous in the same way:

(5) John thinks that man is a fool.

Perhaps, then, demonstrative descriptions must always have scope over attitude verbs, and this is something that would need to be explained at some point. But an explanation of this would do nothing to disguise the fact that the theory appears to make the wrong prediction in connection with (2) when the person I am indicating is Donnellan, who has in fact written on descriptions but is drinking a Martini. It predicts that my utterance is false, but this doesn't seem like a natural thing to say.

There are further technical problems with this approach. Unlike quantification into positions inside definite descriptions and (other quantified NPs), quantification into positions inside demonstrative descriptions seems to be very unnatural. While (6) is naturally interpreted as (7), (8) does not seem to have a legitimate interpretation—but see below—unless the "demonstrative" is simply interpreted as a definite description, in which case (8) is also read as (7) and the referential hypothesis is irrelevant:

(6) [Every guitarist]$_1$ likes the guitar he$_1$ is playing
(7) [every x_1: guitarist x_1][the x_2: guitar x_2 & x_1 is playing x_2] x_1 likes x_2
(8) ? [Every guitarist]$_1$ likes that guitar he$_1$ is playing.

If the function of the descriptive material in a demonstrative description is to steer the hearer to a particular individual who is (or is being made) salient in some way or other, and if the material does not contribute to the semantical value of the NP, then the relativization of a unique guitar per guitarist in (6) cannot be mirrored in (8).

Actually, matters are more complicated. It *does* seem to be possible to bind a pronoun in such an environment when the antecedent is semantically singular as in (9) and (10):

(9) Keith$_1$ likes that guitar he$_1$ is playing
(10) The guitarist likes that guitar he$_1$ is playing.

This suggests that the real issue concerns *relativity* rather than binding *per se*. This seems also to be supported by the felicity of the following point (due to Ernie Lepore). Suppose the same (token) guitar is being played by every guitarist at the same moment; one could just about get away with pointing at the guitar in question and uttering (8). That there is still a real difference between demonstratives and descriptions reveals itself in the fact that the second sentence of (11) is ambiguous between strict and sloppy readings while the second sentence in (12) is not:

(11) Keith$_1$ likes the (actual) guitar he$_1$ is playing. So does Ron.
(12) Keith$_1$ likes that guitar he$_1$ is playing. So does Ron.

I believe there is something artificial about both accounts of demonstrative descriptions just sketched: as stated, each presupposes that a single proposition is expressed by an utterance of 'that *F* is *G*'. Perhaps a better picture of what is going on will emerge if we say that both a descriptive proposition *and* a singular proposition are expressed. Only when both are true or both false do we feel pulled to judge the utterance true or false. Indeed, I suspect that just such a synthesis is required if we are ever to get to the bottom of the semantics of singular terms, and that those who are moved deeply by Fregean substitution problems have been feeling the attraction of the general proposition while those moved more by the sorts of modal considerations that Kripke and Kaplan have stressed have been feeling the attraction of the singular proposition. Might it not be the case that a general proposition typically does the communicative work in epistemic environments while a singular proposition normally does it in modal environments? And might this not be a reflex of a distinction between epistemology/psychology and metaphysics? (When we investigate our thoughts about things we are interested in the properties or features that we use to identify them and the concepts under which we take them to fall; when we investigate the nature of things themselves, we are interested in the things themselves and the properties they actually, necessarily, and accidentally possess.)

How might we explore this idea? Again, the course of least resistance seems to be one that treats the meaning of an expression as a sequence of instructions: (i) an initial array of lexical information provides a sequence of instructions that, in conjunction with syntactic information, "yields" an initial (ground floor) proposition (or propositional matrix) that is general in nature, i.e., a proposition built around the properties that might be used to identify something; (ii) after the generation of the initial proposition, any lexical instructions that cannot operate until such a proposition is generated come into play, effectively yielding a secondary array of lexical information which, in conjunction with syntactic information and semantic content of the initial proposition, yields a *parasitic* proposition that is singular in nature, i.e., a proposition built around an object; (iii) the two propositions will typically end up ranked as a direct result of contextual factors (perhaps of the sort that Searle (1975) has articulated in connection with primary and secondary speech acts).

On such an account, we might begin to construct a theory of demonstrative noun phrases by thinking of the semantics of 'that F is G' in the following way (this is not meant to be a final account). In the first instance, lexical instructions conspire with the syntax (another set of instructions) to yield the ground-floor proposition that we can describe using the formal language sentence (13), in which 'the' is Russellian and 's' stands for the speaker:

(13) [the x: s is indicating x & Fx] Gx.

Once this proposition is obtained, the lexical instructions tell the hearer to look for the unique object satisfying the description (if there is one) and obtain the corresponding singular proposition about the satisfier, a proposition we might describe using the formal language sentence (14), in which α is directly referential:

(14) $G\alpha$.

(For the moment, let us put aside what the hearer is meant to do in cases where nothing seems to satisfy '*s* is indicating *x* & *Fx*'.) I am not sure what it means to entertain a singular proposition except in so far as one entertains it in a certain way. The idea here would be that, when all is going well, the proposition described by (13) provides a minimal specification of the object that the proposition described by (14) is about. With demonstratives, typically, it is the singular proposition that carries the conversational weight; but in exceptional circumstances that can change, as Nunberg (1977) and others have shown.[18]

Where a demonstrative description occurs in a sentence containing a modal operator or a verb of propositional attitude, issues of scope arise. As far as recovering the ground floor proposition is concerned, the hearer is in a similar situation to someone who hears an utterance of a sentence containing a description and a modal operator or psychological verb ('the first person into space might have been American', 'John thinks the man who lives upstairs is a spy'). The difference (perhaps) is that the default setting for a demonstrative description is for it to be understood with large scope over nonextensional items (perhaps this is also the case for definite descriptions, the real difference being only that it is easier or more common to override the default in connection with such phrases). As far as the higher-order proposition is concerned, the hearer is being instructed to look for the actual satisfier. A modal environment will likely push the interpreter to focus on this singular proposition built around the actual satisfier.

There is a Searlean flavor to this proposal: (13) is a means to (14), and *conventionally* so. It is part of the lexical meaning of 'that' that the hearer is *meant* to find the indicated object (if there is one) and the satisfier of the subsequent noun complex (if there is one), and that this should be the same object. (The account can be extended naturally to utterances of sentences containing the simple demonstratives 'this' and that', or indexical pronouns such as this 'I' and 'you': a singular and a general proposition would be expressed (again, the former via the latter); in typical communicative exchanges, the singular proposition carries the conversational weight, especially when the pronoun in question occurs in a modal environment.

Let us turn now to failure of fit cases, which were used earlier to motivate the multiple proposition approach to demonstrative descriptions. There are many sorts of examples and scenarios that need to be examined, but there is space here for only a few, best introduced through dialogue:

Dialogue I   *A:*   That goat hasn't moved since we sat down
              B: That isn't a goat, it's a ram.
Dialogue II   *A:*   That goat hasn't moved since we sat down
              B: That isn't a goat, it's a shadow.

Dialogue III *A:* That goat with a bell around its neck is limping
           B: It's not a bell, it's a thick beard.

It is not difficult to come up with all sorts of contexts involving these dialogues (*A* and *B* sitting in a field containing a ram and no other visible animals, a field containing a ram and a goat, a field containing no visible animals, a field full of goats, only one of which has a bell-shaped beard, and so on; *A*'s utterance accompanied or not by a gesture; . . .). And reflection reveals that the preliminary account of demonstrative descriptions sketched above will need to be repaired if it is to do justice to our judgments of truth and falsity. First, the absence of an object indicated by the speaker and satisfying the main noun 'goat' seems worse than the absence of an object indicated by the speaker and satisfying subordinate predicates—the depth of predicate embedding seems also to have an effect. Second, hearers do seem to manage to latch onto the objects that speakers *intend* in failure of fit cases, so any finally acceptable account must be integrated with a pragmatic theory that explains how this is accomplished.

Questions about Direct Reference and Semantic Innocence are now seen in a new light. It would be wrong, on this view, to say that a phrase of the form 'that *F*' is directly referential; but the singular proposition described by (14) is a proposition that contains an object and not any properties used to identify it, i.e., α is directly referential. I am inclined to think this is the best way to proceed, that the work Fregeans want done by senses is already being done by the *other* proposition, the one described by (13), and that to this extent the directly referential understanding of the proposition characterized in (14) is all that is needed. Frege's remarks about coloring, when examined and developed in a larger context, lead very naturally to a theory that allows us to junk senses.

Does this theory respect Semantic Innocence? So far, yes. A demonstrative description does not change its meaning in different linguistic environments. What can change is (a) the referent (this is just the point that they are *context*-sensitive, not *environment*-sensitive), and (b) the relative conversational weight attached to the singular and general propositions.

§9. Definite Descriptions Revisited

A usefully anachronistic way of viewing the debate about the semantics of descriptions is as follows. (i) From the standpoint of untutored semantic intuition, descriptions appear to be devices of *reference;* but syntactic intuition might suggest viewing them as devices of *quantification,* the word 'the' functioning as a quantificational determiner much like 'every', 'some', 'a', and 'no'. Frege was moved more by the semantic intuition, Russell more by the syntactic.[19] (ii) As part of a broadside against formalized semantics,

Strawson argued that Russell's Theory of Descriptions fails to take into account that referring is something *speakers,* rather than expressions, do (he had other objections of course). (iii) Reflection upon nonextensional contexts, the structure of propositions, the relationship between reference and intention, anaphoric relations, and the possibility of successfully communicating something about an individual while misdescribing it, led Donnellan (1966) and others to view matters as more complex than either Russell or Strawson thought. Sometimes descriptions are used in the way Russell's theory predicts, but at other times something closer to Strawson's speaker-reference theory seems to provide a more realistic picture. When 'the *F*' is used in the Russellian way, the proposition expressed is general; when it is used referentially the proposition expressed is singular, the referent of the description functioning as a component of the proposition expressed, as it is put on some accounts.

Although Donnellan's distinction turns out to be neither exclusive nor exhaustive, his examples of referential usage and his own positive suggestions have forced philosophers to confront the issues involving descriptions anew, to realize that more theoretical machinery was needed if anything like a comprehensive account was to surface. No one disputed the philosophical and linguistic significance of Donnellan's examples, the most notorious of which involved using a description 'the *F*' to communicate something about someone who was not in fact *F.* But there was, and still is, disagreement about the precise location, within an overall account of linguistic communication, of the machinery that is needed to explain them. Roughly, there is a division between those who locate the machinery in the general (Gricean) principles of a theory of communicative capacities and those who locate it in a theory of word meaning. Over the years, an enormous interest in this topic has arisen, especially in California. Indeed, with anachronism and poetic license the battle lines can be drawn more or less geographically, as is customary in California: North (San Francisco to Sacramento, mereologically attached to New Jersey) vs South (La Jolla to Palo Alto, mereologically attached to Maryland and Massachusetts). South argues that Donnellan's distinction is of semantical and lexical relevance; North argues that the distinction requires no departure from a unitary Russellian theory, apparent evidence to the contrary explained away by appeal to an antecedently motivated Gricean distinction between what is said and what is meant in some other way (e.g., conversationally implicated).

I want to go west, to explore the idea that North and South have both been assuming something that it may not be a good thing to assume, viz. that a single proposition is expressed by an utterance of a sentence containing a description.

On Russell's quantificational account as embodied in the axiom given earlier, if I utter

(1) The man drinking water has written on descriptions

intending to draw my hearer's attention to a particular individual (Donnellan), who is in view, then my utterance expresses a general proposition
to the effect that exactly one man is drinking water and every such man has
written on descriptions. The singular proposition that Donnellan has written on descriptions is part of what is meant but not part of what is said, general Gricean considerations helping to bridge the gap between the two.
This is the view I defended at length in *Descriptions*. I came down in favor
of the Russellian-Gricean account for one main reason: it seemed to provide an explanation of why we do not feel inclined to deliver a clear ver-
dict as to truth or falsity when the description used is not satisfied by the
intended or demonstrated object. Suppose I utter (1) and the man to whom
I intend to draw my hearer's attention is not drinking water. *Pace* Donnellan, I think it is quite clear that even if the man in question has written on
descriptions we do not have a clear intuition that my utterance is true. The
Russellian-Gricean seemed to me to be able to explain this fact: *something
went right and something went wrong:* what was said was false, what was
meant (or at least part of what was meant) was true. If you are wedded to
the idea that an utterance expresses a single proposition, this is surely the
better way to go.

I think we are now on course for a much better explanation than the one
that results from combining Russell with Grice. Both the unitary Russellian
account and the ambiguity theorist's account of the semantics of descriptions might be viewed as wrongheaded because they take seriously the idea
of *the* proposition expressed. I suggest the following. When a description is
used nonreferentially, there is a single proposition expressed and it is the
general proposition with quantificational truth conditions given by Russell.
More precisely, the word 'the' has as its lexical meaning an *initial* set of instructions that leads to an initial proposition that is *general*. Once that
proposition has been constructed, a further set of lexical instructions in-
structs the hearer to attempt, in favorable conditions, the construction of a
parasitic proposition, a singular proposition about the object uniquely satisfying F (if there is one) or being otherwise indicated. When these conditions are met we have a candidate "referential" use of the description. So
on the ground floor we have the general proposition given by (2), with the
singular proposition given by (3) piggy-backing:

(2) [the x: man x & x is drinking water] x has written on descriptions
(3) α has written on descriptions.

(Of course (2) and (3) belong to a formal language whose formulae are designed to express exactly one proposition.)

Not only does this revised approach explain our judgments and reluctance to offer judgment in failure of fit cases, it may also help to explain why Donnellan focused on such cases in his original paper: Donnellan realized that some utterances of sentences containing descriptions seemed not to be clearly false although Russell's account predicted falsity. Very naturally, he turned to embrace the view that such utterances were, well, if not false then *true*. If one is in the grip of the idea—and I think we have been—that an utterance expresses a single proposition, this is a natural first move. But the existence of coloring, conventional implicature, and the knotty case of demonstrative descriptions suggest we liberate ourselves from this position.

The important difference between demonstratives and descriptions is that it is part of the meaning of 'that' that the speaker has in mind some object or other that the hearer is meant to identify; it is part of the meaning of 'the' that the speaker *may* have such an object in mind. Of course, any finally acceptable account constructed along these lines will have to take into account the sorts of considerations adduced in the last section concerning failure of fit.

§10. Proper Names

Some view proper names as directly referential; others view them as having Fregean senses. Still others hold that a descriptive theory of names can still succeed, despite the battering it was given by Kripke (1980). I suspect we are ultimately going to need a hybrid theory and that a sequential analysis involving multiple propositions might do the trick.

Foucault (1969) has suggested a hybrid account according to which names have both a designative function and a descriptive function. I think there is something right about this idea, something right about McDowell's idea about reference axioms, and something right about metalinguistic theories of names.

Utterances of the following sentence will express a truth:

(1) Vivlos is in Greece.

And since 'Vivlos' and 'Tripodes' are two names, both current, for the same town in Greece—we can substitute 'Tripodes' for 'Vivlos' in (1) to produce another sentence, utterances of which will also express a truth:

(2) Tripodes is in Greece.

If you talk to the villagers, you find there is something like a coloring difference between 'Tripodes' and 'Vivlos' (Fregeans will also say there is a difference in sense, but the village is hitherto free of Fregeans). 'Vivlos' is an older name, which regained currency during the Greek civil war. Older villagers are aware of quasi-political overtones to the choice of name in conversation (as are local map-makers and the office that erects road signs). Of course, all of this presupposes knowledge of the fact Tripodes *is* Vivlos. Perhaps names carry coloring simply by virtue of *being* names. The act of naming is loaded—people squabble about names all the time—children's names, country names, street names.

I am drawn to the idea that the ground-floor proposition expressed by an utterance of a sentence containing a name is *descriptive* and *metalinguistic*. An idea first suggested by Russell (1911) can be adapted to form part of a sequential semantics. Russell's suggestion, which at first blush seems obviously circular, was to view a name *N* as equivalent to a definite description that mentions *N*. On such as account, "Cicero" might be treated as equivalent to "the individual called 'Cicero'" or something of that ilk.[20] There are two things I would like to do to convert this suggestion into something useful. Firstly, I propose introducing a basic *sortal* noun in connection with each name; that is I want to work with descriptions like 'the *individual* called "Cicero"', 'the *place* called "Vivlos"', 'the *thing* called "Hesperus"', and 'the *event* called "Bloody Sunday"' (these four categories will suffice). Secondly, I propose that the descriptive proposition is just the initial proposition generated, the ground-floor proposition. So the name 'Cicero' has two sets of instructions as part of its meaning, one for generating the initial, ground-floor proposition and another for generating a second, singular proposition. For example, an utterance of 'Cicero is asleep' will express the propositions given by (3) and (4), where α is rigid and, perhaps, directly referential:

(3) [the x: x is an individual & (actually) x is called 'Cicero']
x is asleep
(4) α is asleep.

(Remember, these formulae are designed to express exactly one proposition each.) I want to suggest that this projects into the logical space in which our attributions of utterances and mental states lie, precisely because the coloring of names is something of which we are so keenly aware.

Verbs like 'believe', 'think', 'doubt', and 'hope' create notorious difficulties for semantics, problems that I suspect will be solved only by appeal to multiple propositions. Consider the following sentence:

(5) On June 18, 1992, Stephen Neale thought he was in Vivlos.

Someone who utters this sentence expresses a truth. On that day I was hiking, looking for a village that, according to my map, was called 'Tripodes', a village I thought might be large enough to have a small taverna. After losing my way for a couple of hours, at around three o'clock in the afternoon I stumbled across a tiny village, whose signs called it 'Vivlos'. I felt confident that the village I had entered was far too small to be marked on my map, and there being no one around—any Greek villager with sense is asleep on June afternoons—headed off for a village I could see in the distance, which I deduced, on the basis of size and location with respect to two hills, must be Tripodes. It wasn't Tripodes—but it did have an excellent taverna. It was not until the next day that I discovered 'Vivlos' and 'Tripodes' were names of the same place—or as some might put it, that Vivlos was Tripodes. Now consider the following sentence:

(6) On June 18, 1992, Stephen Neale thought he was in Tripodes.

Someone who utters (6) would, I think, normally be taken to be expressing a falsehood. (If I had thought the village I was in was Tripodes why would I have left in search of Tripodes?) We want, remember, to *explain* my behavior in *this actual case.* Such an example creates serious problems for traditional theories that respect Semantic Innocence and Direct Reference.

It is my suspicion that philosophers are divided on how to view the semantics of sentences like (5) and (6) because it is so easy to engineer scenarios in which judgments of truth and falsity are malleable or unclear. But now think of utterances of (5) and (6) as expressing sequences (actually pairs) of propositions, some of which may be true, others of which may be false, and that our intuitive judgments as to the truth or falsity of the utterances depend upon the perceived truth values of those propositions relevant to particular communicative purposes. The propositions characterized by (7) and (8) are both true:

(7) On June 18, 1992 [the x: x is a place & x is (actually) called 'Vivlos'] Stephen Neale thought he was in x
(8) On June 18, 1992 Stephen Neale thought [the x: x is a place & x is (actually) called 'Vivlos'] he was in x.

And obviously the reading with the scope of the description as in (8) is the one that interests us here; switching the description for one containing "'Tripodes'" yields a falsehood (not so the same substitution in (7).

Thanks to Kripke (1980), we know that a *complete* account of the semantics of proper names in terms of descriptions is out of the question; but in contextually specifiable circumstances a judgment of the truth-value of an utterance containing a name, whether subordinated to a psychological verb or not, may be shaped by the perceived truth-value of a general proposition determined by the trivial description. (Or it may, as in many modal statements, be shaped by the singular proposition constructible from the general proposition.) To say this is *not* to say that the description gives the *sense* of the name in Frege's sense. Rather it involves a rejection of Fregean sense on *at least* the grounds of redundancy. Clearly, there is much work to be done before a sequential approach to singular terms can be properly evaluated, but I am inclined to think that the stock problems involving, e.g., names, propositional attitudes, identity, the contingent *a priori*, and negative existentials will not go away within approaches that restrict themselves to a unique proposition expressed. We have been attracted modally to singular propositions and we have been attracted epistemically to general propositions. We need a semantic theory sophisticated enough to associate both types of proposition with utterances of sentences containing singular terms, and a pragmatic theory that explains how we are led to focus on one rather than the other in concrete situations. Just how dependent upon context our uses of proper names is can be made clear by comparing dialogues involving names of (e.g.) close friends, historical characters, fictional characters, and authors.

§11. Conclusion

Within the framework I have sketched, an utterance of a sentence may express one or more propositions. An initial array of lexical information provides a sequence of instructions that, in conjunction with syntactic information, creates an initial proposition. Once this has been generated, any remaining instructions kick in and a secondary array of lexical information conspires with syntactic information and semantic content of the ground-floor proposition to yield one or more "parasitic" propositions. In such cases—which may be far more widespread than I have been assuming—propositions expressed may be ranked in various ways determined by contextual factors. Semantic theories founded upon these ideas will be immune to the usual technical problems besetting presuppositional theories, and at the same time ought to make predictions that accord much better with our intuitive judgments of truth and falsity, which it is the business of semantics to explain. The strength of one's inclination to judge an utterance true or false is a function of the truth or falsity of those propositions expressed by the utterance relative to the situation under consideration. Typically, it is only relative to situations in which the members of a contextually weighted subset of the propositions expressed are true that we are strongly inclined to say that an utterance itself is true; and it is only relative to situations in which the members of a contextually weighted subset of the propositions are false that we are strongly inclined to say that the utterance is false. I am inclined to think that we will not get much further in semantics and the philosophy of language until we adopt a multiple proposition framework. The present discussion is, of necessity, highly programmatic and compressed. It would be an enormous undertaking to work out a rigorous compositional theory of the sort I envision, but I hope the general shape of such a theory has been made clear.

Notes

1. For simplicity, I have ignored the fact that quantified as well as referential noun phrases may function as direct objects. On a Fregean account, whereas a referential noun phrase is of the category N, a quantificational noun phrase (e.g., 'every man') is of the category S/(S/N): in either case the result of combining a noun phrase with a one-place predicate is a sentence. A quantificational noun phrase, on this account, refers to a function from functions from objects to truth-values to truth-values: $(O \rightarrow V) \rightarrow V$.

2. The matter of what a sentence refers to when it is doubly (triply, . . .) embedded as in 'Phaedo doubts Socrates believes Plato is wealthy' has attracted some attention. Some have argued that it still refers to its customary sense, i.e., a mode of presentation of its customary reference; others have maintained that it must refer to a mode of presentation of a mode of presentation of its customary reference. In fact, neither party is right: once the possibility of multiple embeddings is introduced, Frege's theory becomes inconsistent.

3. This fact makes a mockery of the claim that the notorious slingshot arguments associated with Frege, Church, and Gödel presuppose Semantic Innocence or Direct Reference.

4. VII/4 [xix/6], Frege to Husserl, 9.12.1906, in Gottlob Frege, *Philosophical and Mathematical Correspondence,* Oxford: Blackwell, 1980, pp. 70–1:

> It seems to me that an objective criterion is necessary for recognizing a thought again as the same, for without it logical analysis is impossible. Now it seems to me that the only possible means for deciding whether a proposition *A* expresses the same thought as proposition *B* is the following, and here I assume that neither of the two propositions contains a logically self-evident component part in its sense. If *both* the assumption that the content of *A* is false and that of *B* true *and* the assumption that the content of *A* is true and that of *B* false lead to a logical contradiction, and if this can be established without knowing whether the content of *A* or *B* is true or false, and without requiring other than purely logical laws for this purpose, then nothing can belong to the content of *A* as far as it is capable of being judged true or false, which does not also belong to the content of *B*. . . . Thus what is capable of being judged true or false in the contents of *A* and *B* is identical, and this alone is of concern to logic, and this is what I call the thought expressed by both *A* and *B*. . . . Is there another means of judging

what part of the content of a proposition is subject to logic, or when two propositions express the same thought? I do not think so.

In Frege's "A Brief Survey of My Logical Doctrines," also written in 1906 (published in English in Gottlob Frege, *Posthumous Writings,* Oxford: Blackwell, 1979, pp. 197–202), he is less precise on the logic of equipollence, offering a closely related psychological or epistemological characterization. Two sentences *A* and *B* are said to be equipollent when " . . . anyone who recognizes the content of *A* as true must thereby also recognize the content of *B* as true and, conversely, that anyone who accepts the content of *B* must straightway accept that of *A*." (p. 197). At the very least, this characterization still invites the thought that mutual entailment is at the heart of the notion. (There is an obvious problem with all of this: if logically equivalent sentences have the same sense, then such sentences ought to be intersubstitutable *salva veritate* in contexts of propositional attitude. But this is simply not the case according to Frege (1892).)

5. I use the term "two-place connective" loosely. As Frege realizes, many expressions that are treated (formally or informally) as two-place sentence connectives—e.g., 'although', 'because', 'before', 'after', 'therefore', 'so' and also 'if' and 'only if'—are better viewed as devices that attach to a single sentence to form another expression. For present purposes, the fiction that they are two-place connectives is harmless and helpful.

6. Everything Frege says about the semantics of (1) carries over to examples like (i) and (ii):

(i)   Napoleon, recognizing the danger to his right flank, personally led his guards against the enemy position
(ii)   Recognizing the danger to his right flank, Napoleon personally led his guards against the enemy position.

7. I do not mean to be endorsing Grice's account of 'and' here. My sympathies lie with Carston's (1988) theory.

8. The way Grice appeals to the maxim of Manner creates an obvious problem for this test.

9. The existence of conventional implicature presents a difficulty for one of Grice's dearest projects: an analysis of the philosophically important notion of *saying*. Grice proposes to analyze the notions of *utterer's meaning* and *sentence meaning* in terms of such psychological notions as intention, belief, and recognition. And, very naturally, he proposes to analyze the notion of *saying* by focusing on the terrain in which there is overlap in utterer's meaning and sentence meaning. Abstracting away from ambiguity and indexicality—both of which create further difficulties for Grice's project—the following captures the main idea behind his preliminary definition of saying (Grice, 1989, pp. 87–88 and pp. 118–121):
By uttering a token *x* (of type *X*), *U* said that *p* iff

(i)   (at least part of) what *U* meant by uttering *x,* was that *p*
(ii)   *X* means "*p*" (in virtue of the particular meanings of the elements in *X* and their syntactic structure).

Grice's unhappiness with this definition (or this sort of definition) derives in large part from the existence of conventional implicature. If *U* sincerely and nonironically utters 'She is poor but she is honest', *U says* only that she is poor and that she is honest; *U* does not say that there is some sort of contrast between poverty and honesty (or between her poverty and her honesty). So for Grice, the conjunction of (i) and (ii) above characterizes not "by uttering a token *x* (of type *X*), *U* said that *p*" but only "by uttering a token *x* (of type *X*), *U conventionally meant* that *p*." On Grice's account, what *U* meant by uttering a token *x* (of type *X*) is broken down as follows:

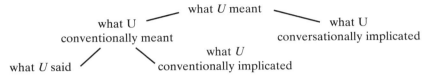

In short, a conventional implicature attaching to an utterance of *X* gives rise to a mismatch between what *U conventionally meant* by uttering *X* and what *U said* by uttering *X* (again, abstracting away from indexicality and other forms of context-sensitivity). In such a case, the latter underdetermines the former, and the gap is bridged by what *U* conventionally implicated by uttering *X*. There is a further complication for Grice: as Sperber and Wilson have argued in detail, the precise content of what *U* said—and, for that matter, what *U* conventionally implicated—by uttering a sentence that means "*p*" is often underdetermined by the fact that the sentence means "*p*."

10. There may be other conceptions that prove to be of utility to a theory of communication—so-called "pragmatic" presuppositions (see, e.g., Stalnaker (1974) and Heim (1988)). In standard cases of alleged semantic presupposition there is a strong inclination to say that *what the speaker said* does the implying (indeed this has motivated some people to promote many presuppositions of the type just exemplified to entailments). In the case of an utterance of (1), one does not feel particularly inclined to say that what the speaker said implied that there was a contrast between e.g., poverty and honesty. An unargued for, but very intuitive, test Grice proposes here is the following:

> If accepting that the implication holds involves one in accepting an hypothetical if *p* then *q* where *p* represents the original statement, and *q* represents what is implied, then what the speaker said (or asserted) is a vehicle of the implication, otherwise not. (1961, p. 127–8)

One does not feel at all compelled to accept the hypothetical *If she is poor but honest then there is some contrast between poverty and honesty, or between her poverty and her honesty*. This observation, together with the observation that what is asserted by uttering this sentence can be false even if what is implied is false, invites the suspicion that talk of "presupposition" is well off target in such cases. Even if the implication were false, i.e., even if there were no reason on earth to suppose that there is any contrast between poverty and honesty, what is stated could still be false, say if she were *rich* and honest.

11. Bach and Harnish (1979) allow for the possibility that a higher-order speech act may function as a commentary upon a lower-order act in these two distinct ways. The idea is being developed in work in progress by Bach.

12. Notice that 'so' can replace 'therefore' in (4) but not in (3). For a discussion of differences between 'so' and 'therefore' see Blakemore (1987).

13. McCawley prefaces his argument by claiming that neither (3) nor (4) can occupy an embedded sentence position:

> (i)   ? John doubts(/believes/hopes/said) that: Bill is a philosopher, therefore he is brave
> (ii) ? It is not the case that: Bill is a philosopher, therefore he is brave
> (iii) ? If Bill is a philosopher, therefore he is brave, then I am mistaken.

(i)–(iii) do seem very odd, and perhaps McCawley is right to say they are ungrammatical rather than just semantically odd in some way yet to be elucidated (the counterparts of (i)–(iii) containing (3) rather than (4) are surely ungrammatical). Suffice to say that an adequate theory of English must explain somehow why replacing 'therefore' by 'and' yields perfectly good English sentences. McCawley's view is that whereas 'and' functions syntactically as a two-place sentence connective, 'therefore' functions as a sentence-modifying adverb (effectively a one-place sentence connective) in (3) and (4), hence the attempted embeddings are grammatically deviant. (Notice that 'whereas' appears to function as a two-place sentence connective in the previous sentence, producing a clause that serves as the complement of 'McCawley concludes that . . .'.) Incidentally, McCawley is incorrect in supposing that Grice's account of 'therefore' treats it as a two-place sentence connective in (4); Grice says nothing that commits him to either that view or the view that it is a sentence-modifying adverb.

14. See, e.g., Sperber and Wilson (1986) and Carston (1988).

15. Although 'although', 'but', and 'on the other hand' are all used to signal the higher-order speech act of contrasting, there are important syntactic differences: as Grice observes, 'but' functions as a two-place sentence connective whereas 'on the other hand' functions as an "embedded enclitic."

16. Frege, as we saw earlier, retains the Principle of Composition in respect of reference in the face of apparent problems introduced by sentential verbs and other devices of subordination by treating a sentence occurring within the scope of such a device as either referring to its customary sense or else contributing to a second proposition (thereby abandoning Semantic Innocence). Since he was not particularly interested in coloring, he says nothing about compositionality in connection with this notion. Similarly, Grice does not examine conventional implicature in connection with embedded sentences; but Karttunen and Peters (1979) have examined the matter in detail and have come up with some generalizations about embedding constructions. For example, they claim that in structures of the form '*A* φs that *p*', we need to distinguish three different classes of sentential verb φ according as the structure (i) *inherits* ('know', 'regret', 'discover', 'forget', 'point out'), (ii) *transforms* ('believe', 'think', 'hope', 'expect', 'doubt', 'fear',), or (iii) *blocks* ('say', 'report', 'claim') the conventional implicatures generated by *p*. These claims are surely incorrect as far as the original Fregean and Gricean examples are concerned. Consider the following:

(i)   a.   Bill knows that Alfred has not arrived yet
      b.   Bill thinks that Alfred has not arrived yet
      c.   Bill said that Alfred has not arrived yet
(ii) a.   Bill knows that she is poor but she is honest
      b.   Bill thinks that she is poor but she is honest
      c.   Bill said that she is poor but she is honest
(iii) a.   Bill knows that Alfred succeeded in cashing a check today
      b.   Bill thinks that Alfred succeeded in cashing a check today
      c.   Bill said that Alfred succeeded in cashing a check today.

17. Intuitive judgments about truth, falsity, contradiction, entailment, and synonymy constitute the basic data for the construction of theories of meaning, just as intuitive judgments about grammaticality are the basic data for the construction of theories of syntax. As Chomsky (1965) and Rawls (1971) have pointed out, even if such judgments are the raw data of linguistic investigations, in certain specifiable circumstances it may be reasonable, and even necessary, to re-examine and reject some of them when they conflict with predictions made by otherwise well-behaved theories. Ultimately, both semantic and syntactic theorizing must aim for a "reflective equilibrium" that weaves together theory and data supplied by intuition.

18. It is sometimes said that demonstratives, indexicals, and descriptions all have both referential and attributive readings. The point underlying such a remark is well taken, but I still find the referential-attributive dichotomy theoretically unhelpful.

19. Russell's theory is often put forward as the paradigm case of a theory that invokes a distinction between *grammatical form* and *logical form,* but ironically there is a sense in which it preserves symmetry: the gap between grammatical form and logical form in the case of 'the *F* is *G*' no wider than it is in the case of 'every *F* is *G*' or 'some *F* is *G*' because 'the' is of the same syntactical and semantical category as 'every' and 'some'.

20. Russell changes his wording in successive works: "the man whose name was 'Cicero'" (1911), "the person named 'Cicero'" (1918), and "the person called 'Cicero' (1919)."

References

Bach, K., and M. Harnish (1979). *Linguistic Communication and Speech Acts.* Cambridge, Mass.: MIT Press.

Blakemore, D. (1987). *Semantic Constraints on Relevance.* Oxford: Blackwell.

Carston, R. (1988). Implicature, Explicature, and Truth-theoretic Semantics. In R. Kempson (ed.), *Mental Representations.* Cambridge, Mass.: Cambridge University Press, pp. 155–181.

Chomsky, N. (1965). *Aspects of the Theory of Syntax.* Cambridge, Mass.: MIT Press.

Church, A. (1943). Review of Carnap's *Introduction to Semantics. Philosophical Review* 52, pp. 298–304.

Davidson, D. (1984). *Inquiries into Truth and Interpretation.* Oxford: Oxford University Press.

Donnellan, K. (1966). Reference and Definite Descriptions. *Philosophical Review* 77, pp. 281–304.

Dummett, M. (1980). *Frege: Philosophy of Language.* London: Duckworth.

Foucault, M. (1969). What is an Author? In D. Lodge (ed.), *Modern Criticism and Theory: A Reader.* London: Longman, 1988, pp. 196–210.

Frege, G. (1892). Ueber Sinn und Bedeutung. *Zeitschrift fur Philosophie und Philosophische Kritik* 100, pp. 25–50. Translated as 'On Sense and Reference' in P. T. Geach and M. Black (eds.), *Translations from the Philosophical Writings of Gottlob Frege.* Third edition. Oxford: Blackwell, 1980, pp. 56–78.

Frege, G. (1918). Der Gedanke. Eine Logische Untersuchung *Beiträge zur Philosophie des Deutsches Idealismus* I, pp. 58–77. Translated as 'Thoughts' in B. McGuinness (ed.), *Collected Papers on Math, Logic, and Philosophy.* Oxford: Blackwell, 1984. Reprinted in N. Salmon and S. Soames (eds.), *Propositions and Attitudes, Oxford: Oxford University Press* (1988), pp. 33–55.

Gazdar, G. (1979). *Pragmatics, Implicature, and Logical Form.* New York: Academic Press.

Gödel, K. (1944). Russell's Mathematical Logic. In P. A. Schillp (ed.), *The Philosophy of Bertrand Russell.* Evanston and Chicago: Northwestern University Press, pp. 125–153.

Grice, H. P. (1961). The Causal Theory of Perception. *Proceedings of the Aristotelian Society,* suppl. vol. 35, pp. 121–52.

Grice, P. (1989). *Studies in the Way of Words.* Cambridge, Mass.: Harvard University Press.

Heim, I. (1988). On the Projection Problem for Presuppositions. In D. Flickinger (ed.), *Proceedings of the Second West Coast Conference on Formal Linguistics,* Stanford, Calif.: Stanford University Press, pp. 114–125.

Kaplan, D. (1989). Demonstratives. In J. Almog, J. Perry, and H. Wettstein (eds.), *Themes from Kaplan.* New York: Oxford University Press, pp. 481–563.

Karttunen, L. and S. Peters (1979). Conventional Implicature. In C. K. Oh and D. Dinneen (eds.), *Syntax and Semantics, vol. 11: Presuppositions.* New York: Academic Press, pp. 1–56.

Kripke, S. (1977). Speaker Reference and Semantic Reference. In P. A. French, T. E. Uehling, Jr., and H. K. Wettstein (eds.), *Contemporary Perspectives in the Philosophy of Language.* Minneapolis, Minn.: University of Minnesota Press, pp. 6–27.

Levinson, S. (1983). *Pragmatics.* Cambridge, Mass.: Cambridge University Press.

McCawley, J. (1993). *Everything Linguists Always Wanted to Know about Logic.* Chicago, Ill.: Chicago University Press.

McDowell, J. (1977). On the Sense and Reference of a Proper Name. *Mind* 86, pp. 159–185.

Nunberg, G. (1977). The Pragmatics of Reference. Doctoral thesis. City University of New York.

Perry, J. (1993). Individuals in Informational and Intentional Content. In J. Perry, *The Problem of the Essential Indexical and Other Essays.* Oxford: Oxford University Press, 1993, pp. 279–300.

Rawls, J. (1971). *A Theory of Justice.* Cambridge, Mass.: Harvard University Press.

Russell, B. (1905) On Denoting. *Mind* 14, pp. 479–493.

———(1911). Knowledge by Acquaintance and Knowledge by Description. In *Mysticism and Logic.* London: George Allen and Unwin, 1917, 152–167.

————(1918). The Philosophy of Logical Atomism. In R. C. Marsh (ed.), *Logic and Knowledge*. London: George Allen and Unwin, 1956. pp. 175–281.

Searle, J. (1975). Indirect Speech Acts. In P. Cole and J. Morgan (eds.), *Syntax and Semantics, vol. 3: Speech Acts*. New York: Academic Press, pp. 59–82.

Sperber, D., and D. Wilson (1986). *Relevance: Communication and Cognition*. Oxford: Blackwell.

Stalnaker, R. (1974) "Pragmatic Presuppositions." In M. K. Munitz and P. K. Unger (eds.), *Semantics and Philosophy*. New York: New York University Press, pp. 197–214.

Strawson, P. (1950). On Referring. *Mind* 59, pp. 320–344. Reprinted in Strawson's *Logico-Linguistic Papers*. London: Methuen, 1971, pp. 1–27.

Strawson, P. (1952). *Introduction to Logical Theory*. London: Methuen.

PART TWO

Philosophy, Semantics, and Pragmatics

3

On Communication-Based
De Re Thought, Commitments
De Dicto, and Word Individuation[1]

Adèle Mercier

Preliminaries

In the old days of descriptivism, reference was thought to be a function of one's *epistemic* connection to a referent, a connection fully established by one's beliefs about the referent, which were taken to be individuative of the content of one's thought. Thus it was thought that when I think of Aristotle, the object of my thought is whoever instantiates (enough or most or a weighted sum of) the properties that constitute my information "about Aristotle." Likewise, it was thought that when I think of water, the object of my thought is whatever satisfies (enough or most or a weighted sum of) the properties of being a colorless, odorless, tasteless, potable liquid originally flowing in rivers and lakes.

Since different people have different epistemic backgrounds and perspectives, it was natural to think, on a view where the connection to referents is epistemic, that different people could attach different senses to their words.[2] And to the extent that the sense of a term is what determines its referent, it was natural to think that different people could mean different referents by the same word, or perhaps stated more precisely, by the same word-*form.* In short, the view was fully supportive of individualism about mental content, and thus about reference.

With Donnellan's "Proper Names and Identifying Descriptions" (1970), Kripke's *Naming and Necessity* (1972) and Putnam's "The Meaning of 'Meaning'" (1975), such views have been—to my mind largely rightly—debunked in favor of a causal theory of reference. But, like Searle in "Proper Names and Intentionality" (1983), I want to argue that the new theory of reference, which has substituted for descriptivism an externalist defense of reference, has still not refuted (some aspects of) individualism (though the aspects I have in mind are not wholly Searle's). I wish to draw attention to individualist contributions to the semantics and metasemantics of words that current views fail to acknowledge.

Under the causal theory, the idea that reference is a function of one's epistemic connection to a referent has been replaced by the idea that reference is a function of one's *metaphysical* connection to a referent. What connects me to a referent, on the post-descriptivist view, are actual facts—causal, historical facts—and not what I *take* those facts to be. To quote Kripke: "On our view, it is not how the speaker thinks he got the reference, but the actual chain of communication, which is relevant" (1972: 93). Since the substance with which I have been causally interacting when I utter the words 'this is water' happens actually to be H_2O (unbeknownst perhaps to me, and indeed, even if unbeknownst to us all), it is H_2O that is individuative of the content of my thoughts "about water." Since the person who was being talked about when I interacted historically with the name 'Aristotle' happened actually to be *Aristotle* (whoever that is), it is *that* person—the person standing at the end of the causal-historical chain that brought the name 'Aristotle' down the generations to me—who is individuative of the content of my thought "about Aristotle." As Kripke puts it: "In general, our reference depends not just on what we think ourselves, but on other people in the community, the history of how the name reached one, and things like that. It is by following such a history that one gets to the reference" (1972: 95).

Viewing reference as a metaphysical rather than an epistemic affair guarantees an externalist view of reference, and to the extent that reference is what individualism is about, it constitutes a refutation of individualism. These views are well-worn and commonplace by now, and I shall take them for granted.

Let us now distinguish between the semantics and the metasemantics of words. The semantics of a word is simply what it means, and in the case of a directly referential term, what it refers to. (Indexicals impose qualifications on this simple statement, but let us forget about indexicals here.) According to causal theorists, the semantics of a term is what is passed down the causal chain. Because it is passed down the causal chain, it is not under the control of the user. As Kaplan puts it : "We are, for the most part, language *consumers*. Words come to us *pre-packaged* with a semantic value" (1989: 602).

The metasemantics refers to the event whereby a term is created, before it is launched down the causal chain. A name can be created by at least one of the following two ways: Its reference can be fixed by description (as when Leverrier coins the name 'Neptune' to refer to whatever it is, unbeknownst to him, that is the cause of the perturbations in the orbit of

Uranus), or its reference can be fixed by ostention (as when Aristotle's mother points to her baby and baptizes it 'Aristotle'). Other words have their meanings fixed by similar processes, subject to complications which we can ignore for the nonce.

Note that reference-fixing by ostention typically reduces in the end to reference-fixing by description. This is because descriptive information is (however implicitly) needed to individuate demonstrations: Aristotle's mother is baptizing the whole baby in her arms, not its nose, and were she to have inadvertently brought the neighbor's baby to the baptismal ceremony, we could still allow, I think, that she had baptized her own son 'Aristotle' (and not re-baptized the neighbor's son). Let's call this the *Principle of the Description-Laddenness of Ostention* (the pedantic language is intended to help recall the principle later).

Note also the greater *autonomy* of the individual with respect to the metasemantics than with respect to the semantics of a name. It is obviously not up to Leverrier *what* the cause of the perturbations in the orbit of Uranus actually is (that's up to God, and for us to find out); so it is not up to Leverrier what *thing* the referent of 'Neptune' is. Nevertheless, it is fully up to Leverrier as the coiner of the term what *sort of word* 'Neptune' is (a proper name for an individual, a kind term, an adjective, and so on). Likewise, though the criteria of transworld identification of Aristotle are not up to Aristotle's mother (they depend on such things as the actual egg and sperm out of which he was conceived), it is fully up to her as the coiner of the name 'Aristotle' to determine what sort of name it is (a generic family name, a proper name for a person, for a time-slice of a person, for an undetached person-part, and so on). The case of kind terms (barring complications for now) is similar. If I point to a liquid while coining the word 'blik', though I am not the expert needed to individuate what the very stuff I've pointed to is (we need a chemist for that), nevertheless I am authoritative about what sort of kind I intend the word to stand for: for example, *this very stuff* (as individuated by our scientific community) and nothing but it, or any liquid relevantly *like* it, or its *color,* or any of its phenomenal properties. My intention will determine what *sort* of word I've coined: a natural kind term, a phenomenal kind term, a color term, and so on. And what sort of word it is will in turn determine, not what *thing,* but what *sort* of thing its referent can be. More on this later.

Finally, note that one central thesis of the causal-historical picture is that semantic events, or the passing of meaning down the chain, massively outnumber (by orders of magnitude) metasemantic events. And while I think this is indeed largely true, I will try to show that much more metasemantic creationism takes place than is allowed for by the current view (and that is where individualism still has a foothold).

Now, suppose you use the word 'water' and I want to know what you mean by that word. There are two readings of what it is that I might want to know. On one reading—call it the object-level reading—I want to know what the *stuff* is to which you're referring by that word. The answer to this question depends on what the stuff that you've been interacting with and calling 'water' happens to be. The question can be rephrased in Twin-Earth-ian language as the question:

> Do you mean *this* stuff? (pointing to H_2O) i.e., Do you inhabit
>   the actual world?
> Or do you mean *that* stuff? (pointing to XYZ) i.e., Do you in-
>   habit Twin-Earth?

And the lesson to be drawn from the demise of the description theory is that this question is a question for metaphysics, not epistemology. It's a matter of causal connection *to the world* (and, in the case of causal connections to kinds, it's also a matter of causal-historical connection to a science or scientific community individuating those kinds). Most importantly for our purposes, it's a question whose answer lies outside the competence of the individual.

Another reading of what it is that I want to know is meta-linguistic. We can put it in terms of the following question:

> Which of the many possible homonymous words 'water' are
>   you uttering by means of this token of the word-*form*
>   'water'?

According to causal theorists, though a different question, this is *also* a question of metaphysics, and *also* a question whose answer lies outside the competence of the individual. It's a question of causal history: In this case, a question about your causal connection *to a language* (or to a community speaking this language). If you speak English, for instance, the word you are uttering is (possibly unbeknownst to you) the word meaning water (whatever substance water may be in the world you happen to inhabit: e.g., H_2O, XYZ, etc.). If you speak French, it is (possibly unbeknownst to you) a different word, namely that word 'water' (pronounced slightly distinctly) which refers to a toilet (whatever toilets may be in the world you happen to inhabit: e.g., bathroom fixtures, religious artifacts, etc.[3]). The choice of homonym available to you depends, as Kaplan might put it, on what word, pre-packaged with what semantic value, is causally available for you to consume in the language you speak. Burge holds a view similar, in relevant respects, to Kaplan's; though he sees your choice of homonym revealed by your propensity to relinquish your (mistaken) beliefs about its referent given corrections from the community.

I shall argue that the second question is a far more nearly epistemological—and individualistic—question than it is fashionable these days to argue. To motivate the need to revisit the issue, I first examine how people have used the new theory of reference to explain how *de re* thought can be communicated through the medium of language. I think the purported explanation is hardly explanatory, and that its weakness sheds light on problems with the causal-historical picture.

On Communication-Based *De Re* Thought

The standard (easy) case of *de re* thought is when the thinker has encountered the object that the thought is about perceptually, or when the thinker has a memory-based thought derived from perception. Several people have raised in recent years the question of whether one can also have *de re* thoughts about things one has *not* encountered, but of which one has merely been informed. Like most such people, I think the answer to this question is that we can (and I will simply be assuming for the sake of the current argument that we can). Unlike most such people, however, I think the answer that is standardly given about *how* we can, is not satisfactory.

The answer that is standardly given about how we can have *de re* thoughts about particulars such as Aristotle, or about kinds such as African dormice, which we have never encountered (or of which we have never encountered samples in the case of kinds) but of which we have merely been informed, invariably appeals to the causal-historical chain of communication, which is often taken as supplying an account of how language transmits information.

Let me cite a few key passages that I take to be widely representative of the current philosophical orthodoxy on this matter. Noteworthy is Kaplan's conception of the role for language in thought, a conception which he amusingly summarizes as *Vocabulary Power as Epistemological Enhancement.*

> The notion that a referent can be carried by a name from early past to present suggests that *the language itself* carries meanings, and thus that we can acquire meanings through the instrument of language.
>
> On my view, our connection with a linguistic community in which names and other meaning-bearing elements are passed down to us enables us to entertain thoughts *through the language* that would not otherwise be accessible to us. (1989: 603)
>
> Contrary to Russell, I think we succeed in thinking about things in the world not only through the mental residue of that which we ourselves experience, but also vicariously, through the symbolic resources that come to us through language.

So how shall I apprehend thee? Let me count the ways. I may apprehend you by (more or less) direct perception. I may apprehend you by memory of (more or less) direct perception. And finally, I may apprehend you through a sign that has been created to signify you. (1989: 604)

Now the question of how I can have *de re* thoughts about you merely by apprehending a sign created to signify you can be refocused as the question: What does it take for the linguistic community to transmit *that* sign (i.e., *its* word for you) to me? Kaplan raises this question in his paper called "Words." He asks:

Take the utterance or inscription received and the utterance or inscription transmitted. What makes it that the transmission is an utterance or inscription of the *same* word as that received? (1990: 101)

And he answers:

The identification of a word uttered or inscribed with one heard or read is not a matter of *resemblance* between the two *physical* embodiments. [So I can say 'Adèle Mercier' and still transmit my name even if the recipient calls me 'Aydelee Murciyur' (as some unused to French names are wont to do).] Rather, it is . . . a matter of *intention:* Was it *repetition?* (1990: 104)

Burge would make it a matter of intending to *defer.*

Of course, now the question boils down to: Under what conditions is an intention to repeat (or to defer) *successful?*

Note that the answer to this question cannot be, on nothing less than pain of circularity, that the intention to repeat has been successful as long as you've repeated a word *with the same semantic value* as the word you intended to repeat. It's not that this rendition of the success conditions of repetition is inherently wrong (indeed, because I'm not a consumerist, I happen to think that some such rendition is largely, albeit partially, right). It's rather that those who are committed to the causal historical chain *as an answer to the second question*—those committed to the view that words come to us pre-packaged with their semantic value—cannot, on pain of circularity, avail themselves of identity of semantic value as a condition of successful repetition. If the condition of successful repetition is that we be able to look inside you, as it were, (or externally observe your behavior) to see what semantic value your word has, then compare it to the semantic value our word has, and judge them to be the same, then it is not the case that the semantic value of your word is properly parasitic on (or deferential to) the semantic value of our word, in just the way it is purported to be by the historical chain picture of the transmission of semantic values. The historical chain has me committed to the semantic value of the word that is being transmitted to me, *whether I know what that value is or not.* So we can't appeal to what *I take* that value to be (or how I behave with the word) in order to ascertain that a successful repetition has occurred.

But if not by the identity of semantic value between the word emitted and that repeated, how do we ascertain that a successful repetition has taken place? Here I think it will be instructive to review how Kent Bach, in his *Thought and Reference* explains the transmission of semantic value from user to user, since no one to my knowledge has attempted to do so with such a degree of exactitude.

> A speaker can actually *display* his *de re* way of thinking of the object and thereby enable the hearer to think of it in the same way. . . . If the speaker is thinking of something by name, he is entertaining a mental token of the name; when he refers to it by name, he produces a physical token of that name; and the audience, upon hearing *that* token, forms a mental token of *the same* name. (1989: 32, my emphasis)

Note that Bach is here *assuming* that successful repetition has occurred, not explaining *how* it has occurred, or *how* the mental token formed by the audience ends up being a token of the same *name,* as opposed merely to being a token of the same name-*form.* Though the audience can presume that the speaker has produced a physical token of a name, and not merely a physical token of a name-form, how is the audience to distinguish the physical token of that name, from the physical token of any other name having that name-form, given that all that distinguishes the name from another of the same form is its semantic value (which is not perceptible and hence is not recoverable from the produced token)?

Bach answers this worry thus:

> *Since* the hearer's mental token of the name 'inherits' the same object as the speaker's, the object of the hearer's thought is determined relationally, not satisfactionally.
>
> A token of a name can function as a *de re* mode of presentation because its reference is determined by its ancestry. (1989: 32)

Note here that so far the relation between the question of *what ancestry the word has* and the question of whether the repetition has been successful, is taken for granted, and left wholly unaccounted for. But here comes the specific proposal:

> The token plays this role by being *of a certain form* (sound or shape), generally the same as the one to which it is linked. Indeed, *that only its form matters* is what *constitutes* its being used as a name. And that is what enables one to

form *de re* thoughts about an unfamiliar object referred to by that name. Since
the token of a name represents *in virtue of its form,* not its meaning, *its repre-
sentational features can be perceived* by the hearer, who can then and there-
after use mental tokens of the same name to think of (or refer to) the same
object. (1989: 33, my emphasis)

What Bach appears to be saying is that it suffices for repetition to be successful (at least in the case of names) that you have repeated the same
form. Since the form, unlike the semantic value, can be perceived by the
hearer, the hearer is in a position to repeat that form, and to repeat it
successfully.

On the Form of Words

Now, of course, as Kaplan has pointed out, we can't make identity of form
too strictly a matter of resemblance between the two physical embodiments of the token (we want to allow 'Aydelee Murciyur' to count as having the *same form* as 'Adèle Mercier'). So we can't take the sound or the
shape too literally as necessary conditions on the formal identity of the
name.

But neither are similarity of sound and shape *sufficient* conditions on
formal identity. Support for this claim requires a discussion of what counts
as the form of a word. I engage in an all-too-brief discussion of this very
vexing question with the use of two cases.

First case:

I claim to know *three* words 'BARK.' I know the *kind* name (or noun)
'bark', as in that which covers the outside of trees. I know the *action* name
(or verb) 'bark', as in the sonorous emissions by dogs. And I also know a
dog whose *proper* name is 'Bark'. These words may seem formally identical, but I claim that they are not.

In some dialects of English, the words 'writer' and 'rider' are pronounced
exactly alike. If speakers of these dialects were illiterate, the words would
no doubt seem to them formally identical. Still, they would not be. The
word 'writer' is formally related to the verb 'to write,' whereas the word
'rider' is formally related to the verb 'to ride'. The verbs 'to write' and 'to
ride' are pronounced differently and entertain distinct relations with other
words in the language (the verb 'to write' countenances an indirect object
with a *recipient* thematic role: I write a letter to Jones, whereas the verb 'to
ride' countenances an indirect object with a *locative* thematic role: I ride a
horse to Jonestown); hence they are formally distinct. By transitivity of formal identity (or distinctness), 'writer' and 'rider' are formally distinct.

My three words 'bark' are formally distinct (despite appearances) as witnessed by the difference in their formal relations with other words in the language. It is an accident of writing conventions (admittedly a very convenient one!) that we do not display the whole 'deep-structure' trees of the sentences we write, or that we do not subscript the syntactic category of words as we write them. If we did, their formal distinctness would be obvious. We can think of Latin as a language which does exactly this: it marks nouns with case endings and verbs with declension suffixes, thereby displaying their formal distinctness. This is information that it would be redundant to display in English, precisely because it is recoverable (for the most part) from the formal relations the words entertain with one another in the sentence, such as their word-order (Latin is largely a free word-order language), and their satellites (nouns are accompanied by quantifiers, verbs aren't; verbs require subjects, nouns don't; and so on).

Now I say to you: [bark-is-pretty]. (Pretend this is spoken, or written in the International Phonetic Alphabet, so you don't have the benefit of perceiving whether my statement involves a capital or lower case 'b'.) And you intend to repeat what I said.

You will be able to use your syntactic knowledge to eliminate the action name from the options, because you know that verbs can't be subjects of sentences unless they are infinitives (in which case I would be having you repeat: *To* bark is pretty) or unless they are gerunds (in which case I would be having you repeat: Bark*ing* is pretty). So you can perceive that I'm not using the action term 'bark' (your syntactic knowledge gives you access to this perception). But there are still two options left. Now go ahead: Intend to repeat what I said.

Am I saying that bark is pretty? Or am I saying that Bark is pretty? If I were to write it down, then you could use your knowledge of spelling conventions to perceive which word I'm using, the initial capital individuating the word as the proper name, the lack of it as the kind name. Unfortunately, that perceptual access is not available to you here (as it would not be in most cases of linguistic transmissions, which are oral). In your attempt at repetition, are you using the kind name? Or the proper name? What *sort* of word are you repeating?

According to Kaplan and Bach, the answer is easy: you are repeating the same sort of word as the word that I said. But this answer is too easy. I claim that you have not repeated my *word,* indeed that you cannot be said to have repeated *any* word, unless you can make a mental commitment as to the sort of word you are repeating (proper name, common noun, verb, and the like). For without thus committing yourself syntactically, you will not be able to use the word productively yourself, to generate sentences using it. You will not know, for instance, whether you ought to say:

> I wonder whether *the* bark will still be pretty tomorrow.

or

> I wonder whether *B*ark will still be pretty tomorrow.

Without such a commitment, what you have repeated is a word-*form*, not a word; you are behaving like a parrot, not engaging in speech. Like a parrot, you will only be able to repeat sentences previously uttered. What you will have learned is a fixed phrase containing the sequence 'bark' (like infants who learn to say 'whatsdat' but cannot use 'what' and 'that' in other phrases). You will not be a linguistically competent user of any *word* 'bark'.

Now, the point of this exercise is simply to illustrate that not all formal features of a word, indeed not even the most important formal features of a word (such as its syntactic features) are features that the hearer can readily perceive. Note that in the case of repetition of phonetic forms, the speaker has an intuition of formal identity; I say to you: "No, not Aydelee Murciyur: A-dèle Mer-cier." And you repeat after me: "Ay-de-lee Mur-ci-yur." I say to an Australian: "bark," and she repeats: "baak." Here, somehow, the differing phonological rules of different idiolects or dialects function to establish the membership of these superficially distinct forms into an intuitive equivalence class, in spite of the objective phonetic distance between them. That's how speakers of distinct dialects manage to understand each other: distinct phones (sounds) are intuited as counting as the same phonemes.[4] But there is more to a word's being the word that it is than meets the ear. And some of the important formal features of the word (like the syntactic class to which it belongs) are sometimes (in some contexts) just as unrecoverable as its semantic value can be. Words (at least in English) don't wear their syntactic classes on their sleeves. But in the case of syntactic features, there typically isn't the same kind of intuitive judgment of formal identity as that available for phonological equivalence, to act as a criterion of successful repetition. Different phones can correspond to identical phonemes, but there is nothing (obvious) akin to that in syntax.[5]

The second case is invoked to show what serious consequences a failure to perceive certain features of the word can have on whether the word emitted is successfully being repeated, or whether it is not in fact some other event—like an inadvertent new metasemantic event—that is taking place.

Second case:

I witness a commotion involving the police, a citizen and an intellectual-looking book thief. It turns out that the citizen has made a citizen's arrest of the book thief, and the police are discussing the merits of the arrest. The word 'Aristotle' keeps recurring in their conversation. I have never heard that word before but I firmly draw from my experience conclusions that I would voice as "that an aristotle is a form of arrest" and "that the thief has been aristotled." I am a properly deferential language user, so the next day I phone my lawyer to inquire what conditions of arrest individuate an aristotle precisely. My lawyer tells me there is no such thing and that Aristotle was an ancient Greek philosopher. I resolve to consult a more knowledgeable lawyer tomorrow.

Meanwhile, am I having thoughts, even *de dicto,* about Aristotle? Here, as always, intuitions will differ. But I find it *very* counterintuitive to maintain that I am. The word that has (admittedly mistakenly) entered my idiolect has been invested by me with a *syntactic commitment* (as a noun, which morphological rules allow to generate as a verb) that is syntactically incompatible with its being a proper name for an animate object. By the syntactic rules of English as well as of my own idiolect, singular nouns require determiners but proper names for animate objects shun them. If it were suggested to me that I was thinking that Aristotle is a form of arrest, the suggestion would strike me not just as false (given my intuitions), but as grammatically ill-formed. I can no more think that *aristotle is a form of arrest* than I can think that *door is an opening in the wall.* These thoughts are missing a logical constituent (nothing less than a quantifier). They are incomplete. It is a matter of syntax that I cannot entertain them.

The word that has entered my idiolect has also been invested by me with a *sortal commitment*—as a (would-be) legal kind term—that is categorially incompatible with its being a proper name for an animate object. I understand the thought that 'Aristotle' is a form of arrest: that is the mistaken thought that the word 'Aristotle' refers in the public language to a form of arrest. But what kind of thought is the thought *de dicto* that Aristotle is a form of arrest? What would it mean to think that there exists something that has both the properties of being Aristotle and a form of arrest, or to think that something is both a form of arrest and a famous ancient Greek philosopher? What propositions would these sentences express such that one could be related to them in thought? These thoughts are so semantically deviant that I am not sure in what sense one can really be said to entertain them. They are nonsense.

Having checked with a convincing number of lawyers, I finally relinquish my understanding of events. How should I describe my own relinquishment? Two suggestions have philosophical currency.

The causal theorist's account goes something like this: I have finally gotten a *better mastery* of the word 'Aristotle' which is the term I have been repeating from the outset; I have finally realized that it is not a common noun but a proper name for an animate object. Whereas before I produced syntactically deviant strings, I now know how to use the word in syntactically well-formed sentences.

The metasemantic creationist's account goes something like this: I have discovered that I failed to repeat the word I intended to repeat and instead metasemantically created a new word, the common noun 'aristotle' meaning a kind of citizen's arrest (with its concomitant verb form yielded by productive morphology). This is a word not shared by others; consequently, I must be very careful when using it to communicate (which means it will soon fade into the dark recesses of unused words). I have also discovered that others use the homonym 'Aristotle,' a proper name for an animate object, and I promptly add this new word to my lexicon, deferring to authorities about its reference.

How shall we adjudicate between these suggestions?

Note that the causal theorist's account countenances a single word, of which the speaker develops progressive mastery. The metasemantic creationist account, on the other hand, countenances two words, of which one is more socially useful than the other. Briefly, three reasons are standardly put forward for preferring a one-word account: One, that it is a requirement of commonality of concepts, and hence of communication; two, that without it, we could not explain progressive mastery of a word; and three, that word-creation is a privilege "reserved to parents, scientists, and headline writers for *Variety*" (Kaplan 1989). I shall not discuss these reasons except to state very briefly why I find none of them convincing.

The third is a popularly held normative belief; but who initiates the existence of new words is an entirely empirical matter, better determined by linguists than by the naive populace. (I surmise without argument here that the most productive creators of new words are not parents and the literati but children and bilinguals.) The first and second reasons stated are dubious for the following reasons: I have just invented a verb 'to aristotle'. It means to perform a kind of citizen's arrest. The verb has vague boundaries, because I made it up and I'm vague about citizens' arrests. Many (perhaps most) words have vague boundaries. (Is wine that has begun turning to vinegar still wine?) Nevertheless, it seems to me that you and I have succeeded in communicating, and in sharing in the concept of an aristotle, as well (or as poorly) as we ever do. It is true that there has been no progressive mastery of a single word; rather, there has been progressive mastery *of the social language,* in the form of a substitution of a socially useless word in favor of a socially useful one. To insist that what we need is always an account of progressive mastery *of a word* is to beg the question in favor of the one-word approach. It is also to miss the important distinction between acquiring more information *about the referent* of a word, and being so confused *about the word* as not to succeed in acquiring it at all.

There is essentially one reason for preferring a two-word account over a one-word account. But it is a very good reason. It is that the vast majority of our words share a causal history with other, formally distinct, words. For example, the verb 'to table' is formally a different word than the noun 'table', as witnessed by the fact that they are not substitutable *salva veritate*. In fact, they are not substitutable *salva formulae* (their substitution destroys well-formedness). The words 'warden' and 'guardian' are different words (it is possible to know one without knowing the other) despite the fact that they are just distinct pronunciations of the same original word. The same holds for the English word 'wasp' and the French word 'guêpe'. And in spite of their near perfect resemblance, the English word 'formidable' is a very different word from the French word 'formidable' (as I startlingly discovered after thanking English-speaking hosts for their "formidable hospitality"). Yet in all these pairs, both words share a causal history—up to their difference, that is. The general problem with the one-word account, or with word-individuation by causal history, is that it yields *way* too few words (and *way* too few languages).

On Formal Identity and Word Individuation

The cases that I have provided above argue to the conclusion that the phonetic or orthographic form of words does not suffice to establish their formal identity. Two words can sound (or be spelled) exactly alike and yet be formally distinct. I now turn to argue that even formal identity is not sufficient to individuate words. Two words can be formally identical and yet be distinct words. The argument begins with a tale of two countries.

Marco Polo is shipwrecked on land that he has explored and knows to be an island. (Liberties with historical detail have been taken in service of the argument.) He utterly ignores the existence of the African mainland, and, let us say, given the geographic information gathered during his travels, he would vehemently deny its existence. So Polo has the following belief: There is no mainland within proximity of this island. A native from a country on the African mainland—a country called 'Madagascar' (allegedly from 'Mogadiscio')—appears (one who felicitously speaks English) and the following happens: Polo introduces himself as coming "from Venice" and as having survived the shipwreck "of the Santa Venezia"; mistakenly assuming that the native lives on the island, he asks her what the name of her country is, to which she replies "Madagascar."

At least a new *word-form* has been transmitted from the native's language to Polo's. Polo has the general semantic intention typical of language learners: he forms a deferential meta-linguistic intention to use the word 'Madagascar' to stand for whatever the native uses it to stand for. At the same time, Polo assigns certain sortal features to the new word in his lexicon. This is something he must do to be able to use the new word-form productively in syntactically well-formed strings. As it happens, the semantic and syntactic contexts in which the question is raised and answered felicitously allow Polo to perceive correctly at least some sortal features of the word-form—namely, that it is a *proper* name, and a proper name for a *land mass*.

But they might not have. The context might have (mis)led Polo to perceive the name 'Madagascar' as a proper name for a ship, say. For instance, he could have (mis)heard the native's hesitative 'euh' before 'Madagascar' as 'the Madagascar' and inferred that the native had (mis)heard his word 'country' as 'dory'. Polo would then have produced syntactically deviant sentences (inserting the determiner 'the' before the name), or more precisely, sentences that would have seemed syntactically deviant to the native while seeming well-formed to Polo. This ought to suffice as proof that Polo's deferential intention is so easily defeasible that his linguistic behavior cannot be individuated by it: if the word we should countenance Polo as using is determined by his deferential intention, then the syntactic rules of Polo's idiolect have to be described as allowing a determiner before a (singular) land mass name, something which (by hypothesis, as in English) they do not allow. But let me not press the point.

Happily, as it happens, Polo has assigned to the word the same formal features as has the native. So he is able to communicate with the native with sentences that seem to both to be syntactically well-formed and semantically non-deviant, like: "When I return home, I intend to tell my people about Madagascar."

The fact that Polo is capable of producing well-formed sentences using the new word shows that he has acquired a new word, though it does not settle the question of *which* new word it is that he has acquired. And here the causal theory is led into a dilemma. If Polo has acquired a different word, a new word 'Madagascar' applying to the island on which he is stranded—call it Madagascar$_2$—then the causal theorist is left with the question of how he could have consumed *that* word, given that it is nowhere around to be consumed. If he has repeated the same word as the native, then his intention *de dicto* is to tell his people about the native's mainland country. But this intention, even *de dicto*, is only quite dubiously attributable to Polo. How can he intend to inform his people of something he not only knows nothing about but whose existence he would vehemently deny? Moreover, the view that he has received *the* word that was being passed down along the chain—call it Madagascar$_1$—is inconsistent with our feeling that the word he has passed down to *us* is Madagascar$_2$, the word whose semantic value is the island, not the one whose semantic value is the country on the mainland.

Polo begins his travel memoirs with the sentence: Madagascar is an island. This sentence expresses a false belief in Polo's idiolect, if the causal-historical picture is right. It expresses a true belief only if he has single-handedly invented the new word 'Madagascar$_2$' and is using that word in that sentence. Had Polo read his memoirs to the native, the original linguistic mistake might have been discovered, and hence corrected, and Polo would have changed the mode of expression of his belief. But he didn't.

Two unfortunate consequences follow from the view that the word picked up by Polo is to be individuated by its causal antecedents, i.e., that he has actually picked up the word 'Madagascar$_1$'. The first results from Bach's view of communication-based *de re* thought. Paraphrasing Bach to fit our case:

> The native has actually displayed her *de re* way of thinking of the object and thereby enabled Polo to think of it in the same way. The native was thinking of something (the country on the mainland) by name, and thus entertaining a mental token of the name; when the native referred to it by name, she produced a physical token of that name; and Polo, upon hearing that token, formed a mental token of the same name. Since the token of the name represents in virtue of its form, not its meaning, and since its representational features were perceived by Polo, he can then and thereafter use mental tokens of the same name to think of (or refer to) the same object (the country on the mainland).

This is indeed a puzzling view. We began our story with Polo vehemently convinced that he was surrounded by nothing but water. He picks up a word from some perfect stranger, and with no new information whatsoever, Ta-Da!, he is not merely (unbeknownst to himself) *referring* to some country on the mainland, but actually able to have a *de re thought* about it. (Take comfort in this story next time you're stranded on some lost island.)

The second unfortunate consequence of the causal-historical picture results from the predictions of the view about what happens when Polo comes home and tells us that he has been stranded on the island of Madagascar. By the historical chain of transmission, Polo is talking about the mainland. So when he says "the island of Madagascar" he is using a semantically anomalous construction, on a par, say, with 'the island of Idaho.' But since we cannot (and, according to the theory, need not) perceive the semantic value of the term, we are oblivious to the semantic anomaly and we promptly form a belief that we express as: Madagascar is an island. This is a false belief given our intention to repeat the same name as Polo was intending to repeat, and given that the semantic value of *that* word is a country on the mainland (Madagascar/Mogadiscio), not an island. So, courtesy of the causal-historical chain, we are all mistaken (even the Malagasy are mistaken!), that Madagascar is an island.

Worse than that, since in virtually all cases we ignore the causal origins of the actual chains of communication linking us to the words we use, in all good conscience, we must be skeptical of virtually *all* sortal claims we typically take very much for granted: That Aristotle was a person, that Canada is a country, that Idaho is not a sort of animal, etc. Since the semantic value of these words is imperceptible but comes pre-packaged with the word down the chain, we have *no* way of checking that the word has not strayed off course. We are at the mercy of lexicography.

This is a reductio of the causal-historical picture, one which Searle has forcefully rendered in his inimitable style, by rhetorically asking if we are ready to accept that our name 'Plato' might turn out to refer to a barstool in Hoboken, New Jersey. Some causal theorists, for instance Kripke, have shown the good sense to use this picture with moderation, witness the presence in Kripke's writings of cautious—though undeveloped—passages such as this:

> The name is passed on from link to link. But of course *not every sort* of causal chain reaching from me to a certain man will do for me to make a reference. There may be a causal chain from our use of the term 'Santa Claus' to a certain historical saint, but still the children, when they use this, by this time *probably* do not refer to that saint. (1972: 93, my emphasis)

And about 'Madagascar', Kripke has this to say:

> Evans has pointed out that similar cases of reference shifts arise where the shift is not from a real entity to a fictional one, but from one real entity to another of the same kind. . . . Today the usage of the name as a name for an island has become so widespread that it surely overrides any historical connection with the native name. (1972: 163)

In an effort to counter the reductio, we now pursue the nature and justification of the "probably" in the Santa Claus quote, and the means available to the causal-historical picture as explanations of *how* the historical connections *can* be "overridden." Continues Kripke:

> So other conditions must be satisfied in order to make this into a rigorous theory of reference. I don't know that I'm going to do this because . . . I'm sort of too lazy. (1972: 93)

I want to point out that some of the conditions that appear to be necessary to make the picture work (all of which involve some measure of individual metasemantic autonomy) are in direct conflict with some of the core tenets of the very picture (consumerism) of which they appear to be necessary conditions.

On Conditions of Existence and Word Individuation

Kripke argues in *Naming & Necessity* for a principle that we can call the Principle that Existence Precedes Essence.[6] It is a common intuition that, though unicorns (and Santa Claus) don't exist, they could exist; the intuition is that it is simply a contingent fact that white horses with horns don't roam our prairies, and that no person satisfies a weighted sum of the properties from among the cluster of properties attributed to Santa Claus; there is no reason to think that such creatures, or that person, don't exist in other possible worlds. Kripke argues against this common intuition:

> Even if archeologists or geologists were to discover tomorrow some fossils conclusively showing the existence of animals in the past satisfying everything we know about unicorns ... that would not show that there were unicorns. (1972: 24)

His point is easy, and, I think, persuasive. In order for me to have modal properties (the possibility of being other than I am in another possible world, as it were), it is necessary that I maintain my identity across possibilities (that *I* be in those other worlds). What makes me *me*, as opposed to anyone else who's merely superficially indistinguishable from me, are my conditions of existence (for example, that I am the product of a certain specific egg and a certain specific sperm). To locate me in another world, you have to find someone in that other world who satisfies my conditions of existence.

Conditions of existence are a function of actuality. We start with the object as given and derive from it the conditions failing which *that* object would not be in existence. In the case of unicorns, if we start with unicorns as they are given to us, namely *as fictitious objects,* we see that it is essential to their individuation that they *have* no conditions of existence. (Or, if you prefer a Meinongian approach, it is part of their conditions of existence as they are given to us that they be fictitious objects.) So the white horned horses in other worlds, though admittedly very unicorn-like, are not our unicorns. What about the creatures discovered by the archeologists? Well, for exactly the same reasons, neither are they. They may be completely unicorn-like, but our unicorns are fictitious objects, and as such they don't leave bones lying around; so whatever bones are being found are not unicorn bones.

Note here that Kripke might have expressed his views about unicorns more cautiously. Since he does not have access to the *actual* chain of communication linking his use of the term 'unicorn' to past uses of that term, *for all he knows,* the word may well have come down to him through a historical chain linking his current use of the term to an original metasemantic event that involved ostention to a certain kind, the bones of which are only now being recovered by archeologists. We might all (except presumably the original coiner of the term) have been wrong all along that unicorns never existed—in which case, of course, the bones uncovered would be unicorn bones. So Kripke might have said, more cautiously, that provided that the actual chain of communication through which the word 'unicorn' was transmitted to him did not tie his current usage to past existing creatures, whatever the archeologists discover are not unicorns.

That is not what he says, though it is probably what he means. He is no doubt assuming that we are right in thinking that the chain of communication leads back only as far as properly fictitious objects. On the other hand, given what he says about Santa Claus—where he acknowledges that children "probably" mean a fictitious object *even if* we know there to be a chain leading back to a previously existing person—we can interpret him as saying about unicorns that even if there is a chain leading back to some previously existing kind, *somehow* we have (probably?) gotten freed from that chain. Otherwise, given that causal-historical word transmission chains leave precious few fossil traces (and none but overly speculative ones beyond a certain past), why wouldn't the discovery of unicorn-like bones strongly suggest to us that the chain *did* indeed lead back to existing unicorns?

In a similar vein, with respect to our use of the word 'Madagascar', Kripke might say that though there *is* a chain leading back to the country on the mainland, somehow we have gotten disconnected from that chain. Kripke says:

> In all cases [where a reference shift occurs], a present intention to refer to a given entity (or to refer fictionally) overrides the original intention to preserve reference in the historical chain of transmission. (1972:163)

He continues: "The matter deserves extended discussion," a discussion to which he never returns.

There appears to be a real tension between the commitments of the causal-historical picture—namely, that reference is a function of the actual chain of communication, a metaphysical, not an epistemic, fact—and the existence of reference shifts—which are imbued with epistemology. The kind of (aborted) reference shift I initiated with 'aristotle', like the kind of (sustained) reference shift initiated by the namers of Bark, depended on what I shall call *commitments de dicto*. I call them thus to emphasize two things: first, that minimal competence with a word requires a mental attitude *about the word* in the form of an assignment to the word of syntactic and sortal categories; second (and consequently), that there are virtually no thoughts that are *purely de dicto*, in the sense of being purely parasitic on the language, with no psychological contribution whatsoever by the language user. It is my understanding (however mistaken) of the word 'aristotle' as being of a certain sort—and the will of the namers of Bark to make a verb into a proper name—that resulted in a shift in the sorts of things that could be their reference. The reference shift in Polo's case depended not on his different understanding of the sort of word it was but on his commitment to use it to refer to the island on which he was standing (on his "present intention to refer to a given entity"). Epistemic considerations pervade both cases. My reference shift is due to my beliefs about the word's syntax; it follows from my interpretation of the syntactic intentions of its users. Their actual syntactic intentions are irrelevant to the word I would have passed down to my children had I not noticed and repented of the errors of my ways. Polo's reference shift is due to his beliefs about the word's semantics; it follows from his interpretation of the native's referential intentions. Their actual referential intentions are irrelevant to the word Polo passed down to us. If language users' intentions to preserve reference (or to defer reference) were truly as resilient as they would have to be for the historical chain picture to provide an explanatory account of word transmission, it would be a mystery how an individual's spontaneous commitments *de dicto* (sortal assignment or intention to refer) could override them.

On Intentions to Refer and Word Transmission

Kripke's only attempt to resolve this tension (that I have been able to locate) occurs in the following passage:

> The phenomenon [of reference shift] is perhaps roughly explicable in terms of the predominantly social character of the use of proper names: . . . we use names to communicate with other speakers in a common language. This character dictates ordinarily that a speaker intend to use a name the same way as it was transmitted to him; but in the 'Madagascar' case this *social* character dictates that the present intention to refer to an island overrides the *distant* link to native usage. (1972: 163, my emphasis)

This passage is far from explanatory. The two facts that need reconciling are these: first, the fact that *Polo* intends to use the name 'Madagascar' the same way as it was transmitted to him (and hence by the causal-historical picture refers to the country on the mainland); and second, the fact that he manages, somehow, to bring home a word that refers to the island instead (in violation of the causal-historical picture). The appeal to the social character of language is singularly unhelpful. It misses the point that our current—social, if you like—intention to refer to an island by our use of the word 'Madagascar' *would not exist* if Polo had not brought home a word

'Madagascar' referring to an island. For had Polo brought home the original word 'Madagascar', we too, by virtue of our commitment to the historical chain, would be referring by its means to the mainland. For we are not, and only Polo is, epistemically close enough to the island to form an overriding "present intention to refer to a given entity."

What really needs explaining is the fact that *Polo* succeeded in overriding the link to native usage, a link that was *not* distant from him but singularly close. Since by hypothesis Polo is alone on the island, the appeal to the social character of language is spurious here.

Even the much bandied about distinction between speaker-meaning and semantic-meaning will not help to elucidate matters here. Say if you will that Madagascar-the-island is Polo's speaker-meaning, and that Madagascar-the-mainland is the semantic-meaning. What needs explaining then is how Polo's speaker-meaning becomes our semantic-meaning.

The problem is that what gets passed down causal-historical chains are semantic-meanings, not speaker-meanings. Surely we don't want to end up saying that, though Madagascar-the-mainland is really our current semantic-referent, we are always, all of us, using Polo's speaker-referent when we speak of Madagascar and that's how we succeed in referring to the island. But if there has been no shift in semantic-meaning from the native's language to Polo's language, then the semantic-referent we have inherited from Polo that has been passed down to us by the chain remains Madagascar-the-mainland.

The problem boils down to explaining how Polo's speaker-referent becomes his semantic-referent, so that it can become our semantic-referent. (It doesn't actually matter where along the chain, if not with Polo, the change occurs; the fact is that the speaker-referent of some consumer or other along the chain has to become a semantic-referent so that it can become our semantic-referent.) But the appeal to the social character of language will not explain how Polo's speaker-referent (or anyone else's) becomes his semantic-referent. The social character of language could possibly play a part in such an explanation only if there existed at some point a social language in which the semantic-referent of 'Madagascar' were Madagascar-the-island. But the problem is that the causal-historical picture itself precludes the generation of such a language, by precluding the generation of individual speakers who could together constitute the speakers of such a language. Simply to stipulate that a new semantic-referent comes into being when a sufficient number of speakers share new speaker-referents is not to explain it.

To begin to explain how Polo's speaker-referent can become his semantic-referent, I claim, we have to look at *individualistic* aspects of Polo's interaction with the *word* 'Madagascar' as it gets transmitted to him. Alternatively or additionally, we have to explain how the speaker-referents of each of the members of the critical mass necessary to bring about a semantic change in the social language can become each of their semantic referents. To begin to do this, and for all the same reasons, we have to look at *individualistic* aspects of each of *their* interactions with the word 'Madagascar' as it gets transmitted to each of them as links in the chain. These individualistic aspects can *change* the word (that is, can subvert the chain), thereby changing its semantic referent. Conversely, where the chain is not broken but succeeds in handing the same word down the generations, it is *because* each individual, as a link in the chain, has individually succeeded in reproducing the same word. Historical-causal chains cannot provide an explanation of word transmission because they exist only in retrospect.

On Commitments *de dicto* and Conditions of Existence

It is in our individualistic interaction with words that commitments *de dicto* play a crucial role. To illustrate how they do, let me start with the coining of a new word. Whenever a new word is coined, whether its reference is fixed by ostention or by description, the coiner is always, however implicitly, investing the word with sortal commitments, that is, commitments as to the sort of word the new word is. When the reference is fixed by ostention, there is always an implicit sort of thing that is being demonstrated, which correlates with the sortal commitment of the word that is being coined (recall the pedantically called Principle of the Description-Laddenness of Ostention). The same goes where the reference is fixed by description. Though Leverrier does not know what thing is causing the perturbations in the orbit of Uranus (he doesn't know if it's a planet, a star, a meteorite shower, a god), as I claimed above, there have to be some sortal conditions on his succeeding to refer. Let me now illustrate why this is so.

Suppose that the universe is unstable, and every two months a new object comes to perturb the orbit of Uranus. By coining the name 'Neptune' for the cause of the perturbations in the orbit of Uranus, has Leverrier thereby named 'Neptune' the *series* of such causes? Is *that* the sort of thing that can be satisfied by his description 'the cause of the perturbations in the orbit of Uranus'? Or is it rather that, on this supposition, Leverrier has simply failed to refer to anything on the grounds that a series of causes (separated by months) doesn't count as a particular, and hence the description fails to be uniquely satisfied? Suppose Leverrier has miscalculated the orbit of Uranus, and there are no perturbations. Is 'Neptune' then just another name Leverrier has invented for Nothing, or is it rather a name he has invented for nothing?

We may not always be in a position to know the answer to such questions. But I maintain that Leverrier *would*—indeed, would *have* to—have some intuitions (if probed) about the sortal conditions that must be met in order for him to succeed in referring to something (and, complementarily, intuitions about the conditions failing which his efforts constitute an abortive attempt at naming). For without such sortal intuitions, Leverrier would not know whether he has coined a proper name, a kind term, or some term of another category, information he needs if he is to use the word productively, that is, in novel sentences. For Leverrier to have such intuitions is tantamount to his having intuitions about what he would have to learn about how the world is, to conclude that he had not succeeded in referring at all by means of the name 'Neptune'.

Even when we do not coin a word ourselves but rather receive it (allegedly) pre-coined—or "semantically pre-packaged" as Kaplan would have it—again, a condition of our being able to use the new word productively is that we commit it to being a word of a certain sort. It will often, perhaps typically, be the case that the preexisting sortal commitments of a word being transmitted down the chain will be recoverable from the sentential context in which the word first appears to us, as when Polo tells us that he has just "returned from Madagascar." Since we understand that one returns from a place, and that since Polo is an earthian explorer, the sort of place he has in mind is probably a land mass, our sortal assignment will likely reproduce that of the transmitted word. 'Madagascar' will then enter our lexicon as a land mass term. We will thus have repeated a word that is formally identical to Polo's, that is, one whose occurrence in a sentence satisfies the same syntactic and categorial restrictions.

Moreover, since we are deferential about the semantic value of this proper land mass name—*and* provided that we do not form a present intention to refer to a given entity—we will thus have repeated a word that is semantically identical to Polo's. We will *consequently* have added a new link in the ongoing chain.

But sortals are often not perceptible. Different sortal kinds can occur in the same syntactic contexts. For example, a sentence such as (1)

(1) I can't wait to return to Madagascar.

is consistent with 'Madagascar' being a person's name as much as a place name. And a language (such as Catalan for example) which puts determiners in front of proper personal names makes using the syntax to distinguish proper names from common nouns unavailable, as in (2):

(2) I'm relieved to have found the John.

In such cases, the hearer may assign to the transmitted word different sortal commitments than those it had in the mouth of the speaker, thereby unwittingly performing a metasemantic act initiating a formally distinct word, that is, one whose occurrence in sentences other than those from which it was transmitted will be subject to distinct syntactic or categorial restrictions.

The exact conditions under which the context of acquisition of a word will maintain or change its sortal commitments may be too complex and aleatory to specify. But I suggest the following as a test for one's *de dicto* commitments. We can call it the Conditions of Existence Test. It consists in consulting one's intuitions about how the world would have to be in order for one to conclude that a word as one uses it is an abortive attempt at referring (even in fiction). The properties one intuits will not suffice to determine the referents of these words. Nor should they, since we do not always know enough about the referents of our words to identify them. But they do constrain the sorts of objects the referents must be. It is indeed because our (current) word 'unicorn' is the sort of word it is that it cannot have as its referent the sort of thing the archeologists are uncovering. It is, in turn, that sort of word (a word assigned to fictitious discourse) not because of metaphysical facts about the actual chain of communication, since for all we know that chain does reach back to existing objects. Rather, it is that sort of word because of some aspect of our epistemic state as the word became fossilized in our lexicon. The relevant aspect of this epistemic state consists in whatever explains our *de facto* assignments of commitments *de dicto*. An explanation of these assignments can only be made on a case by case basis, if at all; but all my argument requires is that we do make them, and I think I have shown why we must. Nothing less than our ability to use words productively depends on it. And if productive use is not the core of word competence, I don't know what could be.

The case of Polo is different from simply deferential cases because of his present intention to refer to the given island on which he is standing. But it is wrong to think simply that Polo's intention to refer to the island is an overriding intention. Polo, after all, does intend to defer, and he would have relinquished his use of the word had he been corrected in a timely fashion. At least at first, he intends to defer more than he intends to refer: he is no Humpty Dumpty. But in the absence of a correction, it is his *belief* that the deferential intention is satisfied which allows the referential intention to take over. It is this belief which is playing the causal role in his assignment of semantic value to the word 'Madagascar', that is, in individuating as new the word 'Madagascar' making its way into his idiolect.

Semantic change is as pervasive a phenomenon as it is because the conflict between referential and deferential intentions is often too subtle for detection. Because linguistic contexts are underspecified, people can easily be (mis)led to believe that their deferential intention has been satisfied, and so the fact that the referential intention has overridden the deferential intention escapes correction. That is how a hearer may reproduce a word formally identical to that transmitted, yet still create a substantively new word.

On Conditions of Existence and the Contingent *A Priori*

It is a contingent fact about Neptune that it ever caused perturbations in the orbit of Uranus. But this (if Kripke is right) is a fact that Leverrier knows *a priori*. He knows this *a priori* precisely because he has used the description to fix the referent of 'Neptune' to whatever satisfies it. He knows it *a priori* in the sense that it is knowledge (in whatever sense we can call it knowledge) that he has gotten simply by his understanding of his own language. Likewise, it is a contingent fact that Canada is a land mass on earth; but in exactly the same way that it makes sense to say of Leverrier that he knows *a priori* that Neptune is the cause of the perturbations, that Canada is a land mass is a fact that I know (in whatever sense we can call it knowledge) *a priori:* not because I am innately endowed with geographic information, but because the word 'Canada' has entered my lexicon *as* a land mass name.

Right now, try as I might, I cannot imagine any way the world might be where the referent of my word 'Canada' fails to be a land mass—though I can easily imagine it to be a different land mass than the one I would identify. (I can also easily imagine a way my language might be where the referent of my word 'Canada' in it would fail to be a land mass term.) It is true that I might right now be wrong about my own stated intuitions. The right example might convince me of that. Intuitions about one's own competence can be more or less refined. Let's just assume that mine are sophisticated enough that my self-knowledge about my word 'Canada' is accurate.

There may well be *some* word 'Canada' that does not refer to a land mass (indeed there is, and it refers to huts); but *that* word 'Canada', though causally connected to my word 'Canada', was never part of *my* language.

If I am being duped by an evil genie into believing that there is actually a land mass under my feet when in fact there are no land masses anywhere, then regardless of what 'Canada' means in the mouths of other people, I think I can safely say about my own competence that I have failed by means of this word to refer.

Conclusion

As the cases of 'Bark' and 'aristotle' show, the phonological (or orthographic) form of a word alone is not individuative of its formal identity. As the case of 'Madagascar' shows, even formal identity is not sufficient to individuate words. We deny this at the cost of denying ourselves an explanation of language variety and semantic change.

Words do not reproduce as if by mitosis, multiplying exact copies of each other. Their reproduction rather mimics genetic reproduction: words are complex, multi-layered and deep-structured objects, some of whose features get passed on from parent-word to child-word, while some do not. This should be no surprise. Since words have to be absorbed by minds in order to be productively used by them, the "copying-fidelity" of word-transmission can only be as accurate (or as inaccurate) as the copying-fidelity of mind-reproduction. Our words are genetically different because (relevant epistemic aspects of) our minds are.

The causal-historical picture has the cart leading the horse. Polo's attempt at repetition of the very word 'Madagascar' which was being transmitted to him by the native has failed. It has failed because Polo inadvertently assigned a different semantic value to the word. *As a consequence,* the historical chain of communication was broken, and a new word came into being. By contrast, our attempt at repetition of the word 'Madagascar' that was transmitted to us by Polo has succeeded. It has succeeded *because* we managed to reproduce Polo's commitments *de dicto.* It is a consequence of this fact that the historical chain of communication remained unbroken, and that the same word was transmitted.

Criticisms of the description theory have shown (to my mind, roughly conclusively) that, at least where we form no intention to refer to a given entity, we do not assign semantic values to our words. But we can use words productively in well-formed sentences even when we do not know their semantic values. However, we cannot use words productively in well-formed (or semantically non-deviant) sentences unless we think of those words as words of a certain syntactic and categorial sort. And what sort of word a word is will affect not what *thing,* but what *sort* of thing it can have as a referent.

Criticisms of the description theory have not shown that sortal assignment is not a matter of individualistic competence. If we "inherited" through the causal-historical chain the sortal commitment of the word along with its semantic value, we could not account for how "real reference can shift to another real reference, fictional reference can shift to real, and real to fictional" as Kripke allows that it can. It is plausible to suppose that it is when people started attributing outlandish supernatural properties to Saint Nicholas that they distorted the semantic context of transmission of the name, which encouraged the recipients to adjust their sortal commitments, thereby transforming the name 'Santa Claus' into the (new) name of a fictitious entity.

Metasemantic events are not the sole privilege of original coiners of words. They reflect the syntactic and semantic adjustments that we each make as we acquire words in our lexicon, without which languages would not be in the constant state of drift in which they inexorably are. Far from showing that reference is strictly a metaphysical matter, where, as Kripke says, only "the actual chain of communication is relevant," these adjustments in our commitments *de dicto* are imbued with epistemological content. Though our beliefs do not *determine* the referents of our words (it was the mistake of descriptivism to purport that they did), they do affect the sorts of words we countenance. And that affects, not their referents directly, but the sorts of things that can be their referents. Commitments *de dicto* reintroduce a measure of individual autonomy, which disrupts the flow (and much of the relevance) of the historical chain.

I apologize for the tortuous route of this argument which I now bring to a close, but I hope that through it you see that Kripke's metaphysical principle that Existence Precedes Essence has a metasemantic (read: epistemic) analog. It is that Commitments Precede Reference.

Notes

1. I am grateful to Bill Demopoulos, Bill Harper, Ausonio Marras, Rob Stainton, Arthur Sullivan, members of the Department of Philosophy Colloquia at Queen's University, at the University of Western Ontario and at McGill University for stimulating discussions on the content of this paper. I am grateful also to the Social Sciences and Humanities Research Council of Canada for a research grant enabling its production.

2. See for example Frege's discussion of the sense of the name 'Dr. Lauben' in "The Thought: A Logical Inquiry."

3. See Burge (1979), where he discusses the case of a community which uses the word 'sofa' to refer to objects that are indistinguishable from our sofas but that are used as religious artifacts. Burge thinks that someone from our community who thinks of sofas as religious artifacts nevertheless has the same concept of a sofa (uses the same word 'sofa') as the rest of us—witness that person's propensity to accept correction.

The present paper provides a different take on the nature of the accepted correction.

4. North Americans and Australians understand each other by understanding that the North American *sound* [ar] and the different Australian *sound* [aa] often have the same *phonemic* value (make the same contribution to individuating words).

5. For example, I surmise that speakers of distinct dialects would have trouble understanding each other if what was a noun for one was a verb for another. Being a noun or being a verb affects the individuation of the word, because it affects its semantic value, as well as its contribution to conditions of well-formedness of sentences in which it appears. The only counterexample I can think of is the adverbial use of 'good' in some dialects (as in "My child is doing *good* in school.") which is understood even by speakers of dialects which restrict the use of 'good' to an adjective.

6. The expression is borrowed from Joseph Almog (and ultimately from Sartre!).

References

Bach, K. 1987. *Thought and Reference.* Clarendon Press.

Burge, T. 1979. "Individualism and the Mental." In *Studies in Epistemology: Midwest Studies in Philosophy,* Vol. 4, edited by French, Euhling and Wettstein. University of Minnesota Press.

Donnellan, K. S. 1970. "Proper Names and Identifying Descriptions." *Synthese* 21: 335–58.

Frege, G. 1918. "The Thought: A Logical Inquiry." In *Philosophical Logic,* edited by P. Strawson, Oxford Readings in Philosophy, Oxford University Press.

Kaplan, D. 1989. "Afterthoughts." In *Themes from Kaplan,* edited by Almog, Perry and Wettstein, Oxford University Press.

———. 1990. "Words." *Proceedings of the Aristotelian Society,* LXIV: 93–119.

Kripke, S. A. 1972. *Naming and Necessity.* Harvard University Press.

Putnam, H. 1975. "The Meaning of 'Meaning'." In *Mind, Language and Reality.* Cambridge University Press.

Searle, J. 1983. "Proper Names and Intentionality." In *Intentionality.* Cambridge University Press.

4

Situations and the Structure of Content

François Recanati

1. Introduction

1.1 Austinian semantics

According to Austin (1971), the meaning of an utterance can be analysed in two factors: the situation s the utterance refers to, and the utterance's descriptive content σ. The utterance is true iff σ adequately classifies s, that is, iff the situation referred to "is of a type with which the sentence is correlated by the descriptive conventions" of the language (1971: 122).

Different interpretations of Austin's view have been put forward in the literature. Two main questions arise in this respect: first, what is 'the situation referred to'? Second, what is the utterance's 'descriptive content'? One common answer to the first question must be ruled out from the outset because it is too uncharitable an interpretation of Austin's view: The situation referred to by an utterance such as 'The cat is on the mat' cannot be the state of affairs represented by the utterance, that is, the cat's being on the mat, for then there would be no way for an utterance to be false—the utterance's descriptive content would be built into the situation referred to. A better interpretation, close to the letter of Austin's writings, takes the situation referred to be a complex consisting of all the entities (things, times, places, etc.) referred to in the utterance. Let us assume that 'the cat' and 'the mat' are referring expressions in such a way that 'The cat is on the mat' refers to the cat c, to the mat m and to the time of utterance τ. The situation referred to, therefore, is the sequence $<c, m, \tau>$, while the descriptive content of the utterance is a Russellian 'propositional function', expressible by the open sentence 'x is on y at t'. Austin's definition of truth thus entails that:

> 'The cat is on the mat' is true iff $<c, m, \tau>$ satisfies 'x is on y at t'

Such an interpretation of Austin was offered (and elaborated) by Herman Cappelen and Josh Dever in a seminar in Berkeley in 1994.

A third interpretation is due to Barwise and Etchemendy (1987). Instead of construing the descriptive content of the utterance as exclusive of all demonstrative elements, as Austin himself does, they construe it as a proposition in the traditional sense, say, as a Kaplanian content. Thus the descriptive content of 'The cat is on the mat' is the singular proposition consisting of the 'on' relation and the above-mentioned sequence:

$$<\text{On}, <c, m, \tau> >$$

The situation referred to, for Barwise and Etchemendy, is the portion of reality the speaker intends to be saying something about. To be sure, this situation is normally indicated by various elements in the sentence, elements which are governed by those 'demonstrative conventions' of which Austin says that they determine the situation referred to. Thus the present tense indicates that the speaker intends to talk about what's going on at the time of utterance, and the referring expression 'the cat' indicates that it is the whereabouts of the cat that the speaker is concerned with. The point of the Barwise-Etchemendy proposal, however, is that the situation talked about need *not* be linguistically articulated. They give the following example:

> If the sentence "Claire has the ace of hearts" is used to describe a particular poker hand, then on the Austinian view the speaker has made a claim that the relevant situation is of the type in which Claire has the ace of hearts. Notice that such a claim could fail simply because Claire wasn't present, even if Claire had the ace of hearts in a card game across town. (Barwise and Etchemendy 1987:29)

The particular poker hand the speaker is commenting on is not linguistically articulated; it is given only by the context. That is why the situation talked about cannot be merely that to which the sentence (token) is correlated by what Austin calls the demonstrative conventions of the language.[1] A more significant departure from Austin, however, is the claim that the entities referred to by the demonstrative constituents of the sentence (e.g., Claire, referred to by the proper name 'Claire') can themselves be constitutive of the descriptive content of the utterance. In the present example, Barwise and Etchemendy take the descriptive content to be the singular proposition that Claire has the ace of hearts. That proposition determines a type of situation, viz. the type of situation in which Claire has the ace of hearts. In Barwise's and Etchemendy's framework, the utterance says of the particular poker hand talked about that it is a situation of that type.

Though it significantly departs from the letter of Austin's writings, the Barwise-Etchemendy interpretation is faithful to its spirit. It entails that the content of every utterance, whether indexical or not, depends upon the context (since it is the context which determines what counts as the situation referred to); a view which certainly was Austin's. Be that as it may, I find the Barwise-Etchemendy view interesting in its own right, and it is that view which I will elaborate in this paper.[2] What I find most interesting in that view is the claim that there are two levels of truth-evaluable content, two propositions which an utterance expresses: a content in the classical, Kaplanian sense (e.g., for the utterance 'Claire has the ace of hearts', the proposition that Claire has the ace of hearts); and an Austinian proposition, to the effect that the situation talked about supports that content.

1.2 The debate over 'what is said'

One reason why I am interested in elaborating the semantic theory suggested by the Barwise-Etchemendy interpretation of Austin is that it connects up with recent discussions in pragmatics, concerning the notion of 'what is said'. In this section I summarize those discussions.

Anyone who has reflected on the sentence meaning/utterance meaning distinction knows that a simple distinction is in fact insufficient. Two equally important distinctions must be made.

(i) First, there is the distinction between the linguistic meaning of a sentence-type, and what is said (the proposition expressed) by an utterance of the sentence. For example, the English sentence 'I am French' has a certain meaning which, *qua* meaning of a sentence-type, is not affected by changes in the context of utterance. This context-independent meaning contrasts with the context-dependent propositions which the sentence expresses with respect to particular contexts. Thus 'I am French', said by me, expresses the proposition that I am French; if you utter the sentence, it expresses a different proposition, even though its linguistic meaning remains the same across contexts of use.

(ii) Second, we have the distinction between what is actually said and what is merely 'conveyed' by the utterance. My utterance of 'I am French' expresses the proposition that I am French, but there are contexts in which it conveys much more. Suppose that, having been asked whether I can cook, I reply: "I am French." Clearly my utterance (in this context) provides an affirmative answer to the question. The meaning of the utterance in such a case includes more than what is literally said; it also includes what the utterance 'implicates'.

'What is said' being a term common to both distinctions, we end up with a triad:

sentence meaning
vs.
what is said
vs.
what is implicated

The distinguishing characteristic of sentence meaning (the linguistic meaning of the sentence-type) is that it is conventional and context-independent. Moreover, in general at least, it falls short of constituting a complete proposition, i.e., something truth-evaluable. In contrast, both 'what is said' and 'what is implicated' are context-dependent and propositional. The difference between 'what is said' and 'what is implicated' is that the former is constrained by sentence meaning in a way in which the implicatures aren't. What is said results from fleshing out the meaning of the sentence (which is like a semantic 'skeleton') so as to make it propositional. The propositions one can arrive at through this process of 'fleshing out' are constrained by the skeleton which serves as input to the process. Thus 'I am French' can express an indefinite number of propositions, but the propositions in question all have to be compatible with the semantic potential of the sentence; that is why the English sentence 'I am French' cannot express the proposition that kangaroos have tails. There is no such constraint on the propositions which an utterance of the sentence can communicate through the mechanism of implicature. Given enough background, an utterance of 'I am French' might implicate that kangaroos have tails. What's implicated is implicated by virtue of an inference, and the inference chain can (in principle) be as long and involve as many background assumptions as one wishes.

The basic triad can be mapped back onto the simple sentence meaning/speaker's meaning distinction by grouping together two of the three levels. There are two ways to do it, corresponding to two interpretations for the triad. The first interpretation stresses the close connection between sentence meaning and what is said; together, sentence meaning and what is said constitute the *literal meaning* of the utterance as opposed to what *the speaker* means.

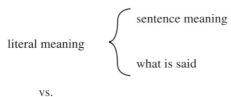

literal meaning $\left\{ \begin{array}{l} \text{sentence meaning} \\ \\ \text{what is said} \end{array} \right.$

vs.

speaker's meaning

The other interpretation stresses the commonality between what is said and what is implicated, both of which are taken to be pragmatically determined:

sentence meaning

vs.

peaker's meaning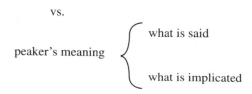
what is said

what is implicated

Essential to this interpretation is the claim that 'what is said', though constrained by the meaning of the sentence, is not as tightly constrained as is traditionally thought.

The first interpretation corresponds to a widespread doctrine which I call pragmatic *Minimalism*. According to that doctrine, 'what is said' departs from the meaning of the sentence (and incorporates contextual elements) *only when this is necessary to 'complete' the meaning of the sentence and make it propositional.* In other words, the distance between sentence meaning and what is said is kept to a minimum (hence the name 'Minimalism'). Thus an indexical sentence-type such as 'He is tall' does not express a complete proposition unless a referent has been contextually assigned to the demonstrative pronoun 'he', which acts like a free variable in need of contextual instantiation. 'Saturation' (or, in Kent Bach's terminology, 'completion') is the contextual process whereby the meaning of such a sentence is completed and made propositional. Other contextual processes—e.g., the inference process generating implicatures—are semantically *optional* in the sense that the aspects of meaning they generate are dispensable: The utterance would still express a complete proposition without them. According to Minimalism, those extra constituents of meaning which are not necessary for propositionality are external to what is said. The only justification for including some pragmatically determined constituent of meaning into what is said (as opposed to what is merely conveyed) is the indispensability of such a constituent—the fact that the utterance would not express a complete proposition if the context did not provide such a constituent.

As an illustration, consider examples (1) and (2), respectively borrowed from Sperber and Wilson (1986) and Kent Bach (1994):

(1) I've had breakfast.
(2) You are not going to die.

Arguably, sentence (1) expresses the proposition that the speaker has had breakfast before the time of utterance. Strictly speaking this proposition would be true if the speaker had had breakfast twenty years ago and never since. That is clearly not what the speaker means (when she answers the question 'Do you want something to eat?' by replying 'I've had breakfast.'); she means something much more specific, namely that she's had breakfast *this morning*. This aspect of speaker's meaning, however, has to be construed as external to what is said and as being merely conveyed, in the same way in which the utterer of 'I am French' implies, but does not say, that he is a good cook. That is so because the 'minimal' interpretation, to the effect that the speaker's life has not been entirely breakfastless, is sufficient to make the utterance propositional without having to bring in the implicit reference to a particular time.

The same thing holds for the other example. Kent Bach, to whom it is due, imagines a child crying because of a minor cut and her mother uttering (2) in response. What is meant is: 'You're not going to die from that cut.' But literally the utterance expresses the proposition that the kid will not die *tout court*—as if he or she was immortal. The extra element contextually provided (the implicit reference to the cut) is not necessary for the utterance to express a complete proposition, hence it does not constitute a component of what is said in the minimalist sense.

Opposed to Minimalism is pragmatic *Maximalism*—the view I have defended and elaborated over the years (Recanati 1993, 1995). According to that view, the relevant distinction is not between mandatory and optional contextual processes, but between those that are 'primary' and those that are 'secondary'. Primary pragmatic processes help determine what is said. Secondary pragmatic processes are inferential processes: they take 'what is said' as input and yield further propositions (the implicatures) as output. Now primary pragmatic processes include not only saturation, but also 'optional' processes such as free enrichment. That is so because, in general, the notion of 'what is said' that is needed to capture the input to secondary, inferential processes already incorporates contextual elements of the optional variety. In the examples above, the speaker implies various things by saying what she does: she implies that she is not hungry, or that the cut is not serious. Those implicatures can be worked out only if the speaker is recognized as expressing the proposition that she's had breakfast *this morning,* or that the child won't die *from that cut.*

Minimalism   **Maximalism**

Sentence meaning   *Sentence meaning*
       | |
saturation   primary pragmatic processes
       | (saturation and optional processes
       | such as enrichment or transfer)
       ↓   ↓
what is said$_{min}$ *What is said$_{max}$*
       | |
optional processes   secondary pragmatic processes
       ↓   ↓
what is communicated   *what is communicated*

What is said in the Maximalist sense corresponds to the intuitive truth-conditions of the utterance, that is, to the content of the statement as the participants in the conversation themselves would gloss it. In contrast, the literal truth-conditions posited as part of the Minimalist analysis turn out to be very different from the intuitive truth-conditions which untutored conversational participants would ascribe to the utterance. Minimalist theorists acknowledge (and sometimes even applaud) this divorce between what is said as a theoretical entity and our intuitions of what is said. Maximalists like myself find it unbearable: insofar as 'saying' is a particular form of meaning$_{nn}$, the statement which is made by uttering a sentence depends upon, and can hardly be severed from, the speaker's publicly recognizable intentions.

1.3 Austinian propositions and minimal content

It has been suggested that the dispute may be verbal to some extent. Why should we not distinguish two notions of what is said: a purely semantic, Minimalist notion, and a pragmatic notion ('what is stated' as opposed to 'what is implied')? If we accept this suggestion (voiced by Nathan Salmon (1991) and Kent Bach (1994)), we end up with four levels instead of three:

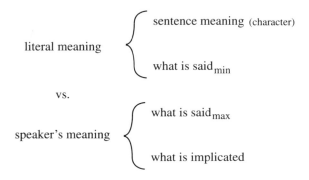

Such a compromise view would seem to be acceptable to both the Minimalist and the Maximalist. The Minimalist wants to isolate a purely semantic notion of content, that is, a notion of the content of a sentence (with respect to a context) which is compositionally determined and takes pragmatic elements on board only when this is necessary. The Maximalist wants to capture the intuitive notion of 'what is said' (as opposed to what is implied) and stresses that what is said in that sense is, to a large extent, determined in a top down manner by the context. Both notions can be had simultaneously if one accepts replacing the traditional triad by a four-level picture:

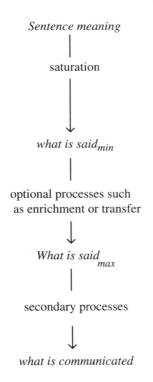

Sentence meaning

saturation

what is said$_{min}$

optional processes such
as enrichment or transfer

What is said$_{max}$

secondary processes

what is communicated

Is the suggested compromise workable? Ultimately I don't think it is, but I agree that we should try to go as far as we can in that ecumenical direction. It is here that Austinian semantics can be most useful. Remember the main claim: An utterance is true iff the situation s it refers to supports the fact σ it expresses. The complete truth-conditional content of an utterance therefore is:

$$s \vDash \sigma$$

This complete content, or Austinian proposition, is distinct from the proposition σ on the right hand side of the support sign ⊨. So there are two levels of content, two propositions which every utterance expresses: the fact σ which is stated, and the Austinian proposition to the effect that the situation of reference supports that fact.

There is much in common between the right hand side σ in the Austinian proposition (I call it the 'nucleus') and Minimalist content. Consider the examples I gave to illustrate Minimalism:

(1) I've had breakfast.
(2) You're not going to die.

In the Austinian framework we can put the meaning constituent generated by free enrichment on the situational side, and keep the nucleus 'minimal' or nearly so. Thus in (1) the speaker refers to a temporally circumscribed situation (viz. the situation on the day of utterance) and characterizes *it* as a situation in which the speaker has had breakfast. In the same way, the mother who utters (2) refers to the specific situation brought about by the child's cut, and characterizes *it* as a situation in which the child does not die. The proposition on the right hand side of the Austinian formula is thus exactly what the sentence seems to express; there is no need to consider the sentence as somehow 'elliptical'. The same thing holds for the cases in which a quantifier is contextually restricted: the contextual domain of the quantifier is nothing other than the situation talked about, in the Austinian framework (Recanati 1996). It follows that the nucleus itself is unaffected by contextual restrictions on the domain of quantification. The Austinian framework, therefore, helps us to implement the compromise view imagined by Salmon and Bach. As in the latter we have four levels, with the notion of 'what is said' split in two:

- sentence meaning
- what is said$_1$: nucleus
- what is said$_2$: Austinian proposition
- what is implicated

Ultimately, I think the equation between nucleus and minimal content will have to be given up (see 5.2 below). Still, there is a rather obvious similarity between them, and interpreting the nucleus in this light—that is, as an approximation of the sort of 'literal content' the Minimalist has in mind—usefully constrains our understanding of situations and the general form which Austinian semantics must take.

2. The 'Support' Relation

2.1 Situations, facts, and worlds

According to Austinian semantics, utterances refer to situations and what they say (their Kaplanian content) is predicated of those situations. But what are 'situations'? When confronted with this question, we should be wary of conflating situations in the ordinary sense and situations in the technical sense. The technical notion of 'situation' we find in situation theory has much wider application than the ordinary notion. Situations, in the ordinary sense, are 'eventualities'—perhaps a specific sub-class of 'stative' eventualities. Eventualities are a special type of entity, distinct from other types (e.g., individual objects, groups, places, or times). But every entity, of whatever sort, is a 'situation' in the technical sense, insofar as we can think of it and store information about it. At least this is how I will elaborate the notion of 'situation' which is at the center of Austinian semantics.

The reason why I keep using the possibly misleading term 'situation' is this. A situation in the ordinary sense supports facts and can be seen as a micro-universe (the world itself being 'the collection of all the facts,' as Wittgenstein wrote). Take the situation here and now as I am writing this. It contains a number of facts: the fact that I am typing on my computer, the fact that my children are playing with a cat and keep interrupting me, and so forth. Situations in the ordinary sense contain entities having properties and standing in relation to one another. That feature is precisely what the technical notion of 'situation' is meant to capture (and to generalize). What characterizes situations in the technical sense is their double nature: They are entities and, *qua* entities, they have properties and bear relations to other entities; at the same time they are like a micro-universe *containing* entities having properties and bearing relations to other entities. We capture this double nature by associating each entity (each situation) with a set of facts (the *factual set* of the entity).

Facts, or states of affairs, are triples consisting of an n-place relation, a sequence of n appropriate arguments, and a polarity which is '+' if the relation obtains between the arguments and '−' if it doesn't. (A fact is negative if the polarity is '−'. By default, a fact is considered as positive; thus I will often omit the '+' sign in what follows.) The items in the sequence of arguments are called the (material)[3] constituents of the fact. Each situation determines a set of facts, namely the set of facts in which the situation itself is a constituent. Thus consider the situation s = London in the 19th century. Suppose it's a fact that: *in 19th century London, poor children used to work hard.* That fact concerns the situation s (it contains it as a constituent), hence it goes into the set of facts which the situation determines. In the same way, the fact that Freud was bald concerns Freud, hence it goes into the set of facts determined by the 'situation' Freud. The set of facts determined by a situation contains all the facts of which that situation is a constituent.

Suppose it was a contingent fact that Freud was bald. We want to capture this contingency. It will not be captured if the set of facts associated with a situation is considered as definitive of that situation. If a situation *is* the set of facts it determines, then it cannot be a contingent fact that a situation contains such and such a fact. That is why we must distinguish situations (entities) from the sets of facts they determine. Situations determine sets of facts only relative to a world.

What is a world? On the present view there are two components in a world *w:* a domain of entities, Dom (w); and a function w from entities (situations) in that domain to sets of facts. The set of facts associated with a situation $s \in$ Dom (w) is the set $w(s)$. The contingency of Freud's baldness is thus captured: the fact that Freud was bald belongs to the factual set actually associated with Freud, but in other possible worlds the factual set associated with Freud would not have contained that fact. Different worlds can associate different sets of facts with the same situations (entities) if the situations in question are in the domains of those worlds. Thus Nixon has the property of resigning in the actual world, but not in other possible worlds in which he exists. This simply means that the fact that Nixon resigned belongs to @(Nixon), but not to w(Nixon), for some world $w \neq @$.

Let us now turn to Austinian propositions. An Austinian proposition says that a situation, s, supports a fact σ. The 'support' relation is relative to a world, hence instead of '$s \vDash \sigma$', we should write:

$$s \vDash_w \sigma$$

In what follows, however, I will subscript the relation only when necessary (i.e., when distinct worlds are simultaneously at issue: see 3.3 and 3.4).

Knowing what situations and facts are, can we define the 'support' relation? The obvious candidate is:

$$s \vDash \sigma \text{ iff } \sigma \in w(s)$$

But that will not do. Consider, for example, the utterance 'Everyone is asleep.' We want σ to approximate the minimal content of the utterance. This means that the contextual restriction (everyone *in group G*) does not affect σ but only the situational component s: 'Everyone is asleep' thus states the same (nonpersistent) fact σ whatever situation we are referring to. But if we accept the definition of 'support' above, we'll have to take σ to be the (persistent) fact that everyone is asleep *in situation s.* That is so because the facts in $w(s)$ contain s as a constituent. Owing to that feature, the definition of 'support' above entails that the contextual restriction of the quantifier affects the nucleus σ. If we want the latter to approximate the minimal content of the utterance, we must change the definition of 'support'. I suggest the following:

$$s \models \sigma \text{ iff } \sigma \in w(s)_r$$

The subscript 'r' indicates that the facts of $w(s)$ have been 'relativised', where relativisation is a form of 'backgrounding'. To that topic I now turn.

2.2 Backgrounding and variable polyadicity

From a given relation R, further relations can be *generated* by increasing or decreasing the arity of R. Consider the relation between the seller and the buyer in a commercial transaction. There are a number of argument roles in that relation: not only *buyer* and *seller,* but also the *goods* to be transferred, the *money,* and so forth. As Fillmore pointed out, verbs like 'buy' and 'sell' cannot be understood without mastering the complete 'frame' which serves to define both (see e.g., Fillmore (1975), (1982), Fillmore and Atkins (1992)). Still, each verb highlights different aspects of the frame, by making different sets of argument roles obligatory to fill. With 'buy', the buyer and the object bought must be specified (linguistically or contextually), but the other argument roles can be left unfilled; with 'sell', it is the seller and the goods which must be specified. The buyer is optional, as the seller in the case of 'buy'. This provides an argument in favour of the view that 'buy' and 'sell' express *distinct* relations, if we agree with Devlin that "part of the complex structure that constitutes a 'relation' is the collection of conditions that determine which particular groups of argument roles need to be filled" (1991: 121). Let us therefore consider that the Fillmorian frame evoked by both 'sell' and 'buy' denotes a complex relation R*, while each of the two verbs denotes a distinct relation R, such that the set of argument roles of R is included in the set of argument roles of R*.

When an argument role is left unfilled, as the *seller* role in 'John bought a house', the existence of an object playing that role is implicit since it is part of the semantic frame evoked by the verb. In such a case, following Fillmore, I will say that the relevant argument role is *backgrounded*. The argument roles which are filled are *foregrounded* (or 'profiled', in the terminology of Langacker (1987)). Leaving an argument role unfilled is equivalent to existentially quantifiying over its values. Thus 'John bought a house' is equivalent to 'John bought a house from someone, who sold it'. 'John has eaten' is equivalent to 'John has eaten something edible.' But it does not follow that 'John has eaten something' and 'John has eaten' say the same thing and involve the same relations. On the view I am defending, 'John has eaten' involves a one-place relation (a property), while 'John has eaten something' involves a two-place relation, one of the arguments of which is unspecified.

Grammatical constructions contribute a lot to foregrounding and backgrounding. Consider (3):

(3) The house was sold.

The commercial transaction frame is evoked, and it is evoked through the verb 'sell' which lexically foregrounds the *seller* role. Yet the passive construction has the well-known effect of backgrounding the argument role associated with the subject term in the active form—here the *seller* role which the verb normally highlights.[4] The grammatical construction can also foreground some aspect of the frame. Thus in (4), the ditransitive construction foregrounds the *buyer* role back despite its being backgrounded by the verb 'sell':

(4) John sold Bill the house.

We cannot say that the relation here is a two-place relation between a buyer and an object bought, on the grounds that these two roles are the roles which the verb 'sell' renders obligatory to fill. The *buyer* role, though it might have been left unfilled without ungrammaticality (had another construction been used), is foregrounded in (4) through the ditransitive construction. In that construction, therefore, 'sell' expresses a three-place relation between the seller, the buyer, and the goods—the same type of three-place relation which the verb 'give' expresses, except that the verb 'give' always (or nearly always) expresses a three-place relation, while 'sell' makes only two argument roles obligatory to fill.

The ditransitive construction turns the two-place relation denoted by the verb 'sell' into a three-place relation. Similarly, adverbial adjuncts turn *n*-place relations (e.g., 'John studies geography') into $n+1$ place relations ('John studies geography at UCLA'). In this framework, the inferential pattern which motivated Davidson's analysis of action sentences can be accounted for by appealing to the (fairly general) principle that, when two relations are related to each other by arity-decreasing/increasing operations such as these, the relation with greater arity entails the other one: R_{n+1} entails R_n. Thus we have the following inference pattern:

> John studies geography at UCLA → John studies geography
> John sold Bill the house. → John sold the house.
> John walks the dog. → The dog walks.
> John eats a banana. → John eats.
> John buttered the toast in the kitchen. → John buttered the toast.

There are exceptions, though. For example, it is not obvious that 'It's raining in Nevada' entails 'It's raining,' at least if 'It's raining' is interpreted in the sense of 'It's raining here and now.' It may be raining in Nevada without there being rain here and now. In general, the $R_{n+1} \rightarrow R_n$

inference pattern becomes problematic whenever the right hand side of the entailment relation is an instance of 'definite null instantiation' (DNI) in Fillmore's sense. DNI is a special case of backgrounding where the backgrounded argument role is contextually filled instead of being un-filled (Fillmore 1986, Fillmore and Kay 1994). I will return to that topic in the next section.

It should be noticed that the 'walk' alternation above is significantly dif-ferent from the other examples. First, the arguments are linked to different grammatical functions on the two sides of the alternation; in contrast the other alternations do not affect linking. More important for our purposes, the 'walk' example does not support an argument pattern which the other examples illustrate. While we have:

> John studies geography. → John studies geography somewhere.
> John sold the house. → John sold the house to someone.
> John eats. → John eats something.

we don't have:

> The dog walks. ↛ Someone walks the dog.

This fact shows that the two-place relation 'walk' in 'John walks the dog' does not belong to the WALK frame. Rather, it belongs to a more complex frame containing the WALK frame as a part. A relation R belongs to a frame Φ iff it can be obtained from the complex relation $R*$ denoted by Φ by decreasing the arity of $R*$. R then corresponds to a particular aspect of the frame which is highlighted or focussed on. When that is the case, the ar-gument roles of $R*$ which are not profiled (replicated as argument roles in R) are still present in the background via the evoked frame. As those back-ground roles are not filled, the general effect is that of quantifying over the values of the role: that explains the inference pattern above. We don't find this inference pattern in the 'walk' case because the argument role corre-sponding to the person walking the walker is not part of the WALK frame; not being part of the evoked frame, there is no reason why it should be im-plicit when we say 'The dog walks.'

2.3 Relativisation

I have just mentioned cases in which the backgrounded argument role is left unfilled. In other cases, however, the backgrounded argument role *is* filled. This corresponds to what Perry (1986) calls 'unarticulated con-stituents.' An argument is unarticulated when it corresponds to an argu-ment role which no linguistic expression is used to fill, but which is nevertheless *contextually* filled. Fillmore and Kay (1994) refer to this process as 'Definite Null Instantiation' (DNI), as opposed to 'Indefinite Null Instantiation' (INI). Compare 'I've eaten' (INI) and 'I've noticed' (DNI). In both cases the object (the thing eaten or the thing noticed) is left implicit. In the case of 'I've noticed', however, the object noticed must be contextually identifiable for the utterance to be felicitous. This is not the case for 'I've eaten', as we have seen: 'I've eaten' can be understood to mean that the speaker has eaten something or other. This sort of reading is not available for 'I've noticed'.[5]

In Indefinite Null Instantiation, the relevant argument role is left unfilled; in Definite Null Instantiation, it is contextually filled. Shall we say— as I did above—that it is backgrounded (because it is left implicit), or that it is foregrounded (because it is filled)? It does not really matter what we say, as long as we make a clear distinction between *three* types of case:

> Unfilled argument roles
> vs.
> Contextually filled argument roles
> vs.
> Linguistically filled argument roles

The operation on facts which Barwise (1989: 253–4) calls 'relativisation' corresponds to the second case. A fact which contains a certain constituent can be turned into a fact not containing that constituent, by appropriately decreasing the relation. The resulting fact is said to be 'relativised to' the constituent in question. This operation makes sense whenever the missing constituent is contextually provided or 'presupposed'.

Relativisation is pervasive in natural language. More often than not, when we state a fact, some constituent of the fact is contextually given and somehow taken for granted. Instead of expressing the more complex fact containing that constituent, what we linguistically express is the simpler fact relativised to that constituent. Barwise gives perspectives as an example. When Holmes says 'The salt is left of the pepper,' he expresses a relativised fact:

> Left-of (salt, pepper)

This fact holds with respect to Holmes's perspective, but that perspective is not a constituent of the (relativised) fact. Rather, it is an aspect of the situation talked about.

Perry's distinction between 'concerning' and 'being about' (Perry 1986) is useful here. A fact is about something iff that thing is a constituent of the fact. The fact

Left-of (salt, pepper, Holmes's perspective)

is 'about' Holmes's perspective in that sense. But Holmes's own words, 'The salt is left of the pepper,' do not express that fact; they express the *relativised* fact that the salt is left of the pepper. The relativised fact 'concerns' Holmes's perspective, but it is not 'about' it.

In Barwise's example, the perspective need not be linguistically articulated because it is given in the context. Similarly in Perry's own example, 'It is raining.' The person who says 'It is raining' talks about a certain location and expresses a relativised fact concerning that location: the fact that it's raining. That fact is distinct from the (apparently) unrelativised fact that *it is raining at that location.* It is felicitous to express the latter type of fact only if the location in question is contrasted with other possible places where it might rain (or not rain). If no contrast is envisioned and only that location is concerned, there is no need to articulate it by expressing the more complex fact.

It is in terms of this notion of relativised fact that I propose that we define the 'support' relation. I said that all the facts in the factual set of a situation contain that situation as a constituent:

$$(\sigma)\ (s)\ (\sigma \in w(s) \supset s \in \sigma)$$

Now a fact σ belonging to a situation s can be relativised to that situation. The relativised fact σ_r holds with respect to s—it 'concerns' s—even if it is not part of $w(s)$ (it does not contain s as a constituent and thus is not 'about' it). I interpret Austinian semantics as the claim that natural language utterances express relativised facts of this sort. That is why I build relativisation into my definition of the 'support' relation. Corresponding to $w(s)$, the factual set of the situation s, there is $w(s)_r$, the set of all the facts of $w(s)$ relativised to s. A situation s supports a fact σ iff $\sigma \in w(s)_r$.

3. δ-Structures

3.1 Mentioning situations

In 2.3 I claimed that the fact linguistically expressed by an utterance is relativised to the situation talked about. But that does not seem always to be the case. Instead of merely saying, 'It is raining,' I can say, 'It is raining here'—thereby making the location I am talking about explicit. Similarly, Holmes could say: 'The salt is left of the pepper *from my perspective*,' thereby making the perspective explicit. As the situation talked about is made explicit in the utterance itself, it becomes a constituent of the fact linguistically expressed. It follows that the fact in question cannot be relativised to that situation, for a fact cannot be relativised to α if it contains α as a constituent.[6] By building relativisation into our definition of $\models$ do we not run the risk of depriving ourselves of the means of accounting for such cases?

We do not. We have no trouble accounting for 'explicit' cases in the framework set up so far, in which only relativised facts are taken to be linguistically expressed. In explicit cases like 'It's raining here' or 'The salt is left of the pepper from Holmes's perspective,' the fact is not relativised *to the situation which is explicitly mentioned in the utterance,* but it is relativised nonetheless—to a different situation.

Let us contrast Holmes's utterance with Watson's:

> Holmes: The salt is left of the pepper.
> Watson: The salt is left of the pepper from Holmes's
>   perspective.

The first utterance presupposes Holmes's perspective and expresses a fact relativised to that perspective. The second utterance makes that perspective explicit by integrating it as a constituent of the fact linguistically expressed. The latter is not relativised to Holmes's perspective, but it is not unrelativised either: it is relativised to a distinct situation, namely the situation *Watson* is talking about. The situation Watson talks about contains Holmes, the salt and the pepper. That is not the same situation as the situation Holmes was talking about in the first place, for the latter contained only the pepper and the salt (it did not contain Holmes).[7] In general, when we make some aspect of the earlier situation explicit by incorporating it into the fact linguistically expressed, the utterance demands a broader situation of reference than the implicit utterance did: it demands (= is felicitous only with respect to) a situation of reference containing the new constituent in its domain.[8]

On the view I am presenting, the fact linguistically expressed by an utterance is relativised to the situation talked about, and there is a principled difference between the situation talked about and the 'mentioned situation' which is a constituent of the linguistically expressed fact. The situation talked about must conform to a specific constraint concerning the size of its domain. The domain of a situation contains the constituents of all the facts in its relativised factual set. Now to assert something is to claim that the fact the utterance expresses belongs to the relativised factual set of the situation talked about. It follows that, when a fact is linguistically expressed, the situation it concerns—that which the speaker is talking about—must contain all the constituents of the expressed fact in its domain, on pains of pragmatic contradiction. Since the mentioned situation is a constituent of the linguistically expressed fact, the situation of reference s' must contain the mentioned situation s in its domain. The mentioned situation is subject to no such constraint: it need not contain itself in its domain.

Consider the 'It is raining' example again. Suppose John is in Condé sur Huisne, and he says: 'It is raining.' His utterance concerns Condé sur Huisne and is true if and only if it's raining in Condé sur Huisne. As Perry emphasized (1986: 216), when we say or think 'It is raining', we need not think *reflectively* about the place we're in, even though that place enters the truth-conditions of what we say. We let the place we are in complete the content of our thought, instead of representing it explicitly. The complete content of John's utterance can therefore be represented as:

Condé sur Huisne ⊨ <<It is raining>>

where Condé sur Huisne is on the situational side, rather than on the side of linguistically expressed content.

If John reflectively thinks of the location he is in, instead of letting it be provided by the context, he will say something different, namely 'It is raining in Condé sur Huisne.' The utterance is now *about* Condé sur Huisne. One difference with the previous utterance is that the situation talked about *must* contain Condé sur Huisne as a constituent, while this was not necessary for the simpler utterance 'It is raining'. Anticipating somewhat, we can represent the content of 'It is raining in Condé sur Huisne' as:

s' ⊨ <<Condé sur Huisne ⊨ <<It is raining>> >>

where the situation s' must contain Condé sur Huisne in its domain. For example, we can imagine that John is talking about the meteorological situation in various places, such as Condé sur Huisne and Cajarc. He says: "In Cajarc, the sun is shining, but it is raining in Condé sur Huisne." Here the situation s' John is talking about contains both Cajarc and Condé sur Huisne in its domain. It is *that* situation which is said to support 'It is raining in Condé sur Huisne'.

At this point, it is worth introducing a technical term instead of using a number of equivalent expressions such as 'the situation talked about', 'the situation of reference', or 'the situation with respect to which the utterance is interpreted'. From now on I will use the technical term 'exercised situation' instead of 'situation talked about' and its cognates. In formulas, I will enclose the expression standing for the exercised situation in square brackets. Thus the Austinian proposition expressed by an utterance will be represented as:

[s'] ⊨ σ

The special case in which a situation is linguistically mentioned and is a constituent of the expressed fact will be represented by iterating the Austinian formula:

$$[s'] \models\; <<s \models \sigma>>$$

Such an iterated Austinian proposition I call a δ-structure. It contains two situations: s', the exercised situation, and s, the mentioned situation; two 'support' relations: one between the exercised situation and the linguistically expressed fact, the other internal to the linguistically expressed fact; and two facts: the fact that s $\models \sigma$ and the fact that σ.

3.2 δ-structures in English

In my version of Austinian semantics, the content of most utterances in ordinary English has the structure:

$$[s'] \models\; <<s \models \sigma>>$$

That is so because utterances are tensed and the tenses I treat as 'mentioning' temporal situations (much as temporal adverbials do). Thus utterances of the form

> (At *t*) it will be the case that *p*

and

> (At *t*) it was the case that *p*

are instances of the schema:

$$[s'] \models\; <<l_t \models \sigma>>$$

where s' is the exercised situation, and l_t, the mentioned situation, is a (past or future) temporal location. Concrete examples are:

(5) Yesterday Paul attended the meeting.
(6) I saw the accident on TV.
(7) When he arrived, Peter was upset.
(8) You will break your neck!
(9) Jane is feeding the rabbits.

Similar examples involving spatial locations are easy to come by:

(10) In Spain, the government is appointed by the King.
(11) Three miles from here, there is an architectural treasure.

Those examples I analyse as

$$[\text{s'}] \vDash\, << l_s \vDash \sigma>>$$

where l_s is the location denoted by 'in Spain' or 'Three miles from here'. (In the first case, the location is geopolitical rather than spatial in a strict sense.) It is an interesting fact that the reference to temporal locations is built into the grammar of the language via the tense feature, while spatial locations are in most cases introduced into the linguistically expressed fact via adverbial adjuncts. But the expressed fact has, in both cases, the same structure, and that is all that matters here.

Beside locations, any type of situation (in the technical sense, that is, any type of entity) can be mentioned in a δ-structure. That is true in particular of individual objects, insofar as they can be treated as situations in the technical sense (2.1). In the present framework, the content of a simple subject-predicate sentence such as 'John is British' is also a δ-structure:

$$[\text{s'}] \vDash\, <<\text{John} \vDash <<\text{British}^0, +>> >>$$

The subject term contributes the mentioned situation (viz. John), and the predicate contributes a 'thetic fact' which that situation is said to support (viz. the fact of being British). Let me explain.

The *factual set* of an individual object is the set of facts involving that object as constituent, while the *relativised factual set* consists of all the facts in the factual set relativised to the object itself. This means that, whatever relation R^n is a constituent of a fact in the factual set of s, the corresponding fact in its relativised factual set will be built around the relation R^{n-1}, with s itself disappearing from the sequence of arguments. The relativised factual set is the set of all such relativised facts. Now consider an individual object, John, and the property of being British. This gives us a fact: $<<\text{British}^1, <\text{John}>,$ $+>>$, a fact which belongs to the factual set of John. The monadic relation British^1 is a constituent of that fact, together with the individual John. If we relativise that fact to John, we obtain a fact with an 0-adic relation and no argument: the fact $<<\text{British}^0, +>>$. The relativised factual set of John thus contains a number of such 0-adic facts, facts relativised to John himself, in the same way in which the relativised factual set of a spatio-temporal location can contain the 0-adic fact $<<\text{Rain}^0, +>>$. (On the 'rain' predicate as 0-adic, see Barwise and Perry (1983: 50–51), and Fillmore and Kay (1994 4.3))[9]

0-adic facts can sometimes be expressed directly, as when we say 'Superb!' about a performance we are watching. An Austinian proposition is expressed, in which the performance is the exercised situation and the nucleus is the 0-adic fact $<<Superb^0, +>>$. This corresponds to what grammarians in the Brentanian tradition called a thetic judgement, and to what others in the Saussurean tradition called a 'monoreme'. Thetic judgements were said to be simple, in contrast to categoric judgements such as that expressed by 'John is British' (or 'This performance is superb.'). Categoric judgements are 'double' in that they involve two ancillary acts: (i) the identification of some entity (or entities), and (ii) the predication of some property or relation holding of that entity (or sequence of entities). Since the second ancillary act is common to the thetic judgement and the categoric judgement, we can analyse categoric judgements as denoting complex facts with two components: a thetic fact, plus a situation which supports it.

$$<<British^1, <John>, +>>$$
$$=$$
$$<<John \models <<British^0, +>> >>$$

On this analysis there is a semantic contrast between the thetic utterance 'Superb!', *concerning* the performance, and the categoric utterance 'This performance is superb', in which the performance is *mentioned* in the utterance itself:

Thetic: [the performance] $\models <<Superb^0, +>>$
Categoric: $[s'] \models <<the\ performance \models <<Superb^0, +>> >>$

This contrast is the same as that between 'It is raining' and 'It is raining here' (3.1). Traditionally, existential sentences ('There are spies') and weather sentences ('It is raining') were considered as expressing thetic judgments. Since those sentences are tensed, the claim that they express thetic judgements is somewhat controversial. A better example is provided by children's one-word utterances (e.g., 'Rain!'). In this type of utterance, some contextually provided topic is globally characterized by means of a 0-adic predicate (Lyons 1975, Sechehaye 1926). Except for this type of case, English sentences express δ-structures of various degrees of complexity— i.e., not only simple δ-structures, but also *iterated δ-structures* conforming to the following pattern:

$$[s_n] \models <<s_{n-1} \models << s_{n-2} \models ... \models \sigma ... >>$$

Iterated δ-structures abound in ordinary discourse. A simple example in which the only mentioned situations are locations is:

(12) Two miles from here, a huge building will be erected.

The structure of this representation is

$$[s_3] \vDash \, <<s_2 \vDash \, << s_1 \vDash \sigma >> >>$$

where σ is the fact that a huge building is erected, s_1 is the temporal situation indicated by the future tense, s_2 is the spatial situation denoted by the phrase 'two miles from here', and s_3 is the exercised situation. If what I said above is correct, a grammatically simpler sentence such as 'Napoleon was ambitious' can be construed as expressing an iterated δ-structure of the same degree of complexity:

$$[s] \vDash \, << l_t \vDash \, <<\text{Napoleon} \vDash \, <<\text{Ambitious}^0, +>> >> >>$$

More complex δ-structures are far from uncommon. A good example (from Recanati 1997) is the English sentence 'The landlord thought that, in 1996, Peter would be penniless', which involves five distinct situations.

δ-structures can also be quantified. In a *quantified* δ-*structure,* no specific situation is mentioned, but a general fact is linguistically expressed. We have:

$$[s'] \vDash \, << Qs: s \vDash \sigma>>$$

where Q can be any (possibly restricted) quantifier. For example the following utterances express universally quantified δ-structures:

(13) Each time he comes, John asks for a break.
(14) John always succeeds.
(15) Everywhere in France, there are communal swimming pools.

(13) and (14) quantify over temporal situations, (15) over spatial situations. Except in (14), the quantifiers are explicitly restricted: (15) mentions all spatial locations within the French territory, and (13) all temporal locations supporting: <<John comes>>.

Finally, we must pay attention to an important difference between the exercised situation and the mentioned situation. The exercised situation is referred to, hence it must exist in the actual world.[10] But the mentioned situation need not be actual; it can be 'virtual', in a sense shortly to be explained. When the mentioned situation is virtual, the δ-structure is an *intentional* δ-*structure.*

3.3 *Intentional δ-structures*

The most obvious example of intentional δ-structure is provided by conditionals. Conditionals mention *hypothetical* situations and state facts concerning them. The content of an utterance like (16)

(16) If he opens the fridge, John will be scared to death.

can be analysed as:

$$[s'] \models \mathord{<\mathord{<}}s \models \mathord{<\mathord{<}}\text{John is scared to death}\mathord{>\mathord{>}} \mathord{>\mathord{>}}$$

where s' is the actual situation in which the conditional holds, and s is an hypothetical situation in which John opens the fridge. By analysing conditionals as δ-structures we capture the commonality between (16) and (17).

(17) When he opens the fridge, John will be scared to death.

(17) is a temporal δ-structure similar to those mentioned above. The difference between (16) and (17) is that s, the mentioned situation, is a virtual situation in (16) and an actual temporal situation in (17).[11]

In earlier writings (Recanati 1996, 1997) I analysed meta-representations—representations about representations—on the same pattern. For example, 'In the film, Robin Hood meets Frankenstein' was analysed as mentioning a *fictional* situation (that depicted by the film) and saying that it supports <<Robin Hood meets Frankenstein>>. In the same way, I analysed 'John believes that *p*' or 'According to John, *p*' as a δ-structure in which the mentioned situation is John's belief-world (the complex situation corresponding to John's beliefs, that is, the world as it is according to John):

$$[s'] \models \mathord{<\mathord{<}} \text{Bel}_{\text{john}} \models \sigma \mathord{>\mathord{>}}$$

('Bel$_{\text{john}}$' is my name for John's belief-world.) In general, I analysed the content of a meta-representation as a δ-structure $[s'] \models \mathord{<\mathord{<}}s \models \sigma\mathord{>\mathord{>}}$, where s, the mentioned situation, is the situation described by some representation given in the exercised situation. The representation can be a film, a book, a picture, an utterance, or a person's mental states (to mention only the most salient types of case). In the examples above, the relevant representations are John's belief state (which represents the world as being thus and so) and the film (which represents a certain complex situation). Other examples include (18) and (19).

(18) In the picture, John is smiling.

(19) John said that Peter would come.

I now see several problems with my earlier analysis of meta-represen-tations. First, it is pretty clear that the representation (the picture, the film, John's mental states, etc.) is actually mentioned in the meta-repre-sentation; it cannot be confined to the exercised situation which the meta-representation concerns. We must therefore introduce the repre-sentation itself into the fact denoted by the meta-representation. The general structure becomes:

(20) $[s'] \vDash <<R \vDash s \vDash \sigma >>$

where s' is the exercised situation, R is the representation, and s is the sit-uation the representation describes.

Once we have taken this step we face the Compositionality problem: how is it possible that a representation such as 'In the picture, *p*' ex-presses a structure like (20), in which two situations are mentioned (the picture R, and the situation s it represents), while a very similar repre-sentation, 'In the kitchen, *p*' expresses a much simpler structure (in which only one situation—the kitchen—is mentioned)? I think this particular problem could be solved by appealing to Nunberg's theory of meaning transfer (Nunberg 1995).[12] However there is another problem which can-not be solved so easily.

On my earlier analysis, as well as on the revised version correspond-ing to formula (20), a meta-representation mentions the virtual situation described by the representation R: it is that situation which is said to support a particular fact σ. Thus 'John believes that *p*' mentions John's belief world and says that it supports the fact that *p;* 'in the film, *p*' men-tions the fictional situation described by the film and says that it sup-ports the fact that *p;* and so forth. The major problem raised by this the-ory is this: what is 'the situation described by the representation'? Is it really a situation (e.g., something to which a world associates a factual set) or is it a complete world? It seems clear that John's 'belief world', for example, *is* a world. Similarly, a work of fiction describes a world, rather than merely some particular situation. There is a clear contrast with conditionals in this respect. While the antecedent of a conditional serves to identify the mentioned situation, in meta-representational sen-tences the sole function of the prefix arguably is to shift the world, with-out indicating any *particular* situation as supporting the fact expressed by the accompanying sentence. When we say 'John believes that kanga-roos have tails,' we present the fact that kangaroos have tails as holding in John's belief-world, but no particular situation is singled out, in con-trast to what happens with conditionals.

Faced with this particular difficulty, we can do several things. We can treat meta-representational sentences such as 'John believes that kangaroos have tails' as expressing *existentially quantified* intentional δ-structures:

$$[s'] \vDash_@ << \exists s \; s \vDash_{bel_{john}} << \text{kangaroos have tails} >> >>$$

On that view John's belief-world is a world, not a situation; it indexes the 'support' relation between the mentioned situation and the fact that kangaroos have tails. The mentioned situation in question is left indefinite instead of being specified—thus we account for the above-noted contrast with conditionals.

Alternatively, we could define, for each world, a 'maximal situation' (that very world, construed as a situation), and say that it is that maximal situation which the meta-representational prefix denotes. That would make the general picture much more complex than it is; for we would have to say either that a world can assign a factual set to another world, or that worlds are self-interpreting, in contrast to partial situations.

There is a third option, which enables us to solve several of our problems at once. We can *give up* the view that the meta-representational prefix (e.g., 'In the film', 'John believes that', etc.) mentions a virtual situation, and construe it instead as doing two things: (i) it mentions a *real* situation—the representation R itself (the film, or John's belief state); and (ii) it shifts the world with respect to which what follows the prefix is interpreted. It is this (very tentative) suggestion which I will pursue in what follows. Appearances notwithstanding, this analysis is compatible with the claim that meta-representations are intentional δ-structures, in which a virtual situation is mentioned. What we give up is only the claim that the virtual situation in question is contributed by the prefix itself.

3.4 World-shifting

When I say that hypothetical or fictional situations are 'virtual', do I mean that they are not in the domain of @? Certainly not. Suppose I utter (21):

(21) If John went to Lyons, he took the 1:30 train.

I am considering a hypothetical situation, viz. a situation in which John went to Lyons. Suppose that John indeed went to Lyons. Then the hypothetical situation turns out to be in the domain of @ (in the sense that @ associates a factual set with that situation). Yet it still is a hypothetical (hence a virtual) situation. So we cannot define a virtual situation as a situation which does not belong to the domain of @, the actual world.

Situations can be in the domain of several worlds; a situation does not essentially belong to the domain of this or that world. But when we mention a situation in a δ-structure, we mention it as supporting a certain fact. Now the 'support' relation *is* relative to a world: a situation s supports a fact σ iff that fact belongs to $w(s)_r$, the relativised factual set of the situation *as determined by a particular world function w*. I therefore suggest the following (tentative) definition:

>   (B)   A situation s mentioned in a δ-structure is virtual (hence the
>   δ-structure itself is intentional) iff s is presented as supporting
>   a certain fact *with respect to a world* w *different from* @ (or at
>   least, different from the world with respect to which the global
>   δ-structure is evaluated[13]). That fact itself I call an 'intentional
>   fact'.

At the end of 3.1 I said that a δ-structure involves two situations, two facts, and two 'support' relations. According to (B), the two facts which we find in an *intentional* δ-structure are not only presented as supported by different situations (the exercised situation and the mentioned situation), that is, as belonging to their respective relativised factual sets, but the relativised factual sets in question are themselves determined by different world functions:

$$[s'] \vDash_@ << s \vDash_w \sigma >>$$

In this formula the two 'support' relations bear different indices. This means that the relativised factual sets they implicitly refer to (via the equivalence between $s \vDash_w \sigma$ and $\sigma \in w(s)_r$) are determined by different world functions, @ and *w*. In non-intentional δ-structures the same world-function is appealed to throughout and need not be explicitly represented.

This analysis works well with conditionals. In (21), the situation s which is mentioned is a hypothetical situation in which John went to Lyons. To say that it is hypothetical is not to say that the actual world associates no factual set with that situation; as we have seen, it may be a fact that John went to Lyons (indicative conditionals are used precisely when the hypothetical situation's being actual is a live option). What makes the situation hypothetical is the world with respect to which that situation is said to support the fact that John took the 1:30 train: that world is not the actual world, but an hypothetical world *hyp* which may be more or less similar to @. The utterance can therefore be analysed as:

$$[s'] \vDash_@ << s \vDash_{hyp} <<\text{John took the 1:30 train}>> \; >>$$

where s, the mentioned situation, is characterized as temporally past and as supporting the fact that John went to Lyons. In a conditional sentence the consequent expresses the fact which is said to hold in the hypothetical situation, while the antecedent characterizes that situation as supporting a 'restricting' fact, a fact which serves to identify the hypothetical situation in question (in our example, the restricting fact is the fact that John went to Lyons).

The word 'if' in a conditional I take to be a *world-shifter:* it indicates that the facts in its scope are evaluated with respect to an hypothetical world distinct from the world with respect to which the global δ-structure is evaluated. The well-known context-sensitivity of conditionals comes from the fact that the world in question can be fleshed out differently in different contexts.

Meta-representational prefixes such as 'In John's mind', 'in the picture', 'in the film', 'according to Paul', 'John believes that', 'John said that', and so forth, are intuitively world-shifters, like the word 'if'. Consider, again, the Robin Hood example, 'In the film, Robin Hood meets Frankenstein'. The meta-representational prefix 'In the film' indicates that the fact expressed by the accompanying sentence ('Robin Hood meets Frankenstein') holds in a fictional universe, in contrast to the fact expressed by the global meta-representation (i.e., the fact that *in the film* Robin Hood meets Frankenstein): the latter holds in the actual world.

On this analysis, meta-representational prefixes such as 'In John's mind', 'in the picture', 'in the film', 'according to Paul', 'John believes that', 'John said that', and so forth, mention a real situation (Paul's mental states, the picture, the film, etc.) as supporting a certain fact, but the fact in question is such that *whichever 'support' relation it internally involves is indexed to the world of the representation.* For example, the utterance

(22) John believes that, in the eighteenth century, kangaroos had tails.

would be analysed as denoting the following fact:

$$<< \text{John's mental state} \models_@ <<18^{th} \models_{bel_{john}} <<\text{kangaroos have tails}>> >> >>$$

where '18th' is the temporal location denoted by the phrase 'in the eighteenth century' (together with the past tense). Now that situation is 'virtual' because it is in some alternative world, namely John's belief-world, that it supports the fact that kangaroos have tails. So the meta-representational prefix, *qua* world-shifter, 'virtualises' the situations which the accompanying sentence mentions.

In that framework the complete content of a meta-representation such as 'In the film, p' or 'John believes that p' has the following structure:

$$[s'] \vDash_{w1} \; <<R \vDash_{w1} \; << s \vDash_{w2} \sigma>> \; >>$$

where s' is the exercised situation, R is the mentioned representation (e.g., the film, or John's mental state), and $<< s \vDash_{w2} \sigma >>$ is the fact denoted by the sentence p which the meta-representational prefix introduces (e.g., 'Robin Hood meets Frankenstein', or 'In the eighteenth century kangaroos had tails'). In contrast, the complete content of a conditional retains the simpler structure:

$$[s'] \vDash_{w1} \; << s \vDash_{w2} \sigma>>$$

where s' is the exercised situation, s is the situation mentioned by the antecedent, and σ is the fact denoted by the consequent. On that view, although the content of both conditionals and meta-representations is an intentional δ-structure, characterized by a world-shift, there is a significant difference between them. In meta-representations, the world-shift itself is represented, that is, it is internal to the fact denoted by the meta-representation; while in conditionals the world-shift takes place without being represented. The fact denoted by the conditional is the fact that $s \vDash_{w2} \sigma$, while the fact denoted by a meta-representation is the fact that $R \vDash_{w1} \; << s \vDash_{w2} \sigma>>$.

That consequence of the analysis is desirable. For, as I said earlier, it is clear that the representation (the picture, the film, John's mental states, etc.) is actually mentioned in the meta-representation; it cannot be confined to the exercised situation which the meta-representation concerns. Yet the analysis of meta-representations which has just been sketched has another, less desirable consequence. A meta-representation is said to mention a real situation (viz. a representation: film, picture, etc.) as supporting an *intentional fact*: a fact such that the 'support' relation it internally involves is indexed to the world of the representation rather than to the world with respect to which the global δ-structure (the meta-representation) is evaluated. But aren't there simple facts which internally involve no 'support' relation? Arguably there are; they are the 'thetic facts' mentioned in 3.2 (e.g., the fact that it is raining). Assuming that there are such facts, it follows from the above analysis that they cannot be intentional: *they cannot be what the complement sentence in a meta-representation expresses.*

That consequence is surprising, but empirically correct as far as I can tell. If I say 'John believes that it is raining,' I ascribe to John the belief that it is raining *in a particular place* (tacitly referred to). So the fact expressed by the complement sentence is not simple (thetic), appearances notwithstanding. This is less clear in an example like 'In the picture, it is raining,' but we could perhaps treat that as an instance of quantified δ-structure.[14] More generally, we could admit that the meta-representational prefix is a world-shifting operator requiring a complex fact to operate on, and handle the counterexamples by arguing as follows. Whenever the fact expressed by the accompanying sentence is not (already) complex, it is made so: thus if a sentence S expresses a simple (thetic) fact σ, embedding it within a meta-representational frame has the result that it expresses the complex fact that: $\exists s \ s \models \sigma$. The world-shifting operator can then operate on *that* fact, indexing the support relation it internally involves to the world of the representation.

4. Complex and Schematic Facts

4.1 Complex facts

In 2.1 I represented facts as triples consisting of an *n*-place relation R^n, a sequence of *n* appropriate arguments, and a polarity. It is in terms of such facts that I defined the 'support' relation: a situation supports a fact iff that fact belongs to the relativised factual set of the situation. But what about *complex* facts in which simple facts enter as constituents? What is it for a situation to support a complex fact? This is the issue I will address in this section.

The first thing we must do is distinguish various forms of complexity. One form of complexity I call δ-complexity. A fact is δ-complex iff its constituents are a situation, the 'support' relation, and a fact which itself can be δ-simple or δ-complex. Adverbial adjuncts are δ-complexifiers in that they mention a situation in which the fact expressed by the remainder of the sentence is said to hold. In 3.2, I argued that tenses themselves are δ-complexifiers. It may be possible to treat moods also as δ-complexifiers, but I will not address this question here.[15] More important for our purposes is the claim I made in the same section, to the effect that simple subject-predicate sentences themselves can be construed as expressing δ-complex facts. Categoric judgements, I said, can be represented as *δ-complexifications* of thetic judgements:

$$\text{Thetic:} \quad [s] \models \ <<R^0, +>>$$
$$\text{Categoric:} \quad [s'] \models \ <<s \models \ <<R^0, +>> \ >>$$

On this analysis a 'thetic fact' is expressed both in thetic and categoric judgements. In categoric judgements the fact in question is not expressed directly by the utterance, but indirectly, as a constituent of a δ-complex fact. In thetic judgements it is directly expressed.

What is it for a situation to support a δ-complex fact? There is an easy answer to that question. A situation s' supports a δ-complex fact $<<s \models <<R^n, <a_1, \ldots a_n>, i>> >>$ if and only if it supports the corresponding 'unrelativised' fact $<<R^{n+1}, <a_1, \ldots a_n, s>, i>>$. There is a complication if the supported fact is intentional, for that forces us to keep track of the world-indices. Still, the equivalence holds.

There is another form of complexity, which I call '⊕-complexity'. '⊕' stands for any connective such as ∨ or & (but not for negation which affects the polarity of the fact, not its complexity). What is it for a situation to support, for example, a conjunctive fact or a disjunctive fact? In situation theory (e.g., Barwise 1989, Devlin 1991) ⊕-complexity is accounted for by extending the definition of 'support' as follows:

$$s \models \sigma \oplus \sigma' \text{ iff } s \models \sigma \oplus s \models \sigma'$$

For example:

$$s \models \sigma \,\&\, \sigma' \text{ iff } s \models \sigma \,\&\, s \models \sigma'$$
$$s \models \sigma \vee \sigma' \text{ iff } s \models \sigma \vee s \models \sigma'$$
$$s \models \sigma \supset \sigma' \text{ iff } s \models \sigma \supset s \models \sigma'$$

A third form of complexity involves quantification. What is it for a situation to support a quantificational fact such as the fact that all men are mortal? There are two approaches to this problem in the present framework.

(i) Quantificational facts can be treated as having the same global structure as simple (non quantificational) facts: $<<R^n, <a_1, \ldots a_n>, i>>$. The difference between quantificational facts and simple facts is simply this: In quantificational facts the relation is a *second-order* relation and its arguments are themselves first-order relations. If such second-order facts are allowed into the relativised factual sets of situations, we do not have to extend the definition of 'support' to account for quantification.

(ii) Alternatively, we can appeal to the same method we use for ⊕-complexity, and extend the definition of 'support' as follows:

(N) $s \models <<Qx\, \sigma(x)>> \text{ iff } (Qx)\, (s \models \sigma(x))$

where 'Q' is an arbitrary quantifier, '$\sigma()$' is a schematic fact, and '$Qx\, \sigma(x)$' is a quantificational fact. It is this approach which I will pursue in the next section.

4.2 Schematic and quantificational facts

Schematisation is a process much like relativisation. *Relativising* a fact $\sigma = <<R^n, <a_1, \ldots, a_n>, i >>$ to one of its constituent arguments consists in backgrounding the argument role corresponding to that argument and generating a fact $\sigma' = <<R^{n-1}, <a_1, \ldots, a_{n-1}>, i >>$. *Schematizing* a fact σ with respect to one of its constituent arguments consists in 'parametrizing' the argument role corresponding to that argument: The arity of the relation is preserved (in contrast to what happens with relativisation), but the relevant argument role is filled only by a place-holder (a 'parameter'). While a relativised fact is a complete fact of arity $n-1$, a schematic fact is an *incomplete* fact of arity n, with one of the argument roles filled by a place-holder.

Being incomplete a schematic fact is not a fact (hence it does not belong to the relativised factual set of a situation), but a function from appropriate values for the argument role to non-parametrized facts. While $\sigma()$ is a schematic fact (hence not a genuine fact), $\sigma(a)$, the value of the schematic fact $\sigma()$ for argument a, is a genuine fact. We are therefore in a position to understand the right hand side in formula (N): '$(Qx) (s \models \sigma(x))$', where Q is an arbitrary quantifier. It says that for Q entity x, the situation s supports the fact which is the value of $\sigma()$ for argument x. Various types of *quantificational facts* can thus be defined through the support-conditions enunciated in formula (N). The following definitions are particular instances of (N):

$$s \models <<\exists x\ \sigma(x)>>\ \text{iff}\ (\exists x)\ (s \models \sigma(x))$$
$$s \models <<\forall x\ \sigma(x)>>\ \text{iff}\ (\forall x)\ (s \models \sigma(x))$$

I will henceforth represent a quantificational fact as $\sigma(Q)$, where $\sigma()$ is a schematic fact and Q is a quantifier ranging over the values of the parametrized argument role in $\sigma()$.

Schematic facts themselves can be schematized. When that is so, the resulting fact is *doubly schematic.* I represent doubly schematic facts thus:

(23) $\sigma()\ ()$

This means that two of the argument roles of the relation $R^{n \geq 2}$ around which σ is built have been parametrized.

Quantificational facts themselves can be schematized:

(24) $\sigma(Q)\ ()$

A schematized quantificational fact like (24) is a doubly schematic fact like (23) in which one of the two parametrized argument roles is 'bound' by the quantifier, the other argument role remaining 'free'. The free argument role in a schematized quantificational fact like (24) can itself be bound by a new quantifier; for example we can have:

$$(\exists x) \, (\sigma(Q) \, (x))$$

or any instance of

$$(Q'x) \, (\sigma(Q) \, (x))$$

where Q' is an arbitrary quantifier. Such a *doubly quantified fact* can be represented as follows:

$$\sigma(Q) \, (Q')$$

Of course, the process can be repeated. A doubly quantified fact can be schematized by parametrizing a third argument role (if the relation around which the fact is built has arity $n \geq 3$):

$$\sigma(Q) \, (Q') \, ()$$

This, in turn, can yield an even more complex quantificational fact:

$$\sigma(Q) \, (Q') \, (Q'')$$

A complex quantificational fact involves (i) a sequence $<Q_1, \ldots Q_n>$ of quantifiers, and (ii) a schematic fact with n parametrized argument roles. I have represented the binding relation between quantifiers and argument roles by putting the quantifier in the relevant argument place. In English that relation is established through the lexical phenomenon of 'linking'. In the semantics of relational expressions (e.g., verbs) different argument roles for the denoted relation are linked to different grammatical functions such as 'subject', 'object' and 'indirect object'. Now quantificational expressions, that is, words or phrases denoting quantifiers, are themselves associated with specific grammatical functions, viz. the functions they fulfil or occupy within the sentence in which they occur. Hence a simple solution to the problem of determining which quantifier binds which argument role:

> *BTL (binding through linking) Principle*
> The quantifier Q contributed by a token θ of a quantificational expression *Quant* binds the argument role linked to the grammatical function occupied by θ.

For example, consider the sentence 'John sold something to Bill'. The verb in this sentence expresses a three-place relation $sell^3$ whose argument roles are borrowed from the commercial transaction frame. The three foregrounded argument roles in this construction are: *seller, buyer,* and *goods*.

In the semantics of the construction the *seller* argument role is linked to the grammatical function 'subject', the *goods* argument role is linked to the grammatical function 'object', and the *buyer* argument role is linked to the grammatical function 'indirect object'. In the sentence, the proper nouns 'John' and 'Bill' respectively occupy the functions 'subject' and 'indirect object', whereas the quantificational expression 'something' occupies the object position. It follows that (i) the referents contributed by the proper nouns 'John' and 'Bill' fill the *seller* and the *buyer* argument roles respectively; and (ii) by virtue of BTL, the quantifier contributed by 'something' binds the *goods* argument role.

4.3 Questions

I have analysed quantificational facts as involving a schematic fact $\sigma()$, and a quantifier Q which binds the (or a) parametrized argument role in the schematic fact. Though they involve schematic facts, quantificational facts themselves are not schematic (unless they are 'schematized quantificational facts'): They are not schematic because the parameter they involve is not 'free'.

Can schematic facts be expressed directly by natural language sentences, without the parametrized argument role being quantified over? I think so. I take the semantic content of *questions* to be such a schematic fact.

There are various sorts of questions: *yes-no* questions ('Is John home?'), *wh*-questions ('Where is John?'), alternative questions ('Will John go or will you come?', 'Will John go or not?'), and so forth. So-called indirect questions, such as 'Paul wonders *where John is*', are not questions in the pragmatic sense, and I will not be concerned with them in what follows. I will consider only the simplest cases: *yes-no* questions and *wh*-questions. I start with the latter.

In 'Who came?', the argument role linked to the subject position is parametrized. No complete fact is therefore expressed, but only a function from parameter values to facts. The role of question-words like 'who', 'what' or 'where' is triple:

   (i) Like quantificational expressions, they occupy a particular grammatical function (subject, object, etc.) and thereby indicate which argument role the question concerns: the question concerns that argument role of the expressed relation which is linked to the grammatical function occupied by the question-word.
   (ii) They provide an indication concerning the sortal nature of the parametrized argument: person (who), thing (what), place (where), time (when), etc.

(iii) Together with word-order and intonation, they indicate that the utterance is a question, that is, an utterance with such and such *felicity conditions*. A question expressing a schematic fact σ() is felicitous only in a context in which it is followed by an utterance providing a value for the parameter. The pair consisting of the question followed by the answer expresses a fact, but the question in isolation expresses only a schematic fact.

In order to stress what is common to questions and quantificational utterances, I represent questions as follows:

σ(?)

The content of both a quantificational utterance σ(Q) and a question σ(?) involves a schematic fact σ(). The difference between quantificational utterances and questions is this: In quantificational utterances the schematic fact is turned into a complete (quantificational) fact. Not so with questions: questions express schematic rather than complete facts.

At this point a question arises. I said that sentences containing quantificational expressions do *not* express schematic facts, but complete facts (namely quantificational facts). That is so, I said, because the parametrized argument role is not free but 'bound' by the quantifier. But question-words also bind an argument role of the relation expressed by the verb: In 'Who came?', the question-word binds the argument role linked to the subject position, exactly as 'Someone came' binds the argument role linked to the subject position. Still, I maintained, questions express schematic facts. How can that be? How can binding affect schematicity in one case but not in the other?

In fact there are two forms of binding, and two senses in which a quantificational expression *Quant* (e.g., 'someone' or 'everything') 'binds' a particular argument role. *Quant* does two things:

(i) It has the effect of parametrizing a particular argument role, namely that which is linked to the grammatical position occupied by *Quant* in the sentence. In this respect there is no difference between a quantificational expression *Quant* and a question-word *Wh*. They both parametrize a particular argument role through the BTL principle. The latter must be reformulated as a general principle concerning parametrization: Both quantificational expressions and question-words parametrize a particular argument role in the relation expressed by the verb, namely that argument role which is linked to the grammatical position occupied by the expression. Expressions

which have this property I call 'parametrizers'. A parametrizer, whether a quantificational expression or a question-
word, 'binds' a particular argument role in the sense of parametrizing it. But quantificational expressions do something
else as well.

(ii) *Quant* denotes a quantifier. That quantifier 'binds' the parametrized argument role in the sense that it quantifies over its values. Binding in this sense has the effect of completing the
schematic fact into a quantificational fact. A question-word
Wh does not 'bind' the parameter in this sense, for it does not
denote a quantifier—indeed it does not denote anything. The
meaning of a question-word is pragmatic: question-words signal that the utterance is a question, that is, an utterance with
certain felicity conditions, and presuppose that those conditions are satisfied. Question-words therefore constrain the
context in which the sentence containing them occurs, but
make no contribution to the content expressed by such sentences (except insofar as they parametrize the argument role
linked to the position they occupy).

So much for *wh*-questions. *Yes-no* questions are a more delicate matter,
because they do not appear to express a schematic fact. According to the
traditional speech-act analysis, a *yes-no* question such as 'Is John home?'
expresses a complete proposition, rather than a propositional function. In
situation theory, however, a fact consists of a relation, a sequence of arguments, *and a polarity.* So far I have been concerned only with one form of
schematicity: that which results from parametrizing an argument role. But
it is also possible for the formal constituents of the fact, viz. the relation or
the polarity, to be parametrized. *Yes-no* questions can thus be construed as
a special case in which parametrization concerns the polarity of the expressed fact. If we use question marks to represent parametrized constituents, the difference between *wh*-questions like 'Who is bald?' and *yes-
no* question like 'Is Paul bald?' comes out as follows:

Who is bald? = $<<\text{Bald}^1, ?, +>>$
Is Paul bald? = $<<\text{Bald}^1, \text{Paul}, ?>>$

This analysis, however, raises a serious objection. As Cornulier (1982)
pointed out in his insightful paper on the semantics of questions, a *yes-no*
question such as 'Is Paul bald?' is not equivalent to its negation: 'Is not Paul
bald?'. The first question asks whether a certain state of affairs (Paul's
being bald) is actual, while the other concerns a different state of affairs
(Paul's not being bald). If the polarity of the expressed fact was parame-

trized in *yes-no* questions, there could be no such difference. 'Is Paul bald' and 'Is not Paul bald' would both have the schematic content mentioned above: <<Bald[1], Paul, ?>>.

To deal with negative questions I think we must complicate the analysis and remember the generalization I made earlier: unless it is a mere interjection, an English sentence always expresses a δ-complex fact <<s ⊨ σ>>. As such a complex fact contains the simpler fact σ as a constituent, two polarities are involved, corresponding to the δ-complex fact <<s ⊨ σ>> and to the internal fact σ respectively. This comes out clearly if we represent δ-complex facts thus:

$$<< \vDash, <s, <<R^{n,} <a_1, \ldots a_n>, i >> >, i >>$$

It is therefore possible to parametrize the polarity of the complex fact <<s ⊨ σ>>, without parametrizing the polarity of the internal fact σ—the latter can be negative as well as positive. This accounts for the non-equivalence of questions and their negations: Both express a δ-complex schematic fact whose polarity (but *not* that of the internal fact) has been parametrized:

> Semantic content of positive questions: $<< \vDash, <s, <<R^n, <a_1, \ldots a_n>, +>> >, ?>>$
> Semantic content of negative questions: $<< \vDash, <s, <<R^n, <a_1, \ldots a_n>, ->> >, ?>>$

5. Informational Structure

5.1 Exercised situations as 'topics'

In the course of this paper I made several assumptions which it is time to scrutinize. Two assumptions are especially important. First, I suggested that we equate the exercised situation and the 'topic' of the utterance in the traditional sense: that which the speaker is talking about. Correspondingly, the nucleus (the right hand side in the Austinian proposition) can be equated with the 'comment': what the speaker says concerning the topic. If this equation is correct, Austinian semantics should connect up with the vast literature on the topic/comment distinction and accommodate its findings (see Lambrecht (1994) for a recent survey).

Second, I implied (and in Recanati (1997) I said) that the exercised situation is necessarily external to the nucleus. If the exercised situation is mentioned and becomes a constituent of the nucleus, then it ceases being the exercised situation and a new exercised situation emerges (see 3.1 above). Let me state this assumption a bit more explicitly:

Principle of Non-Redundancy
The exercised situation must be distinct from any situation
mentioned in the utterance.

The Principle of Non-Redundancy can be abridged as: $[s'] \neq s$, where $[s']$ is
the exercised situation and 's' is the mentioned situation. It can be read as
saying that the topic cannot be part of the comment.

The Principle of Non-Redundancy raises two problems. The first problem concerns the cases in which a situation is reflexively about itself. In
'Situations, Sets and the Axiom of Foundation', Barwise gives seven examples of such reflexive situations, including Gricean intentions, the
Cartesian *cogito,* self-referential and 'specular' representations, and
common knowledge (1989: 177–200). I myself analysed *perspectives* as
reflexive situations (Recanati 1997: 70n). But if there are reflexive situations, why is it not possible for a situation to be both exercised and
mentioned?

As I pointed out in 3.1 the reason why it seems that a situation cannot be
both exercised and mentioned is this: A situation is exercised when it is presented as supporting the fact which the utterance expresses. Now a situation cannot support a fact which contains that situation itself as constituent,
because a fact which is relativised to an entity α cannot contain α as a constituent. Hence it seems that we cannot have it both ways: Either we give
up our definition of the support relation in terms of relativisation, or we
stick to the Non-Redundancy Principle and give up the hope of accounting
for reflexive situations.

There is a way out of this dilemma. We can deny that a fact cannot be relativised to an entity α if it contains α as a constituent. For a fact can contain the same entity twice, if the entity in question fills two distinct argument roles in the fact. Let us imagine that that is the case. We can relativise
the fact in question to α, by suppressing one of the two argument roles
filled by α, without automatically suppressing the other. In such a situation,
the fact is relativised to α yet it (still) contains α as a constituent. That is
precisely what happens when a situation s is reflexive. The unrelativised
fact involving s is the fact that: *in situation* s, $F(s)$. The situation s occurs in
that fact twice. Through relativisation, we obtain the simpler fact which the
situation supports—the fact that: $F(s)$.

Let us assume that reflexive situations can indeed be handled in that
manner. It follows that the Principle of Non-Redundancy is not unrestrict-
edly valid, yet we need not give it up. Reflexive situations are rather special cases; and non-reflexive situations are sufficiently typical for a generalization such as the Principle of Non-Redundancy to be worth making. If
we want a more universal principle, we can modify the Principle of Non-
Redundancy as follows:

Principle of Non-Redundancy (modified)
Unless it is reflexive, the exercised situation must be distinct
from any situation mentioned in the utterance.

From now on I shall ignore reflexive situations, hence I will stick to the un-
modified version of the Principle of Non-Redundancy.

The Principle of Non-Redundancy raises a second problem, one which
arises even if we disregard reflexive situations. So far, I have assumed that
a situation is mentioned just in case it is linguistically *articulated* in the sentence. As we have seen, a situation can be articulated in many different
ways: through tenses, adverbial expressions, attitudinals ('John believes
(that)', etc.), or singular terms in subject position. Let us make this auxiliary assumption explicit:

(M1)   A situation s is mentioned in an utterance *u* if and only if
       there is something in the uttered sentence which denotes s
       (possibly in a context-dependent manner).

If we interpret the Principle of Non-Redundancy in the light of (M1),
it says that the exercised situation cannot be articulated, that is, denoted
by something in the sentence, without ceasing to be the exercised situation. In conjunction with the equation of topics and exercised situations,
this entails that *topics cannot be articulated*. Now that consequence conflicts with well-documented findings in the theory of informational
structure.

In the informational structure literature, examples are given and
analysed in which some constituent of the sentence identifies the 'topic'
while other constituents contribute to the 'comment'. Think of the following contrast (from Recanati (1996: 463–464)):

(25)   What's new in the class?
       Mary is in love with John.
(26)   How is Mary?
       She is in love with John.
(27)   How is John?
       Mary is in love with him.

In the first case the topic is the situation in the class; that topic is mentioned
in the question, but not in the answer. As the topic of the answer is not
mentioned in that answer itself (but only in the question), the Principle of
Non-Redundancy is respected. In the other two examples, however, the
topic—Mary and John respectively—are articulated in the answer, through
the pronoun.

In order to identify the topic, a sentential constituent must be unstressed. Thus in (28)

(28) *Mary* is in love with John.

Mary cannot be the topic. Whatever is stressed is 'in focus' and cannot be (part of) the topic. Other ways of putting in focus are word order, cleft-constructions, and so forth. Now pronouns are always unstressed, and this suggests that the referents of pronouns are somehow constitutive of the exercised situation, of the 'topic'. Whatever we think of this suggestion, which will be pursued below (5.2), it is pretty clear that, in examples such as (26) and (27), the topic is articulated in the utterance. Hence we cannot maintain the Principle of Non-Redundancy (interpreted in the light of (M1)) if we equate the exercised situation and the topic in the traditional sense.

To solve that difficulty, I suggest that we replace (M1) by a weaker interpretation of what it means for a situation to be mentioned:

(M2) A situation s is mentioned in an utterance *u* if and only if s is a constituent of the nucleus of *u* (i.e., of the right hand side of the Austinian proposition expressed by *u*).

Interpreted in the light of (M1), the Principle of Non-Redundancy is unacceptable because it conflicts with well-established findings in the theory of topics. Interpreted in the light of (M2), however, the Principle of difference is fine. It says—and says only—that the exercised situation must be *external to the nucleus*. If a situation is a constituent of the nucleus, it cannot be the exercised situation (the topic); if an expression identifies or articulates the topic, it cannot contribute to the nucleus.

Interpreted in the light of (M2), the Principle of Non-Redundancy prevents the exercised situation from being 'mentioned', but it does not prevent it from being 'articulated'. If the topic is articulated, however, the expression which articulates it cannot at the same time contribute to the nucleus. (This is reminiscent of Austin's analysis of performative utterances. According to Austin the performative prefix does not contribute to the propositional content of the speech act, but only to its force.)

The effect of the Principle of Non-Redundancy can be described in the framework set up previously. If the situation denoted by a sentential constituent is elected as 'topic' (exercised situation), it is automatically banned from the nucleus. This is an instance of 'backgrounding'. The mechanism through which the topic is backgrounded from the nucleus is that which I discussed in 2.3: The nucleus is *relativised to* the topic. Thus if we consider the 'Mary is in love with John' example, we see that the nucleus covaries with the topic: In the first case ('What's new in the class?') the nucleus is the fact that Mary is in love with John; in the second case ('How is Mary?') the nucleus is the property of being in love with John; in the third case ('How is John?') the nucleus is the property of being loved by Mary. The Austinian propositions respectively expressed are:

[The situation in the class] $\models$ <<Love^2, <Mary, John>, +>>
[Mary] $\models$ <<Love^1, John, +>>
[John] $\models$ <<Loved-by^1, Mary, +>>

5.2 Nucleus vs. minimal content

On the view I have just sketched the nucleus can no longer be equated with the utterance's 'minimal content'. The nucleus results from a process of *relativisation to the topic* ('t-relativisation') which can only take place when the topic has been contextually identified. As the 'Mary is in love with John' example shows, that process is non-minimalist (optional), for the sentence expresses a complete proposition (the proposition that Mary is in love with John) before that process occurs. We must therefore give up the picture we started with. Instead of the picture in Figure 1,

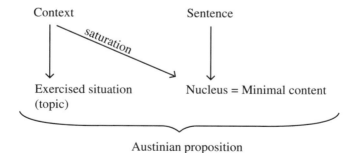

Figure 1

we now have the picture in Figure 2.

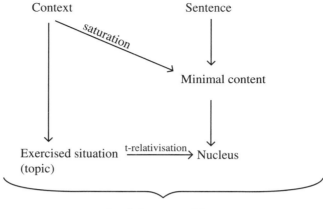

Figure 2

Once the nucleus is seen as resulting from the operation of a non-mini-malist (optional) pragmatic process, namely t-relativisation, we have no reason to consider it as unaffected by other optional processes like enrichment or transfer. The non-minimal character of the nucleus must be fully acknowledged, as in Figure 3.

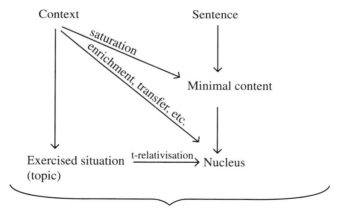

Figure 3

I conclude that the minimalist construal of the nucleus, which was adopted at the beginning of this paper as a working hypothesis, must be rejected if we want to accommodate well-known observations concerning informational structure. This, in itself, does not settle the debate over what is said: it is still possible to accept or alternatively to reject Minimalism as a general doctrine. Minimalism posits an intermediary level of 'minimal' truth-evaluable content between the meaning of the sentence-type and what is said in the intuitive sense. In Figure 3 there still is such a level of minimal content, but it is no longer equated with the nucleus. Instead of three levels of meaning (sentence meaning, what is said$_{min}$, what is said$_{max}$) there are four:

• Sentence meaning

• Minimal content (what is said$_{min}$)

• Nucleus

} what is said$_{max}$

• Austinian proposition

As far as I am concerned, I see no reason to maintain such a complicated picture. We are much better off if, giving up Minimalism, we get rid of the intermediary level of minimal content. If we do, we are left with the following picture:

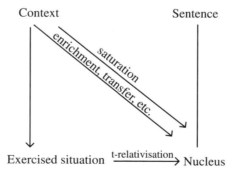

Context   Sentence

enrichment, transfer, etc.   *saturation*

Exercised situation $\xrightarrow{\text{t-relativisation}}$ Nucleus

Figure 4

The only levels of meaning thus posited are: the meaning of the sentence-type; the nucleus; and the complete Austinian proposition. I think all important semantic and pragmatic phenomena can be accounted for in a framework with only these three levels.

The picture can still be greatly simplified. In Figure 4 we see that the nucleus is affected by the context in two ways: (i) directly, through the usual primary pragmatic processes (saturation, enrichment, transfer); (ii) indirectly, through the topic which itself affects the nucleus via t-relativisation. The simplification I have in mind is made possible by the following principle:

> *CTT ('context through topic') Principle*
> The context acts on the nucleus only through the topic (exercised situation).

This is a bold conjecture which I cannot argue for here (no more than I can argue in favour of Maximalism). Figure 5 displays the picture which would result from accepting CTT.

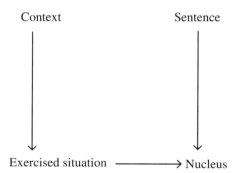

Figure 5

According to CTT, all primary pragmatic processes, whether mandatory (saturation) or optional (enrichment, transfer, t-relativisation), proceed from the exercised situation. This is clear at least in the case of t-relativisation, which is obviously topic-dependent. In the case of enrichment too, the topic (the situation talked about) appears to be the controlling factor. If we are talking about a policeman regulating the traffic, the sentence 'He stopped three cars this morning' will be understood as entailing that the cars were stopped by means of an appropriate signal to the driver, rather than, say, by pressing the brakes (Rumelhart 1979). In this typical instance of top-down enrichment, it is the knowledge of the situation talked about which enables an interpreter to correctly recover the intended meaning.[16]

That enrichment is topic-dependent has been noted many times in connection with so-called 'incomplete quantifiers' (see e.g., Recanati (1986: 60–61), Neale (1990: 115–116)). So we can admit the CTT as far as enrichment is concerned. But what about saturation? Saturation is supposed to be rule-dependent rather than topic-dependent. Let me summarize the traditional view concerning the saturation of indexicals:

> *Indexicals and saturation: the traditional view*
> It is a semantic rule (e.g., the rule that 'I' refers to the speaker) which determines the contextual value of an indexical. The situation talked about is irrelevant here. Different indexicals depend upon different aspects of the context of utterance, but that *context* is distinct from the *situation talked about*. The context includes such things as the speaker, the hearer, and the time of utterance. It can contain the situation talked about as a particular parameter, but it is distinct from it.

This view is known to be defective or at least exaggerated. Saturation is much more topic-dependent and much less rule-dependent than it suggests. Genitives provide a classical example of the need for contextual saturation: an utterance including the phrase 'John's book' does not express a complete proposition unless a particular relation has been identified as holding between the book and John. Now which particular relation is contextually singled out clearly depends on the situation talked about. The same thing holds for demonstratives: what a demonstrative like 'he' or 'this' refers to is highly topic-dependent. In general, semantic underdetermination can be overcome only by the participants' knowledge of the exercised situation. (See, e.g., Clark (1992) on 'contextual expressions'.) It is only 'pure indexicals'—admittedly a very limited category—which are immune to that sort of topic-dependence.

The traditional view can easily accommodate the topic-dependence of (impure) indexicals, however. The only thing one has to do is to take the topic on board as one contextual parameter among others. Thus we could rephrase Austinian semantics within a Kaplanian sort of framework, by treating the meaning of a sentence as a function from extended Kaplanian contexts to Austinian propositions (where an 'extended Kaplanian context' is a Kaplanian context containing the exercised situation along with the standard parameters).

The CTT represents a totally different option: All contextual features relevant to the determination of what is said are construed as aspects of the exercised situation. Exercised situations thus *replace* Kaplanian contexts.

This view is perfectly compatible with the notion that indexicals are rule-governed. The 'rules' governing indexicals are essentially *constraints on their use;* and these constraints, in turn, can be described as *constraints on the exercised situation.* Thus a referential expression (be it an indexical or a proper name) can be construed as demanding that the exercised situation contain an appropriate referent. Here 'demands that' can be replaced by 'is felicitously used only if'. The Familiarity Theory of Definiteness (Hawkins 1978, Heim 1988) can be reformulated within that sort of framework, but I will not go into this matter here.

5.3 Topics and truth-conditions

According to Peter Strawson (1977: 93), the failure of reference entails a 'truth-value gap' only when the referring expression contributes the 'topic' of the utterance. Consider, for example, utterances (29) and (30).

(29) The King of France visited the Exhibition yesterday.
(30) The Exhibition was visited by the King of France yesterday.

As there is no King of France, both (29) and (30) suffer from reference failure; but in (29) the topic is the Exhibition, while in (30), presumably, the topic is the King of France.[17] Hence the failure of reference is felt as more damaging in (29) than it is in (30). As the object which the speaker attempts to talk about and characterize in (29), namely the King of France, does not exist, the characterization of that object as having visited the Exhibition yesterday is 'neither correct nor incorrect'. In (30), however, the object talked about and putatively characterized, namely the Exhibition, un-doubtedly exists; the failure of reference only affects the characterization which is offered of that object.

I think Strawson is right in his observation that our intuitions concerning falsity and truth-value gaps in cases of reference failure depend a lot on the topic of discourse.[18] Apparently Stephen Neale thinks this is a reason for disregarding those intuitions, for, he says,

> Surely the truth-value of what one says depends upon whether the world is as one has said it is; to let the decision as to whether one has said something false or said nothing at all depend upon such things as what is the primary or over-riding focus of the discourse at any given moment—to the extent that such a notion is even theoretically manageable—is to give up this idea. Indeed it is to give up doing serious semantical work altogether . . . (Neale 1990: 28)

I think Neale is moved by the putative fact that (29) and (30), which dif-fer only by their respective 'topic', express the same proposition.[19] How then could they fail to have the same truth-value? There is the world on the one hand, and a single proposition—that which both (29) and (30) express—describing the world as being thus and so on the other hand. If the world is as described by that proposition, (29) and (30) are both true; if not, they are both false. How could extraneous matters such as the 'point' of the statement affect the truth-value of the utterance?

Neale's remark concerning the alleged truth-conditional irrelevance of topics objects not only to Strawson's treatment of truth-value gaps but also to my version of Austinian semantics. If Neale is right, the view I have sketched is badly mistaken: it presents itself as a theory of truth and content, while in fact it's only a theory about 'topics' and related pragmatic issues.

Neale is not alone in thinking that topics have no (direct) relevance to truth-conditions; that claim is almost universally accepted among philosophers. This is because we have rather strong intuitions, for example the intuition that an active sentence and its passive counterpart (e.g., (29) and (30) above, or 'John kissed Mary' and 'Mary was kissed by John') say the same thing and are true in the same circumstances, despite their difference in informational structure. In the same way, the sentence 'Mary is in love with John' was presented above in three different contexts characterized by a variation in the topic of the utterance:

(25) What's new in the class?
Mary is in love with John.
(26) How is Mary?
She is in love with John.
(27) How is John?
Mary is in love with him.

Intuitively, it seems that 'Mary is in love with John' in (25), 'She is in love with John' in (26), and 'Mary is in love with him' in (27) all have the same truth-conditions, despite the difference in their respective topics. The fairly strong intuitions we have concerning those examples suggest a general principle:

> *Invariance Principle*
> The truth-conditions of an utterance are invariant under topic change.

Evidently, this principle conflicts with the theory I have sketched.

Despite our intuitions to the contrary, I think the Invariance Principle is misguided. There are cases in which a change in topic affects the intuitive truth-conditions of the utterance: All the cases in which the topic is unarticulated ('extrasentential topic cases', as I call them) fall in that category. It is when the topic is articulated in the sentence ('sentential topic cases') that we have strong intuitions in support of the Invariance principle; but I will show that those intuitions themselves can easily be accounted for without accepting the Principle.

Let us start with extrasentential topic cases. Consider the Barwise-Etchemendy example I mentioned earlier in this paper (1.1). Commenting on the poker game I am watching, I say "Claire has the ace of hearts." Let us call the poker game in question '*pk*1'. Now suppose that, unbeknown to me, another poker game is taking place elsewhere; let us call it '*pk*2'. According to Barwise and Etchemendy, my utterance is true iff *pk*1 supports <<Claire has the ace of hearts>>. Thus if I am mistaken and Claire is not a participant in the game I am watching (*pk*1), my utterance is false, even if Claire is a participant in the game *pk*2 and has the ace of hearts there. The truth-conditions of my utterance are therefore different from what they would have been had *pk*2 been the topic of my utterance instead of *pk*1. My actual utterance is about *pk*1 and expresses the Austinian proposition (31); the counterfactual utterance would have been about *pk*2 and would have expressed the Austinian proposition (32):

(31) $[pk1] \vDash$ <<Has^2, <Claire, the ace of hearts>, +>>
(32) $[pk2] \vDash$ <<Has^2, <Claire, the ace of hearts>, +>>

Our intuitions in cases like this go against the Invariance Principle, to a certain extent at least. We *do* have the intuition that the actual utterance is not straightforwardly true if Claire is not a participant in *pk*1. (In contrast, the counterfactual utterance would be straightforwardly true in such circumstances.) To be sure, we do also have the intuition that, in some sense, what is said is true even in such a case, provided Claire has the ace of hearts somewhere. Traditional semantics handles those conflicting intuitions by saying that the first one concerns what is 'conveyed' by the utterance, while the second one—the only one that matters to semantics—is about what is strictly and literally said. Austinian semantics handles those intuitions quite differently, by distinguishing two sets of truth-conditions, corresponding to the two levels of semantic evaluation (the nucleus and the complete Austinian proposition). At the nuclear level, the utterance is true in a situation s iff Claire has the ace of hearts in s. Those nuclear truth-conditions are the same in (31) and (32), because the nucleus is the same: this captures the invariance intuition. But the Austinian truth-conditions are not invariant under topic change: (31) is true iff Claire has the ace of hearts *in pk1*, while (32) is true iff Claire has the ace of hearts *in pk2*.

Let us now consider cases in which the topic *is* articulated in the sentence itself. When that is so, which constituent is topicalized does not seem to affect the truth-conditions even at the 'Austinian' level: they remain invariant, in accordance with the Principle. Thus (29) and (30) have the same overall truth conditions, (26) and (27) have the same overall truth-conditions, and so forth. But our invariance intuitions can be accounted for by saying that the Austinian propositions respectively expressed are *equivalent*. This equivalence is indeed guaranteed by the fact that (owing to the Principle of Non-Redundancy) the nucleus is systematically relativised to the topic. Thus the Austinian propositions expressed by 'She is in love with John' (where Mary—the referent of the pronoun—is the topic) and 'Mary is in love with him' (where John is the topic) are equivalent, even though structurally they are quite different:

$$[\text{Mary}] \vDash \; \text{<<Love}^1, \text{John}, +\text{>>}$$
$$[\text{John}] \vDash \; \text{<<Loved-by}^1, \text{Mary}, +\text{>>}$$

The first Austinian proposition says of Mary that she has the property of loving John; the second Austinian proposition says of John that he has the property of being loved by Mary. Though equivalent, those propositions are different, as their constituents (the exercised situation and the nucleus) are different. Exactly the same thing can be said of the Strawsonian examples (29) and (30).

I conclude that topics are truth-conditionally relevant, appearances to the contrary notwithstanding. In extrasentential topic cases, the nuclear truth-conditions are invariant under topic change, but the Austinian truth-conditions systematically vary. In sentential topic cases, the Austinian truth-conditions are invariant (because the Austinian propositions are equivalent) but, owing to the primary pragmatic process of relativisation, the nuclear truth-conditions co-vary with the topic.

Notes

1. Note, however, that we could include among the 'demonstrative conventions' of the language those conventions which concern non-linguistic aspects of the utterance (such as the direction of the gaze of the speaker, and so forth). See Beeson (1979).

2. The basic insight underlying that view can also be found in McCarthy (1993).

3. The *formal* constituents of a fact are the *n*-place relation and the polarity.

4. See Tesniere (1969) for pioneering remarks on these matters. (The passive is a 'recessive construction', according to Tesniere, i.e., the opposite of causative constructions which increase the number of argument roles.) See also Goldberg (1995: 57—58) for a distinction between two forms of constructional backgrounding: *shading* and *cutting*.

5. The same distinction can be found in Prandi (1992: 48–49, footnote).

6. See 5.1 for a qualification.

7. Well, perhaps it did contain Holmes after all. The situation is complicated by the existence of reflexive situations. See §5.1 below and Récanati (1997), where I suggest that perspectives are reflexive situations.

8. Situations, like worlds, have domains. The domain of a situation s (with respect to a world w) contains all the entities (situations) which are constituents of the facts in $w(s)_r$.

9. Of course, the relativised factual set of John will also contain monadic facts such as <<Married-to[1], <Josephine>, +>>, and other n-adic facts derivable through relativisation from $n+1$-adic facts in the factual set.

10. The cases in which a non-actual situation is used as exercised situation are cases of simulation, in which we do *as if* the situation was actual.

11. I will characterize 'virtual situations' properly in the next section. For the time being I rely on an intuitive understanding of what it is for a situation to be virtual rather than actual.

12. Briefly: While 'my car is parked out back' predicates a certain property of the car (the property of being parked out back), 'I am parked out back' predicates a different (and more complex) property of a different subject: it ascribes to the speaker the property of 'having a car which is parked out back'. The predicative expression 'is parked out back' thus undergoes a transfer of meaning (Nunberg 1995). In virtue of the same type of process, 'In the picture John is smiling' could be considered as ascribing to the picture a more complex property than 'In the kitchen, John is smiling' ascribes to the kitchen.

13. This qualification is needed to deal with the cases of 'projection' in which some previously mentioned situation is used as exercised situation (Récanati 1997).

14. Alternatively, we could appeal to what I call the 'Meinongian pretense' to account for that example: see Récanati (forthcoming), §5.5.

15. Arguably, moods indicate the world which indexes the 'support' relation in the Austinian proposition. Thus 'Close the door' says that whatever situation is at issue supports the fact of your closing the door, where the 'support' relation is relative to your wish-world. On this analysis moods are *not* δ-complexifiers.

16. In the example I have just mentioned a minimalist would argue that the entailment at issue is not 'semantic': the proposition literally expressed is the proposition before enrichment, namely the minimal proposition that the policeman stopped the cars in some way or other. Maybe so. But there are cases in which the proposition literally expressed is so vanishingly abstract as to hardly make sense. Thus in *Desire,* a film by Frank Borsage (1936), the following dialogue takes place:

> - Pedro!
> - Yes sir.
> - Take the plate to the kitchen and disarm the fricassee.

What does the complex phrase 'disarm the fricassee' literally mean? It is hard to tell. To make sense of that phrase, we must know the situation talked about. In the film, the exercised situation contains the following facts: (i) Gary Cooper (the speaker) is handing a fricassee plate to the waiter (Pedro); (ii) the fricassee plate contains a gun; (iii) that gun has just fallen from the hands of someone during a brief fight around the dinner table. With respect to that situation, the phrase 'disarm the fricassee' makes sense: it means that the waiter must remove the gun from the plate. This is, again, a typical instance of top-down enrichment; and it clearly involves the situation talked about. (Other examples in the same vein can be found in Searle (1978) and (1980); see also Travis (1975), (1981)). Whether a minimal proposition can still be isolated in such examples is a central issue for the debate over what is said, but not one I can deal with in the limits of this paper.

17. Normally (though not invariably) the subject term identifies the topic.

18. Strawson's claim about topics and truth-value gaps should be carefully separated from his claim concerning the semantic role of definite descriptions. If we are uncertain that definite descriptions are singular terms, we should use examples involving names rather than descriptions. Suppose we have heard of a city in Spain, called Torpedo, with certain properties. Unbeknownst to us, the city does not exist (the person who mentioned it was joking, but we did not realize it). John, who has also heard of the city, expressed the desire to visit it while in Spain. A couple of days after his departure, I ask my friend: "Where do you think John is presently?" She answers: "John is either in Valencia or in Torpedo, depending on how much time he spent in France." Suppose that in fact John is still in France. Then we are prone to consider my friend's utterance as false, even if we know that Torpedo does not exist. For we are talking about John's present location, and what is said about his location ('either in Valencia or in Torpedo') is clearly incorrect. The non-existence of Torpedo does not make it any less incorrect as a characterization of John's current location. Contrast this case with the case in which we are talking, not about John, but about Torpedo. I say to my friend: "Torpedo is very small." Is this true or false? According to Strawson, "if we know of the reference-failure, we know that the statement cannot really have the topic it is intended to have and hence cannot be assessed as putative information about that topic" (1977: 93). The speaker makes neither a correct nor an incorrect statement about Torpedo, for there is no such thing as Torpedo.

19. (29) and (30) also differ at the level of grammatical form, but this is irrelevant. A difference in context is sufficient to induce the relevant difference in topic, without any accompanying grammatical difference. It is that sort of case which Neale has in mind.

References

Austin, J. L. 1971. *Philosophical Papers,* 2nd ed. Oxford: Clarendon Press.

Bach, K. 1994. "Semantic Slack: what is said and more." In *Foundations of Speech Act Theory,* edited by S. Tsohatzidis. London: Routledge: 267–291.

Barwise, J. 1989. *The Situation in Logic.* Stanford: CSLI.

Barwise, J. and J. Etchemendy. 1987. *The Liar: An Essay on Truth and Circularity.* New York: Oxford University Press.

Barwise, J. and J. Perry. 1983. *Situations and Attitudes.* Cambridge, Mass: MIT Press/Bradford Books.

Beeson, F. 1979. "J. L. Austin on Descriptive and Demonstrative Conventions." *Studies in Language* 3: 1–36.

Clark, H. 1992. *Arenas of Language Use.* Chicago: The University of Chicago Press & CSLI.

Cornulier, B., de. 1982. "Sur le sens des questions totales et alternatives." In *Langages* 67: *La Signalisation du Discours,* edited by F. Recanati. Paris: Larousse: 55–109.

Davidson, D. 1967. "The Logical Form of Action Sentences." Reprinted in *Essays on Actions and Events,* Oxford: Clarendon Press, 1980: 105–122.

Devlin, K. 1991. *Logic and Information.* Cambridge: Cambridge University Press.

Fillmore, C. 1975. "An Alternative to Checklist Theories of Meaning." *BLS* 1: 123–131.

Fillmore, C. 1982. "Frame Semantics." In *Linguistics in the Morning Calm,* edited by Linguistic Society of Korea. Seoul: Hanshin: 11–138.

———. 1986. "Pragmatically Controlled Zero Anaphora." *BLS* 12: 95–107.

Fillmore, C. and B. Atkins. 1992. "Toward a Frame-Based Lexicon: the Semantics of RISK and its neighbors." In *Fields, Frames and Contrasts: New Essays on Semantic and Lexical Organization,* edited by A. Lehrer and E. Kittay. Hillsdale, N.J.: Lawrence Erlbaum: 75–102.

Fillmore, C. and P. Kay. 1994. *Construction Grammar Coursebook.* University of California, Berkeley.

Goldberg, A. 1995. *Constructions: A Construction Grammar Approach to Argument Structure.* Chicago: The University of Chicago Press.

Hawkins, J. 1978. *Definiteness and Indefiniteness.* London: Croom Helm.

Heim, I. 1988. *The Semantics of Definite and Indefinite Noun Phrases.* New York: Garland.

Lambrecht, K. 1994. *Information Structure and Sentence Form.* Cambridge: Cambridge University Press.

Langacker, R. 1987. *Foundations of Cognitive Grammar,* vol. 1. Stanford: Stanford University Press.

Lyons, J. 1975. "Deixis as the Source of Reference." In *Formal Semantics of Natural Language,* edited by E. Keenan. Cambridge: Cambridge University Press: 61–83.

McCarthy, J. 1993. "Notes on Formalizing Context." *Proceedings of the Thirteenth International Joint Conference on Artificial Intelligence,* vol. 1. San Mateo: Morgan Kaufmann Publisher: 555–560.

Neale, S. 1990. *Descriptions.* Cambridge, Mass: MIT Press/Bradford Books.

Nunberg, G. 1995. "Transfers of Meaning." *Journal of Semantics* 12: 109–132.

Perry, J. 1986. "Thought without Representation." Reprinted in *The Problem of the Essential Indexical and Other Essays,* New York: Oxford University Press, 1992: 205–225.

Prandi, M. 1992. *Grammaire philosophique des tropes.* Paris: Minuit.

Recanati, F. 1986. "Contextual Dependence and Definite Descriptions." *Proceedings of the Aristotelian Society* 87: 57–73.

———. 1993. *Direct Reference: From Language to Thought.* Oxford: Blackwell.

———. 1995. "The Alleged Priority of Literal Interpretation." *Cognitive Science* 19: 207–232.

———. 1996. "Domains of Discourse." *Linguistics and Philosophy* 19: 445–475.

———. 1997. "The Dynamics of Situations." *European Review of Philosophy* 2: 41–75.

———. Forthcoming: "Context-Shifting in Metarepresentations."

Rumelhart, D. 1979. "Some Problems with the Notion of Literal Meaning." In *Metaphor and Thought,* 2nd edition, edited by A. Ortony. Cambridge: Cambridge University Press, 1993: 71–82.

Salmon, N. 1991. "The Pragmatic Fallacy." *Philosophical Studies* 63: 83–97.

Searle, J. 1978. "Literal Meaning." *Erkenntnis,* 13: 207–24.

———. 1980. "The Background of Meaning." In *Speech Act Theory and Pragmatics,* edited by J. Searle, F. Kiefer and M. Bierwisch. Dordrecht: Reidel: 221–32.

Sechehaye, A. 1926. *Essai sur la structure logique de la phrase.* Paris: Champion.

Sperber D. & D. Wilson. 1986. *Relevance: Communication and Cognition.* Oxford: Blackwell.

Strawson, P.F. 1964. "Identifying Reference and Truth-Value." Reprinted in Strawson 1977: 75–95.

———. 1977. *Logico-Linguistic Papers.* London: Methuen.

Tesnière, L. 1969. *Éléments de Syntaxe Structurale,* 2nd edition. Paris: Klincksieck.

Travis, C. 1975. *Saying and Understanding.* Oxford: Blackwell.

———. 1981. *The True and the False: the Domain of the Pragmatic.* Amsterdam: Benjamins.

PART THREE

Linguistics and Philosophy of Science

5

Moral Competence

Susan Dwyer

1.

In *Knowledge of Language,* Chomsky writes:

> There is reason to believe that knowledge of language, which provides an un-
> bounded range of propositional knowledge and enters into complex practical
> knowledge, should be regarded as a system of principles that develops in the
> mind by the fixing of values for certain parameters on the basis of experience,
> yielding systems that appear to be highly diverse but that are fundamentally
> alike in deeper respects. . . . We might speculate that the same is true in other
> areas where humans are capable of acquiring rich and highly articulated sys-
> tems of knowledge under the triggering and shaping effect of experience.
> (1986: 272)

My aim in this paper is develop one such line of speculation.[1] I argue that
at a certain level of abstraction there are striking parallels between the exercise and development of moral competence, on the one hand, and the exercise and development of linguistic competence, on the other. The parallels motivate pressing the so-called linguistic analogy well beyond the
epistemological use to which Rawls (1971: 46–7) puts it and into substantive service as a psychological hypothesis. Facts about the abilities that
comprise mature moral competence and the conditions in which those abilities develop strongly suggest that children come equipped with something
akin to Universal *Moral* Grammar. Of course, synchronic and diachronic
variability in moral codes tend to raise doubts about the universality of
moral principles. However, such variability occurs overwhelmingly at the
level of particular moral judgments; for example, contemporary Americans
would likely judge that it is impermissible for their children to torture animals for fun, whereas Hopis in the 1950s (apparently) thought otherwise
(Brandt 1954). But the recognition of a distinction between moral and con-

ventional domains, and the belief that moral considerations are imbued with special force and authority appear to be universal features of human life (Song, Smetana, and Kim 1987; Turiel 1983). Thus I argue for the utility of a further appropriation from linguistics. Variability in human languages exists against a background of deep commonality and is explained in terms of the notion of parameter-setting; a similar explanation might be available in the case of morality.

2.

Moral agency is usefully characterized as a cluster of abilities; for example, the ability to recognize that a situation requires a moral response, the ability to decide which of a range of moral responses is appropriate, and the ability to make moral evaluations of one's own and others' characters and actions. These sorts of recognitions, decisions, and judgments differ in both form and content: 'I ought to recycle my newspapers'; 'He is untrustworthy'; 'I am ashamed'; and so on. In addition, moral agents tend to experience moral reasons as especially compelling; they are able to act on such reasons, often in the face of strong countervailing (prudential) considerations; and they are able to provide justifications of their conduct in light of such reasons. More abstractly, moral agents are able to construct a conception of the good and of their relation to it—in short, to develop a character. Finally, all these abilities appear to be open-ended. That is, agents are able to make relatively confident discriminations, evaluations, and judgments in a wide range of actual and hypothetical, novel and familiar cases.

I employ the term "agent" advisedly: moral behavior is a species of intentional behavior. Whether the explanation of moral behavior always requires the attribution of desires in addition to specifically moral beliefs is a vexed question in moral psychology (Smith 1994). Internalists argue that moral beliefs by themselves motivate the agents who have them (McDowell 1978, 1979), whereas externalists deny this (Brink 1986). In what follows I will be primarily concerned with the acquisition of moral beliefs. But I shall have cause to return to the internalism/externalism debate when I consider some objections to the linguistically-inspired model of moral competence that I propose.

3.

How do children, in the normal course of events, acquire the beliefs the attribution of which appears to be required for the explanation of the manifestation of adult moral abilities? This question becomes especially pressing when we reflect on three facts: (i) children less than 4 years of age exhibit some fundamental moral abilities; (ii) ordinary adult moral life is subtle and complex; and (iii) many moral situations we encounter and deal with as adults are unique.

Several studies (Much and Shweder 1978; Nucci 1981; Smetana 1981; Turiel 1983) have found that preschool children discriminate between moral transgressions (e.g., stealing a pencil, pushing someone off a swing) and transgressions of nonmoral rules (e.g., wearing pajamas to school). This discrimination is manifested in two ways. First, children's spontaneous re-actions to transgressions of each type differ: they are more likely to initiate physical responses to actors who have broken a moral rule than to those who have broken a "merely" conventional rule. Second, children offer dif-ferent types of verbal responses to various transgressions: in the case of a moral transgression children will advert to the pain or injury experienced by the victim of an act, and they will often employ the notions of rights and fairness (Nucci and Turiel 1978); whereas in the case of nonmoral trans-gressions, children are inclined to focus on issues of social order and disor-der, and on the explicit commands of their caretakers or teachers. And while there is some disagreement about how the boundaries between the moral and conventional domains are inscribed cross-culturally (Shweder and Sullivan 1993), it appears that young children in different cultures judge the same types of actions (e.g., breaking promises, destroying an-other's property) as moral transgressions (Shweder, Mahapatra, and Miller 1987). It also appears that, contrary to Piaget (1932) and Kohlberg (1981), children attach significance to moral rules above and beyond, and some-times independently of any punishment that might be thought to follow their being broken.[2]

These results show that children are sensitive to some fairly subtle nor-mative demands. And we would like to know how they come to grasp them. One story that enjoys a considerable amount of pre-theoretical plausibility is that moral development occurs by learning by example or mimicking. This is how one leading social learning theorist puts it:

> The capacity to learn by observation enables people to acquire rules for gen-erating and regulating behavioral patterns without having to form them grad-ually by tedious trial and error. . . . By observing others, one forms rules of be-havior, and on future occasions this coded information serves as a guide for action. . . . Throughout the years, modeling has always been acknowledged to be one of the most powerful means of transmitting values, attitudes, and pat-terns of thought and behavior. (Bandura 1986: 19, 47; cited in Wren 1992: 58)

But this will not do as an explanation of moral development, since the process by which such development is said to occur—modeling—goes com-pletely unanalyzed. How does mere observation enable a child to acquire knowledge of and/or internalize moral rules?

We can distinguish two tasks the child faces. First there is the matter of telling the difference between rule-governed behavior and accidentally-regular behavior. Suppose that in the Smith-Jones household there is a rule, unbeknownst to 2-year old Lisa, that glass containers go in the right-hand side of the recycling box and plastic containers go in the left-hand side of the box. Now imagine that left-handed Jones is in charge of laying the breakfast table, which results in the cereal box being placed in a particular orientation on the table each morning. Young Lisa will observe two very regular sequences of events or dispositions of objects. But how, absent explicit instruction, will she learn to discriminate between the rule-governed behavior concerning recyclables and the merely accidental placement of the cereal box? Secondly, assuming that the latter question is answered, how do children learn to distinguish between rule-governed behaviors themselves, for example, between keeping promises and laying the dinner table correctly. The social learning theory is utterly silent on both counts. The fundamental mistake here, I believe, is the assumption that all the information the child needs to achieve moral maturity is available in her environment. But this is far from obvious, as I shall now show.

Given the inadequacy of the observational model of moral learning, one might try to explain moral development in terms of the explicit moral instruction children typically receive. But again it is unclear how such instruction (by itself) can account for the moral abilities children manifestly have and/or develop. First, consider the usefulness of the positive moral instruction we offer children. Usually this takes two forms: either post-hoc evaluations ('You ought not to have broken your sister's train.'), or unexplained imperatives ('Keep your promises.'). Post-hoc evaluations are evaluations of *particular* instances of morally assessable behavior, and rarely involve appeal to a general rule. The child knows that she ought not to have broken her sister's train, but what of her brother's slot cars, or her sister's teddy bear? Moreover, such evaluations are not different in form from, and are perhaps less frequent than, nonmoral evaluations of behavior ('You should have put the fork on *this* side.'). Unexplained imperatives certainly convey more generality, but when we impart them to children we do not ordinarily draw attention to the fact that moral generalizations are *ceteris paribus* generalizations. 'You ought to tell the truth' we instruct our kids; we do not state and explain the several exceptions. Thus, the moral generalizations we offer to children are fairly coarse-grained, offering only limited guidance to children in their future actions.

It is also worth noting that there is a vast amount of moral knowledge that is unavailable to children. While children test the limits of the permissible, so to speak, they do not engage in the full range of behaviors that would stimulate their caretakers to impart a good deal of moral information. Similarly, children are not exposed to examples of every possible situation in which a particular judgment is appropriate. And it is not until the adolescent is enrolled in Moral Philosophy 101 that she even ponders whether it is permissible for the authorities to hang an innocent man in order to avoid a bloody riot.

Absent a detailed account of how children extrapolate distinctly moral rules from the barrage of parental imperatives and evaluations, the appeal to explicit moral instruction will not provide anything like a satisfactory explanation of the emergence of mature moral competence.[3] What we have here is a set of complex, articulated abilities that (i) emerge over time in an environment that is impoverished with respect to the content and scope of their mature manifestation, and (ii) appear to develop naturally across the species.

4.

In terms of these features, moral competence looks analogous to linguistic competence. And this similarity encourages us to mine the resources of linguistic theory in order to provide an explanation for the development of moral competence. It is now well-recognized that first-language acquisition can only occur if human infants are already in possession of a considerable store of linguistic knowledge. But despite the familiarity of this point, it will be helpful to rehearse some of the main considerations in favor of it, if only to fix discussion and bring out more fully the parallels I am urging between ethics and linguistics.

The intuitive idea behind the poverty of the stimulus argument is easy to grasp. We focus on the nature of the linguistic input a child receives—the primary linguistic data—and on the sorts of mistakes that the child is apt to make. Consider questions formed from declarative sentences:

(1) The dog is on the sofa.
(2) Is the dog on the sofa?
(3) The dog which has fleas is on the sofa.
(4) Is the dog which has fleas on the sofa?

Clearly, question formation is sensitive to the structure of the relevant declarative; (3), unlike (1) contains a complex noun phrase. A structure *insensitive* rule for question formation (in English) might be

R Locate the first verb and move it to the front of the sentence.

But (R) would deliver

(5) *Has the dog which fleas is on the sofa?

which is not a well-formed sentence of any language. In particular, children do not utter sentences like (5), despite never receiving explicit instruction about how to form simple questions, and the absence of overt phrase markers. This suggests that they operate with a complex, structure sensitive rule for question formation, when, on the assumption that they are not exposed to many sentences with embedded clauses (like (3)), all the evidence they have is consistent with the simpler one (R) above.

Children do not merely pick up their language from those around them, nor can we explain first-language acquisition in terms of trial and error learning. Another simple example illustrates. Suppose a child hears instances of the following types of well-formed sentences of English:

(6) Alice said that the Queen insulted the Mad Hatter.
(7) Alice said the Queen insulted the Mad Hatter.
(8) Who will forgive her?
(9) Who will she forgive?

On the basis on such evidence, the child would be likely to conclude (i) that 'that' is optional before a complement clause—(6) and (7), *and* (ii) that both object and subject positions can be queried—(8) and (9). If the child were to engage in simple hypothesis formation, we would expect her to utter sentences like (10),

(10) *Who did Alice think that insulted the Mad Hatter?

for a grammar in which 'that' is optional before complement clauses and in which both the object and subject positions may be questioned is the simplest[4] grammar consistent with the data. But, again, children do not produce utterances like (10); in a very real sense, the most obvious hypothesis never occurs to them.

Of course, children do make mistakes and thereby provide the adults around them with some opportunities for explicit instruction. But it is noteworthy that caretakers typically pay more attention to *what* a child is saying than to *how* she is saying it (Demetras, Post, and Snow 1986). When overt correction does take place, it usually concerns rather superficial stylistic matters—what we might call 'fourth grade grammar' (compare 'I seen a fish.' and 'I saw a fish.'), and on those occasions when children *are* corrected on a matter of grammar, they can be remarkably resistant to instruction (MacNeill 1966).

The examples just discussed are just a minuscule portion of the available evidence on first-language acquisition which demonstrates that children acquire competence in their language despite having access to only degenerate and partial linguistic data. *No* traditional learning theoretic explanation of this fact is available (Chomsky 1959; Fodor 1980). Thus we must posit that the child is in possession of a considerable store of innate knowledge which permits the acquisition of her language in the face of the paucity of data available to her. This knowledge is taken to be part of *every* child's genetic endowment.

The logic of the poverty of the stimulus argument drives us to posit an innate epistemic endowment, and several decades of work in theoretical linguistics has begun to reveal what that content of this knowledge is. One thing is very clear: whatever the principles of Universal Grammar are, they must be *specific* enough for a particular child to acquire her native tongue, and *general* enough that *any* child in *any* linguistic environment can acquire a (humanly possible) language. The point can be put problematically: if every human child is endowed with the *same* innate knowledge (Universal Grammar), how do we explain the fact that there are many *different* human languages?

It is important to be clear about precisely what 'different' means in this context. Human languages differ from one another in more or less interesting ways. So, for example, variation in vocabularies is a rather superficial fact, to be explained on the basis of various historical contingencies. More intriguing and deeper differences (and commonalities) are exemplified by facts like the following. All human languages are *configurational;* but English is a right-branching (Head-first) language while Japanese is left-branching (Head-final). Hence in (11)–(13) the complement prepositional phrase 'at Charles' comes after the Head, irrespective of whether this is a verb, noun, or an adjective.

(11) Mallory *swore* at Charles.
(12) Mallory's *amazement* at Charles.
(13) Mallory is *mad* at Charles.

And while all languages have subjects, it is not the case that these must be overt, or pronounced in the sentences of all languages. In English one must always pronounce the subject of a sentence, but Italian and Spanish permit sentences with no overt subject in the main clause. Thus only (14) is permissible in English, but in Italian, versions of both (14) and (15) are permitted—(16) and (17).

(14) I am going to the cinema.
(15) *Am going to the cinema.
(16) Io vado al cinema.
(17) Vado al cinema.

The presence of such variation against the backdrop of deep similarities is captured and explained in current linguistic theory via the theory of *pa-*

rameters (Chomsky 1981; Hornstein and Lightfoot 1981; Lightfoot 1991). The basic idea is very simple. It is hypothesized that some principles of Universal Grammar contain variables that are initially unspecified; specific values for these variables are determined by the linguistic input to which each child is exposed. A useful metaphor is that of a switch: in an English-speaking environment the Head Position Parameter will be set to *Head-first,* while if the same child were to grow up in a Japanese-speaking environment, that parameter would be set to *Head-final.*

The specification and attribution to children of innate principles which are subject to parametric variation represents a significant step toward explaining (i) how the achievement of mature linguistic competence is possible in the face of an impoverished stimulus environment *and* (ii) how it is that human languages, while essentially similar, differ in interesting ways. For, taking the Head Position Parameter as our example, notice that an English-speaking child will be able to set this parameter on the basis of exposure to any of wide variety of triggering data—*any* sentences of the forms in (11)–(13) will do. Moreover, supposing that parameter is set on the basis of hearing sentences like (13), the child will not have to 'learn' independently that verbs precede their objects, or that prepositions precede their complements, for these are necessary concomitants of the parameter being set a particular way. Thus the operation of parameter-setting makes the task of language acquisition dramatically simpler for the child. And it should be obvious how postulation of parametric variation accounts for differences between human languages; linguistic variation just *is* parametric variation.

To summarize, language acquisition is simply not possible without the assumption of some innate endowment. And the very general (though deep claim) that *something* must be innate is given specific and substantive content by the articulation of linguistic rules, principles, and parameters. The child's possession of Universal Grammar renders her particular linguistic community (perhaps surprisingly) largely irrelevant to the fact that she 'learns' to speak *a* language, but highly relevant to *which* language she comes to speak.

5.

I have sketched two parallels: first between the structure and scope of our mature linguistic competence and that of our mature moral competence, and second, between the conditions in which we manage to develop our moral and linguistic abilities. In my view, these parallels suggest that the two sorts of ability might admit of a similar type of explanation. Thus I propose that we all come into the world equipped with a store of innate moral knowledge which, together with our experience, determines our mature moral competence. And given cross-cultural variation in individual moral judgments, it would appear that the postulation of *moral* parameters is not entirely out of order. We might imagine that some of the principles of Universal Moral Grammar contain variables which are initially unspecified, and that these come to take a specific value in light of the moral community in which each child grows up. Just as in the case of language, the discovery of these principles and parameters is a thoroughly empirical matter. And while a child's moral community will be essential to the explanation of the particular moral judgments she is wont to make, any community will do for the development of her moral abilities simpliciter.

The case for moral parameter-setting would be strengthened by the identification of a bona fide example. Since, at least to my knowledge, no-one has yet undertaken the search for moral parameters, I am left to speculate.

To begin, let us return to linguistics. When it comes to giving content to the notion of Universal Grammar it helps to distinguish two levels of analysis. At one level, we are concerned with features of human language that are universal—for example, the fact that all human languages are configurational. At a second, we are interested in features that are relative to particular classes of languages—that is, in the effects of parameter-setting. It is crucial, however, to understand that the variability at the second-level is constrained by first-level features. As we have just seen, the existence of the Head Position Parameter and its dual degrees of freedom (Head first/Head final) only makes sense given the fact that languages are configurational. If languages did not exhibit systematic phrase structure, the notion of a Head position itself would be unintelligible.

This gives us a hint about how to proceed in the case of morality. What we need to do is identify those features of morality that appear to be universal and those that are apparently specific to particular moral communities. I have already adverted to research that strongly supports the idea that the demarcation of two normative social domains (viz., the moral and the conventional) is universal (Sung, Smetana, and Kim 1987; Turiel 1983). Human children are clearly equipped from birth with knowledge that allows them to tell the difference between mere noise and human speech; similarly, we might speculate that they are also in possession of some knowledge that primes them for recognizing two normative social domains.

As for the more specific level, we need to turn to descriptive ethics, comparative religion, and anthropology to see what sorts of local variations exist and to determine whether these variations are capturable in terms of parameter-setting. A full discussion would take me too far afield, but here are some suggestions. Consider the criteria for being a person, that is, for being an individual with elevated (the highest?) moral status. During some historical periods, beliefs about these criteria precluded the attribution of personhood to women and slaves; today there is disagreement about whether animals, human fetuses, and children have full moral status. Furthermore, cultures differ with respect to their social ontology: contemporary North American and European cultures tend to take the individual as the primary ethical unit, whereas some others grant metaphysical and ethical priority to the community as a whole. This might explain why the concept of a right appears to have no application in some moral communities (Haidt, Koller, and Dias 1993; Triandis 1989, 1991). And it would be surprising if prevailing religious beliefs and practices, material conditions like extended famine, and political factors such as radical disparities in socioeconomic status did not substantively influence local moral judgments about life and death, distributive justice, and so on (Hursthouse 1991), and give rise to both inter- and intracultural moral disagreement (Wainryb and Turiel 1995).

6.

Such speculations are all well and good, but it will be objected that, quite apart from the absence of firm empirical evidence for moral parameters, there are a number of theoretical objections that threaten the plausibility of my proposal. The likelihood of such objections is increased, given the interdisciplinary nature of the view, since an almost inevitable consequence of bringing together developmental psychology, linguistics, and philosophy is that one will encounter opposition from all directions. In this paper I cannot provide exhaustive coverage and response to such opposition. But I want to mention three discipline-specific worries about the moral parameters model that appear to be related.

Linguists may doubt whether moral competence is a competence in the Chomskian sense. Typically, moral agency involves *doing* the right thing—or, at the very least, *being motivated* to do the right thing. In other words, moral competence, unlike linguistic competence, appears essentially to involve a performative element. Developmental psychologists might argue that the moral parameters model is empirically inadequate, on the grounds that it is silent on the role of emotions and empathy in moral development. And finally some moral philosophers may complain that the model is committed to an overly 'intellectualist' picture of moral competence; such competence is properly construed as knowledge-how—perhaps, as a form of *understanding,* and hence it involves something above and beyond the (propositional) grasp of rules (Blum 1994; McDowell 1978; Schick 1991).[5]

Underlying all three objections is the idea that morality is practical. Moral judgments (beliefs) appear to be special in the following sense: If an agent judges that it is right that she $\emptyset$ in circumstances C, then she is motivated to $\emptyset$ in C. And if moral beliefs differ from nonmoral beliefs in having the property of motivating the agents who have them, it is arguable that the conditions of their acquisition are unique as well. The last two sentences express what is at the heart of a particular version of ethical internalism.[6] So one way to defend the moral parameters model would be to reject internalism. However, this will not be my strategy. To be sure, it is a controversial view which requires careful articulation in order to be plausible; but I am largely sympathetic to it. Rather I shall try to defend the moral parameters model against each of the three objections in a way that does not beg any obvious questions concerning the internalism/externalism debate.

7.

One way to counter skepticism about whether moral competence is a competence in the relevant sense is to show that a competence/performance distinction makes sense within the realm of the moral. As a first step, however, let us briefly consider the competence/performance distinction as it is constructed in linguistics.

While linguists are concerned to explain human linguistic capacities, linguistic *theory*—the articulation of the content of Universal Grammar, the theory of parameters, etc.—is not a theory about what comes out of actual speakers' mouths. It is not that the theory somehow floats free of the phenomenon it is constructed to explain. For the phenomenon to be explained is precisely speakers' linguistic competence, not their many and varied utterances. Nor is it that actual linguistic behavior has *no* bearing on linguistic theory; although saying what the relation is between speakers' actual linguistic behavior and linguistic theory is complicated. At the most general level, of course, theoretical linguists are motivated by empirical observations of language users: it appears that all and only humans are language users; natural languages universally exemplify a finite set of features (despite the wide variety of languages, the set of humanly possible languages appears to be constrained). More locally, linguists collect speakers' judgments about target sentences such as (18)

(18) *John and Bill admire pictures of himself.

and use the elicited acceptability judgments to test various hypotheses about syntactic structure. English speakers will unanimously judge that (18) is not-okay, and such data can be used to confirm or disconfirm a theory about anaphors. But it would be a mistake to think of such a theory as a mere systematization of speakers' acceptability judgments about sentences of the relevant kind. Linguists are concerned to articulate rules and principles of *grammatical* constructions, knowledge of which is thought partly to explain speakers' acceptability judgments. Linguistic theory trades in idealizations, and while actual speakers' acceptability judgments may deviate from linguists' grammaticality judgments—as they do with respect to so-called garden path sentences and sentences with multiple embeddings—this is not straightforwardly evidence of any lack of competence on the part of speakers. Of course, some explanation is called for. But there are plenty to choose from, including: the limitations of human parsing mechanisms; inattention; drunkenness; a desire to annoy; and so on. And, of course, a particular speaker's linguistic competence can fail to be manifest for reasons like the absence of a larynx.

Returning now to the moral case. It is a commonplace that ethical theory is not intended to be a merely a systematization of the moral judgments that people actually make, far less is it thought to be a summary of what people do. Ethical theory is concerned with articulating the principles of right action,[7] and as Kant warned, we cannot straightforwardly ascertain what we ought to do from what we do do. In other words, ethical theory is concerned with moral competence, with giving an account of what makes moral judgment and behavior possible. Individuals' moral judgments—their moral intuitions—are data for moral theory in the same way that speakers' acceptability judgments are data for linguistic theory, in the sense that moral intuitions about a particular case can lend support to, or detract from, a given ethical principle (Dwyer 1997). To take a familiar example: a crude version of utilitarianism is discredited by the fact that most people judge that it would be wrong to hang an innocent man, even if doing so would prevent the deaths of one hundred other innocent people.

To maintain the parallel between ethics and linguistics, sense needs to be made of people's deviations from moral competence. Recall that the model I have proposed implies that the development of moral competence—like the acquisition of an idiolect—is something that happens to every human child raised in a human environment. But it is clear that we all make moral mistakes.[8] Not just in our actions (when we lie or break a promise), but also in our judgments (when, in the absence of some relevant information, we judge an impermissible action to be permissible). Having a moral idiolect does not guarantee that an agent will always do what is right; the connection between moral belief and action is defeasible. And our moral judgments are analogous to our acceptability judgments about sentences; just as many English-speakers judge garden path sentences to be not-okay, many moral agents make errors in moral judgment. The output of our moral competence can be sullied by inattention, drunkenness, a strong nonmoral desire for power, and so on; and in such instances we can generally be brought to see our mistakes. It is intriguing to consider the existence of either a moral equivalent to a parsing mechanism—the limitations of which might explain other deviations from competence—or specific organs necessary for the manifestation of moral competence. But whether or not we can make sense of these things, the general plausibility of a moral competence/performance distinction appears to be in good shape.

8.

Perhaps, however, moral competence does require the existence of some further capacity or capacities. It is here that one might invoke the ideas that a capacity to recognize and experience certain emotions is required for the development of moral agency. If the moral parameters model has no room for the involvement of emotions in moral development, it invites the charge of empirical inadequacy. But the legitimacy of the charge depends a great deal on precisely what role emotions are thought to play in the initial acquisition of moral beliefs. (The affective dimensions of adult moral life— that is, of the manifestation of moral competence—are discussed in the next section.)

One radical view with which the moral parameters view is plainly at odds is a crudely resuscitated version of eighteenth century moral sense theory. According to one proponent,

> Children do not learn morality by learning maxims or clarifying values. They *enhance their natural sentiments* by being regularly induced by families, friends, and institutions to behave in accord with the most obvious standards of right conduct—fair dealing, reasonable self-control, and personal honesty. A moral life is perfected by practice more than by precept; children are not taught so much as habituated. (Wilson 1993: 249, my emphasis)

On this view, moral agency is not really *agency* at all. We are to assume that humans have an innate affective constitution and that moral development is no more and no less than the disciplining of emotional reactions. In short, there is little or no room for *judgment.*

Ironically, Wilson is motivated to propose this behavioristic view of moral development by observations not unlike the ones with which I began this paper (section 3): morality is a universal feature of human life, very young children exhibit some moral behavior, so it is natural to suggest that something must be innate. But like all poverty-of-the-stimulus type arguments, a lot hinges on how one conceives of the mature or final state of the ability in question. While I do not argue for it here, I assume the truth of moral cognitivism. When Alice says that eating nonhuman animals is wrong, she expresses a belief that is either true or false; and when Gertrude replies that there is nothing morally problematic about eating milk-fed veal, she and Alice have a genuine disagreement. So I grant that the moral parameters model is (probably) inconsistent with moral noncognitivism.

But since noncognitivism faces a host of serious (and, I think, fatal) objections of its own, I will not consider it further.

Of course, one need not be an emotivist to hold that emotions play an important role in moral development. An intuitively plausible view is that moral agency requires the ability to empathize with others, where the capacity to recognize and experience certain emotions is a psychological prerequisite for empathy (Thompson 1987).[9] Moreover, attributions of praise and blame—a central feature of moral life—require the assessment of others' intentions. And a considerable body of evidence suggests that early affective capacities are implicated the child's developing conception of other minds (Gordon 1996).

Of more interest, perhaps, is recent work that is beginning to uncover the ways in which infants and young children use emotions—theirs and others—to regulate behavior (see Thompson (1987) for a review). In particular, there is some reason to think that, from about two years of age, children rely on emotional cues to distinguish between various sociomoral domains. Earlier (section 3) I alluded to research that shows that very young children reliably distinguish between the moral domain and the conventional domain. Building on this work, Arsenio and Lover (1995) propose a four stage model of how children move from observations of the emotional consequences of certain actions to the construction of general moral principles. Roughly: children notice certain regular affect-event links; they form mental cognitive representations of these links, which they then deploy in anticipating the possible outcomes of various actions; and finally they learn to coordinate conflicting affect-event links (e.g., they resolve the tension between the satisfaction of victimizers who get what they want and the unhappiness of their victims).

Now the moral parameters model does not mention emotions. But it does not preclude affective capacities from playing a role in moral development. The main thrust of the moral parameters model is that children's environments are impoverished with respect to the moral capacities they manifest and/or develop. It is for this reason that I think we must attribute a considerable store of innate moral knowledge to children. The research I have summarized certainly implies that the moral environment might be richer than I supposed earlier. Indeed, it is quite plausible that affective cues help children distinguish between moral transgressions and conventional transgressions. But it is hard to see how the deployment of emotional capacities could facilitate children's grasp of the distinction between rule-governed behavior and accidentally-regular behavior. The moral parameters model can accommodate a range of views about the role of emotions in moral development. It would be seriously threatened only if it was shown that an emotion-based model better solved the acquisition problem.

One final remark about emotions and moral development is in order. It might be that only creatures with affective capacities develop moral competence. A species with no emotional life, which employed no emotional concepts might fail to have a moral life or grasp moral concepts. I think this is a plausible view. But the truth of a 'necessary coinstantiation' hypothesis would not entail emotivism, nor any particular (weaker) thesis regarding the role of emotions in the development of moral competence.

9.

While we await further empirical evidence for such theses, we cannot deny the obvious role that emotions play in adult moral life, or, as I prefer to put it, in the *application* of moral knowledge. Sherman (1990) sums it up nicely:

> ... a necessary condition for acting rightly will include recognition of the morally relevant features of situations, or what has been called moral salience. Often this will involve a sensitivity cultivated through emotional dispositions. Not only do we notice, but we notice with a certain intensity or impact that would be absent if emotions weren't engaged. We focus in ways we wouldn't otherwise. ... In addition to this perceptual role, the emotions play a role in communicating to others an agent's interest and concern ... the emotional tone of one's action may make a moral difference. (pp. 150–1)

I agree. But it might be thought that concessions here ultimately undermine the very model of moral development I am trying to defend. Let me explain.

The general sentiment expressed by Sherman is a common theme in much contemporary moral psychology that takes its inspiration from Wittgenstein and Aristotle (e.g., Blum 1994; McDowell 1978, 1979). This work denies that moral knowledge—often construed as the virtuous person's knowledge about how to live—is codifiable. Moral life is too complex; the determination of right action in any circumstance depends too much upon the particular facts of that situation; and moral expertise is more a matter of knowledge-how than of knowledge-that. In short, what the virtuous person knows cannot be formulated exhaustively in any set of rules or principles, no matter how fine-grained those rules and principles are.

As I have presented it, the moral parameters model focuses on how children recover specifically moral rules from the social environments in which they grow up. But the considerations above suggest that there are no moral rules of the requisite kind to be recovered. In this regard it is noteworthy that McDowell—a well-known proponent of the uncodifiablity thesis—also recognizes that there is an acquisition problem. He writes:

We are inclined to be impressed by the sparseness of teaching which leaves someone capable of autonomously going on in the same way. All that happens is that the pupil is told, or shown, what to do in a few instances, with some surrounding talk about why that is the thing to do; the surrounding talk . . . falls short of including actual enunciation of a universal principle, mechanical application of which would constitute correct behaviour in the practice in question. Yet pupils do acquire the capacity to go on, without further advice, to novel instances. Impressed by the sparseness of teaching, we find this remarkable. (1979: 341)

Quite so. However, McDowell thinks we will make little progress in explaining moral development if we replace the question,

. . . 'How is it that the pupil, given that sparse instruction, goes on to new instances in the right way?' with the question 'How is it that the pupil, given that sparse instruction, divines from it a universal formula with the right deductive powers?'. (1979: 341)

Rather we should focus on a community's shared forms of life and the ways in which these are subtlely communicated to children.

In moral upbringing what one learns is not to behave on conformity with rules of conduct, but to see situations in a special light, as constituting reasons for acting; this perceptual capacity, once acquired, can be exercised in complex novel circumstances, not necessarily capable of being foreseen and legislated for by a codifier of the conduct required by virtue, however wise and thoughtful he might be. (McDowell 1978: 21)

A full discussion of all that is involved here is beyond the scope of the present paper. But let me enter the following brief remarks in defense of the moral parameters model. First, I do not propose that moral knowledge is exhausted by explicitly formulated and absolute rules. In a relatively broad sense of "moral knowledge," I agree that there are better and worse ways to apply moral rules, to resolve ethical tensions, and so on. Contemporary Kantians can and do admit that one needs some skill in applying the categorical imperative procedure (Wallace 1991: 460–1); and following Ross (1930) we can make sense of the idea that moral generalizations are *ceteris paribus* generalizations (Pietroski 1993). Nothing in the moral parameters model rules out an individual's acquiring increased moral sophistication as she matures. The point is: she needs something to build on, and that something must be conceived, in part, as innately given.

Secondly, the insistence that morality is essentially practical does not preclude thinking of moral development in terms of the triggering and filling out of some innate cognitive structures. As I mentioned above (section

2), I am sympathetic to the brand of internalism which holds that if an agent judges that it is right that she Ø in C, then she is motivated to Ø in C. The central idea here is that moral beliefs differ from nonmoral beliefs in having the property of motivating the agents who have them. In other words, what underpins the practicality of morality is still a set of cognitive states—namely, beliefs.

Finally, I am not sure how the Wittgensteinian appeal to shared forms of life helps at all in *explaining,* rather than merely redescribing, moral development. Talk of 'whirls of organism' and 'being brought to see things is a certain light' might be useful metaphors to get us thinking about moral development, but such metaphors do nothing to render that process less mysterious or remarkable.[10]

10.

To sum up. Paying attention to the universalized particularity of moral agency—that is, to the fact that morality is a universal feature of human life that manifests itself in different ways in different socio-cultural niches—and noting the relative impoverishment of the moral data available to children, I have proposed a model of what makes moral agency possible that relies heavily on an analogy between the development of linguistic abilities and moral abilities. The central idea is that human beings are equipped with Universal Moral Grammar, a set of abstract principles, some of which are parametized.

While much more needs to be said by way of fleshing out the theory of moral parameter-setting, I hope that what I have said is sufficient to make the idea worth exploring. If the account is on the right track, then we would have the beginnings of an explanation of the cultural variation in moral judgment which is thought to pose such a problem for a realist, or objectivist moral theory. Crucially, it will be an explanation which depends upon the existence of deep commonalities between the world's residents, or morality's clientele. With an account of parameters in hand, the response to the relativist will not (simply) take the form of showing how widely divergent practices in different cultures can be interpreted as manifestations of the various 'locals" adherence to the same very general principle (e.g., one ought to respect one's elders). For I doubt that the content of the principles of Universal Moral Grammar, if such there be, is even as fine-grained as this. But more importantly, the idea of moral competence—understood in the way I recommend—provides an empirically motivated argument for the systematicity of moral consciousness. And offers the hope that we may be able to read off our moral theory from our moral practices. In this sense, I am recommending a thoroughly 'naturalistic turn' in ethics.

Notes

1. Many people have provided helpful comments on earlier versions of this paper; special thanks to Mark Baker, David Brink, Andrew Brook, Andy Burday, David Crocker, Marguerite Deslauriers, Elizabeth Ennen, John MacNamara, James McGilvray, Paul Pietroski, Robert Stainton, and David Wasserman.

2. In talking about this cluster of studies together I am glossing over important disagreements between their proponents. Turiel appears to hold that the acquisition of moral knowledge is no different in principle to the acquisition of non-moral knowledge—both take place via observation and induction—thus assuming that moral properties can be directly observed (see Turiel, Killen, and Helwig 1987). Shweder, on the other hand is more inclined to a projectivist view: what counts as a morally relevant feature of a situation is in large part determined by the evaluator's culture (see Shweder and Haidt 1993; Shweder and Much 1991). Finally, I have omitted any mention of research which tries to explicate moral competence in terms of social competence (e.g., Dunn 1988). Some sort of desire for sociability might be part of the explanation of certain motivational components of moral behavior, but it seems not to be part of an explanation of the content of young children's moral beliefs.

3. A number of recent studies have seriously undermined the plausibility of training accounts of moral development, especially those that stress parental discipline. See Grusec and Goodnow (1994) and Hay (1994).

4. The notion of simplicity at work in the 'pick up' hypothesis is *pre-theoretic* simplicity; in the absence of any substantive linguistic theory we ask, what would be the most straightforward rule to extract from the input? But there is a *theoretical* sense of 'simplicity'. As we will see below, it is children's possession of some rather (pre-theoretically) complex knowledge that makes acquiring a language a relatively 'simple' matter for them.

5. Other concerns that I do not tackle here include the following: (i) The linguistic analogy and talk of moral competence suggests the existence of a moral module, where the hallmark of modularity is 'information encapsulation' (Fodor 1983). But this appears to imply that persons are far more morally conservative than they seem, and to threaten the rational status of moral behavior. Also, moral modularity apparently automatically excludes the involvement of an agent's affective systems in her moral psychology. (ii) Whatever structure and systematicity we can discern in moral life is radically unlike that which we find in natural languages. Hence one might worry about the aptness of the poverty of the stimulus argument in the moral domain. (iii) The moral parameters model appears to be committed to a form of moral realism that some might argue is at odds with certain 'facts' about value pluralism.

6. 'Internalism' actually picks out a number of different theses; see Smith (1994) for discussion.

7. This characterization will strike some philosophers as overly narrow. Virtue ethicists, for example, tend to abjure the formulation of general moral principles. But even for them, ethics is about how to live rightly, albeit where living rightly is not a matter of conforming one's behavior to a set of principles of right action, but rather involves developing virtuous behavioral dispositions (e.g., compassion, resoluteness, courage, etc.).

8. It might be objected that this discussion rests on an unjustified assumption: the existence of moral truth, or correctness. For how else can there be moral *errors?* The logical point must be conceded. But the notion of error does not presuppose any particular account of moral truth or correctness. And in any case, my present aim is not to convert moral nihilists.

9. Empathy is not a purely affective state; it is not simply emotional contagion, but rather involves inferences about the mental states of others on the basis of observed emotional displays (Hoffman 1983; Strayer 1987). Moreover, it is not to be confused with sympathy (Chimsar 1988), for experiencing concordant emotions in response to what one perceives is another's emotional state need not involve any particular motivational component—for example, one can empathize with someone's jealousy without being positively disposed to alleviate it.

10. The uncodifiablity thesis has emerged in another context which might be thought to provide a more empirical (rather than conceptual) challenge to the moral parameters account of moral development. Churchland (1995) and Clark (1996) argue that moral development involves the acquisition of concepts, where this involves the construction of a hierarchy of prototypes on the basis of repeated exposure to examples. It is a familiar point about classical definition that our grasp of concepts resists codification, but both Churchland and Clark wed this plausible claim to a thoroughly physicalistic conception of the mind, in the form of connectionism. Of course, moral competence depends upon the functions of our brains in some sense. However, any move to locate moral competence in specific neural networks is, so far as I can see, wholly fantastic. In particular, Churchland's connectionist model threatens to assimilate moral 'thinking' to brute input-output functions, and thus treads dangerously close to logical behaviorism.

References

Arsenio, W. and A. Lover. 1995. "Children's Conceptions of Sociomoral Affect: Happy Victimizers, Mixed Emotions, and other Expectancies." In *Morality in Everyday Life: Developmental Perspectives,* edited by M. Killen and D. Hart. Cambridge: Cambridge University Press.

Bandura, A. 1986. *Social Foundations of Thought and Action.* Englewood Cliffs, N. J.: Prentice Hall.

Blum. L. 1994. *Moral Perception and Moral Particularity.* Cambridge: Cambridge University Press.

Brandt, R. B. 1954. *Hopi Ethics: A Theoretical Analysis.* Chicago: Chicago University Press.

Brink, D. 1986. "Externalist Moral Realism" *Southern Journal of Philosophy* 24, *Supplement:* 23–42.

Chimsar, D. 1988. "Empathy and Sympathy: The Important Difference." *Journal of Value Inquiry* 22: 257–266.

Chomsky, N. 1959. Review of Skinner, *Verbal Behavior. Language* 35: 26–58.

———. 1981. *Lectures on Government and Binding.* Dordrecht: Foris.

———. 1986. *Knowledge of Language.* New York: Praeger.

Churchland, P. M. 1995. *The Engine of Reason, the Seat of the Soul: A Philosophical Journey into the Brain.* Cambridge, MA: MIT Press.

Clark, A. 1996. "Connectionism, Moral Cognition, and Collaborative Problem Solving." In *Mind and Morals: Essays on Ethics and Cognitive Science,* edited by L. May, M. Friedman, and A. Clark. Cambridge, MA: MIT Press.

Demetras, M., K. Post, and C. Snow. 1986. "Feedback to First Language Learners: The Role of Repetitions and Clarification Questions." *Journal of Child Language* 13: 275–92.

Dwyer, S. 1997. "Learning from Experience: Moral Phenomenology and Politics." In *Daring To Be Good: Essays in Feminist Ethico-Politics,* edited by Bat-Ami Bar On and Ann Ferguson. London and New York: Routledge.

Dunn, J. 1988. *The Beginnings of Social Understanding.* Oxford: Blackwell.

Fodor, J. A. 1980. "On the Possibility of Acquiring more Powerful Structures." In *Language and Learning: The Debate between Jean Piaget and Noam Chomsky,* edited by M. Piatelli-Palmirini. Cambridge, MA: Harvard University Press.

———. 1983. *The Modularity of Mind.* Cambridge, MA: MIT Press.

Gordon, R. M. 1996. "Sympathy, Simulation, and the Impartial Spectator." In *Mind and Morals: Essays on Cognitive Science and Ethics,* edited by L. May, M. Freidman, and A. Clark. Cambridge, MA: MIT Press.

Grusec, J. and J. Goodnow. 1994. "Impact of Parental Discipline Methods on the Child's Internalization of Values: A Reconceptualization of Current Points of View." *Developmental Psychology* 30: 4–19.

Haidt, J., S. H. Koller and M. G. Dias. 1993. "Affect, Culture, and Morality, or Is It Wrong to Eat Your Dog?" *Journal of Personality and Social Psychology* 65: 613–628.

Hay, D. F. 1994. "Prosocial Development." *Journal of Child Psychology and Psychiatry* 35: 29–71.

Hoffman, M. 1983. "Affective and Cognitive Processes in Moral Internalization." In *Social Cognition and Social Development: A Sociocultural Perspective,* edited by T. Higgins, D. N. Roble, and W. W. Hartrup. Cambridge: Cambridge University Press.

Hornstein, N. and D. Lightfoot, editors. 1981. *Explanation in Linguistics: The Logical Problem of Language Acquisition.* London: Longmans.

Hursthouse, R. 1991. "Virtue Theory and Abortion." *Philosophy and Public Affairs* 20: 223–246.

Kohlberg, L. 1981. *The Philosophy of Moral Development.* San Francisco: Harper & Row.

Lightfoot, D. 1991. *How to Set Parameters: Arguments from Language Change.* Cambridge, MA: MIT Press.

MacNeill, D. 1966. " Developmental Psycholinguistics." In *The Genesis of Language: A Psycholinguistic Approach,* edited by F. Smith and G. A. Miller. Cambridge, MA: MIT Press.

McDowell, J. 1978. "Are Moral Requirements Hypothetical Imperatives?" *Proceedings of the Aristotelian Society* 52, *Supplement:* 13–29.

———. 1979. "Virtue and Reason." *The Monist* 62: 331–50.

Much, N. and R. Shweder. 1978. "Speaking of Rules: The Analysis of Culture in Breach." In *New Directions for Child Development, volume 2: Moral Development,* edited by W. Damon. San Francisco: Jossey-Bass.

Nucci, L. 1981. "The Development of Personal Concepts: A Domain Distinct from Moral or Societal Concepts." *Child Development* 52: 114–121.

Nucci, L. and E. Turiel. 1978. "Social Interactions and the Development of Social Concepts in Preschool Children." *Child Development* 49: 400–407.

Piaget, J. 1932. *The Moral Judgment of the Child.* London: Routledge & Kegan Paul.

Pietroski, P. M. 1993. "*Prima Facie* Obligations and *Ceteris Paribus* Laws in Moral Theory." *Ethics* 103: 489–515.

Rawls, J. 1971. *A Theory of Justice.* Cambridge, MA: Harvard University Press.

Ross, W. D. 1930. *The Right and the Good.* New York: Oxford University Press.

Schick, F. 1991. *Understanding Action: An Essay on Reasons.* Cambridge: Cambridge University Press.

Sherman, N. 1990. "The Place of Emotions in Kantian Morality." In *Identity, Character, and Morality,* edited by O. Flanagan and A. Oksenberg Rorty. Cambridge, MA: MIT Press.

Shweder, R. and J. Haidt. 1993. "The Future of Moral Psychology: Truth, Intuition, and the Pluralist Way." *Psychological Science* 4: 360–365.

Shweder, R., M. Mahapatra, and J. Miller. 1987. "Culture and Moral Development." In *The Emergence of Morality in Young Children,* edited by J. Kagan and S. Lamb. Chicago: University of Chicago Press.

Shweder, R. and N. Much. 1991. "Determinations of Meaning: Discourse and Moral Socialization." In *Thinking Through Cultures: Expeditions in Cultural Psychology,* edited by R. Shweder. Cambridge, MA: Harvard University Press.

Shweder, R. and M. A. Sullivan. 1993. "Cultural Psychology: Who Needs It?" *Annual Review of Psychology* 44: 497–523.

Smetana, J. 1981. "Preschool Children's Conceptions of Moral and Social Rules." *Child Development* 3: 211–226.

Smith, M. 1994. *The Moral Problem.* Oxford: Blackwell.

Song, M., J. Smetana, and C. Y. Kim. 1987. "Korean Children's Conceptions of Moral and Conventional Transgressions." *Developmental Psychology* 23: 577–582.

Strayer, J. 1987. "Affective and Cognitive Perspectives on Empathy." In *Empathy and Its Development,* edited by N. Eisenberg and J. Strayer. Cambridge: Cambridge University Press.

Thompson, R. A. 1987. "Empathy and Emotional Understanding: The Early Development of Empathy." In *Empathy and Its Development,* edited by N. Eisenberg and J. Strayer. Cambridge: Cambridge University Press.

Triandis, H. C. 1989. "The Self and Social Behavior in Differing Cultural Contexts." *Psychological Review* 96: 508–520.

———. 1991. "Cross-cultural Studies of Individualism and Collectivism." In *Nebraska Symposium on Motivation, Vol. 37: Cross-cultural perspectives,* edited by J. J. Berman. Lincoln: University of Nebraska Press.

Turiel, E. 1983. *The Development of Social Knowledge: Morality and Convention.* Cambridge: Cambridge University Press.

Turiel, E., M. Killen, and C. C. Helwig. 1987. "Morality: Its Structure, Function, and Vagaries." In *The Emergence of Morality in Young Children,* edited by J. Kagan and S. Lamb. Chicago: University of Chicago Press.

Wainryb, C. and E. Turiel. 1995. "Diversity in Social Development: Between or Within Cultures?" In *Morality in Everyday Life: Developmental Perspectives,* edited by M. Killen and D. Hart. Cambridge: Cambridge University Press.

Wallace, R. J. 1991. "Virtue, Reason, and Principle." *Canadian Journal of Philosophy* 21: 469–495.

Wilson, J. Q. 1993. *The Moral Sense.* New York: The Free Press.

Wren, T. 1991. *Caring About Morality.* Cambridge, MA: MIT Press.

6

Simplicity and Generative Linguistics[1]

Peter Ludlow

Since the beginning of generative linguistics, appeals to simplicity have played a central role in discussions of theory choice. But what *is* simplicity and why is it a good thing to have in a linguistic theory?

In asking this question, I am not so much concerned with technical uses of the term 'simplicity' within particular linguistic theories. While there have been a number of formal definitions of simplicity within specific linguistic theories (see, for example, Chomsky 1975, Chomsky and Halle 1968), for the most part these efforts have not been (and were not intended to be) utilized in theory choice across linguistic frameworks. My interest in this paper is not with such technical uses of the term 'simplicity', but rather with appeals to simplicity that are designed to argue for one theory over another—with simplicity as a criterion for theory choice.

Much writing in linguistic theory appears to be driven by a certain common wisdom which has it that the simplest theory is either the most aesthetically elegant or has the fewest components, or that it is the theory which eschews extra conceptual resources. This common wisdom is reflected in a 1972 paper by Paul Postal entitled "The Best Theory," which appeals to simplicity criteria for support of a particular linguistic proposal. A lot of linguists would wholeheartedly endorse Postal's remark that, "[w]ith everything held constant, one must always pick as the preferable theory that proposal which is most restricted conceptually and most constrained in the theoretical machinery it offers" (137–138).

This claim may seem pretty intuitive, but in this paper I want to argue that it stands in need of clarification, and that once clarified, the claim is much less intuitive, if not obviously false. As an alternative, I will propose that genuine simplicity criteria should not involve appeal to theoretical machinery, but rather a notion of simplicity in the sense of "simplicity of use." That is, I'll try to show that simplicity is not a genuine property of the object of investigation (whether construed as the human language faculty or something else), but is rather a property that is entirely relative to the investigator, and turns on the kinds of elements that the investigator finds perspicuous and "user friendly."

Let's begin by considering Postal's thesis that the simplest (and, other things being equal, the best) theory is the one that utilizes less theoretical machinery. It may seem natural to talk about "theoretical machinery," but what exactly *is* theoretical machinery? Consider the following questions which arise in cross-theoretical evaluation of linguistic theories. Is a level of linguistic representation part of the machinery? How about a transformation? A constraint on movement? A principle of binding theory? A feature? How about an algorithm that maps from level to level, or which allows us to dispense with levels of representation altogether? These questions are not trivial, nor are they easy to answer. Worse, there may be no theory-neutral way of answering them.

The problem is that 'machinery' can be defined any way we choose. The machinery might include levels of representation, but then again it might not (one might hold that the machinery delivers the level of representation, but that the level of representation itself is not part of the machinery). Alternatively, one might argue that levels of representation *are* part of the machinery (as they are concrete data structures of some sort), but that the mapping algorithms which generate the levels of representation are not (as they never have concrete realization). Likewise one might argue that constraints on movement are part of the machinery (since they constrain other portions of the machinery), or one might argue that they are not (since they never have concrete realization).

Even if we could agree on what counts as part of the machinery, we immediately encounter the question of how one measures whether one element or another represents *more* machinery. Within a particular well-defined theory it makes perfect sense to offer objective criteria for measuring the simplicity of the theoretical machinery,[2] but measurement across theories is quite another matter.

For example, if we concede that both mapping algorithms and levels of representation are candidates for being theoretical machinery, is there some reason to suppose that a level of representation counts as more machinery than a mapping algorithm which allows us to avoid that level of representation? If so by what measurement?

To illustrate the problem, following Williams (1986) and other authors,[3] one might argue that scope relations among operators can be accounted for via scope indexing rather than moving the operators to form LF representations which encode those relations. That is, rather than represent the scope possibilities of (1) via the two LF representations in (2) and (3),

(1) Every man loves some woman.

(2)

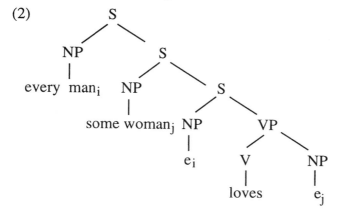

(3)

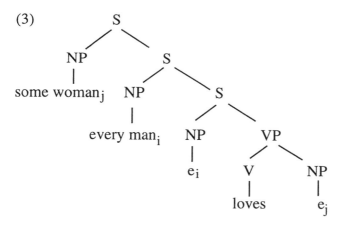

one might argue that the scope relations can be captured by a scope indexing method where the scope possibilities represented in (2) and (3)
might better be captured as in (2') and (3'), where the ordering of the indexes to S indicates the relative scopes of the quantified noun phrases.[4]

(2')

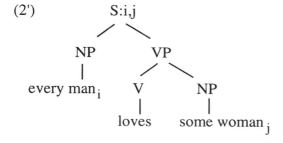

(3')

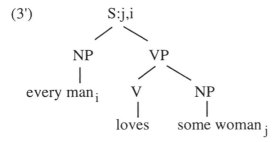

None of the authors cited here have advocated indexing proposals on grounds of simplicity, but one does hear arguments in the oral tradition which reason in this fashion. Perhaps there is some empirical way to distinguish these proposals (I have my doubts), and perhaps there is a sense in which the second proposal is semantically incoherent (I have my suspicions), but is there any clear sense in which the indexing proposal utilizes "less machinery" than the quantifier raising strategy? One can imagine arguments here. One might say that with the scope indexing strategy we can dispense with an entire level of representation. Or, one might argue that by dispensing with movement, we are making do with less onerous mechanisms. Or, one might argue that the second proposal allows us to carry on with "simpler" structures—ones without Chomsky-adjoined NPs. All such arguments are baseless.

While perhaps less ink is spilt by typesetters in putting (2') and (3') on paper, there is no basis for saying that the theory behind those structures is less complex than the theory which gave us (2) and (3). Arguably, we still need some "mechanism" which will tell us how to interpret an indexed structure, and arguably that mechanism shall have to flout certain constraints (such as strict compositionality) which allow a compositional semantics to deal easily with structures like (2) and (3)[5]—not a fatal result, but one which arguably forces us to introduce new "machinery" into the semantics.

Even if one is allergic to talk about "semantics," there is little justification for suggesting that one of these theories utilizes less machinery than the other. In each case there is a rich background theory which tells us how we are to interpret either the LF representations or the scope index representations, and that interpretive background theory (whether we want to think of it as semantical or not) is going to have a certain kind of complexity of its own—perhaps one which would swamp any considerations about the relative complexity of representations like (2) and (2').

This is not to concede that (setting aside the interpretive background theory) (2') is a simpler representation than (2). Even this claim can be challenged. Indeed, the two representations carry the same information, and appear to be notational variants of each other. Differences in notation can be significant, but it would take a very careful and intricate argument to show that given two apparent notational variants, one is simpler than another, or that one involved more machinery than the other.

Just to be perfectly clear, I am not saying that a move to scope indexing forces us to introduce extra theoretical machinery. I'm saying that there is no answer to the question of which has the most machinery, since across theories there is no neutral way of defining theoretical machinery, or measuring its relative complexity.[6]

The scope indexing case provided a concrete illustration of how difficult it is to make claims about machinery, but if we turn to a domain like mathematics we can make the same point at a more abstract level. Consider geometry. We might suppose that here at least, where everyone is restricted to the vocabulary of geometry, it should be easy enough to determine which of two theories is the simplest.

Prima facie, we might suppose that the simpler geometrical theory is the theory with the fewest axioms, but caution is necessary here. As Hempel (1966: 42) notes, there is no unambiguous way of counting axioms or basic concepts. For example, consider the statement that "for any two points there is a straight line containing them." Is this one axiom? As Hempel notes, one might think of it as a conjunction of two: that there is at least one such line, and that there is at most one such line. Similar considerations carry over to talk of basic concepts. In the absence of some neutral way of characterizing what is truly basic, there is no way to count the number of basic concepts in play.

Even if we could agree on what counts as a basic axiom or basic concept, we may find that the axiom system with fewer axioms is far from the simplest theory. For example, the system with the fewest axioms may lead to difficulty in theorem proving in the early stages, so the complexity of the computational task of theorem proving needs to be factored in as well if we are really interested in an overall measure of simplicity.

But we can't stop there. Even assuming that difficulty in theorem proving is not an issue, is a system with fewer axioms always the simplest? Not according to many measures of simplicity in the philosophy of science literature. Sober (1975), for example, has argued that everything depends on the "naturalness" of the axioms (basic elements of the theory). If we trade in five natural axioms for four unintuitive axioms then according to Sober we have achieved no great gain in simplicity. So, by some accounts, even if we have a definition of machinery and a way of quantifying the amount of machinery, we do not have a simpler theory simply by having fewer theoretical elements.

However, one might argue that there is still a clear case in which we can say that one theory has more machinery than another—the case where theory A logically entails theory B, and where theory B has additional components. In that case, one might think Postal is clearly right in making the following claim:

> Given two distinct theories of the same domain, one may make a clear choice between them if certain logical relations hold between these theories. In particular, if the theoretical machinery of one theory is included in that of the second, but the second has, in addition, certain additional theoretical machinery, then, all other things being equal, the first, most conceptually restricted is to be chosen. That is, the conceptual elaboration of the second theory can only be justified on the basis of direct empirical arguments showing the need for this extension. In general, this support will take the form of evidence showing that certain facts in the domain cannot be explained using only the original apparatus provided by the first theory, but that the facts in question do receive a formulation in terms of the additional theoretical apparatus provided by the second. (1972: 137)

But even this claim is false. It is easy to imagine cases which would serve as counterexamples. For example, suppose (counterfactually) that after much labor it had been possible to prove that Euclid's fifth postulate could be derived from the first four. Would it follow that we should choose the four axiom system over Euclid's? That depends in great measure on our interests in using geometry, but clearly for low level theorem-proving we may find our lives as theorists much simpler if we simply assume the fifth postulate as an axiom, rather than go through the arduous task of proving it before we carry out other basic operations.

Postal's conceptual argument thus founders. The particular linguistic case that Postal has in mind fares no better. Postal argued that a particular general approach to linguistic theory (Generative Semantics) was simpler because it eliminates a class of nontransformational mapping rules. The contrast is thus between an organization of the grammar as in (4), similar to Standard Theory proposals like that of Katz and Fodor (1963), and (5), which is consistent with Generative Semantic theories as advocated in Postal (1972).

(4)

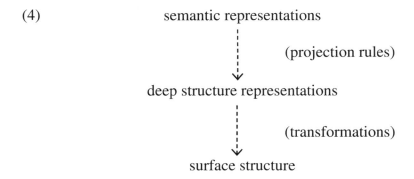

(5)   semantic representations

(transformations)

surface structure

According to Postal's reasoning, the theory which has fewer kinds of rules (in this case the theory diagrammed in (5), which has transformations only) is more "homogeneous" and hence is to be preferred unless there are *strong* empirical considerations favoring the Standard Theory alternative. In Postal's words:

> What I wish to suggest briefly is that because of its *a priori* logical and conceptual properties, this theory of grammar . . . is the basic one which generative linguists should operate from as an investigatory framework, and it should be abandoned, if at all, only under the strongest pressures of empirical disconfirmation. (1972: 135)

Here Postal deserves high marks for being honest enough to put this reasoning in print, when many other linguists simply whisper the same sorts of claims to their graduate students. Unfortunately, honesty is not enough; the reasoning is as wrong as it can be. Overlooked by Postal is the complexity of the additional transformations needed in (5), the utility of intermediate deep structure representations to theorists, and the methodological virtues of constraining the class of transformations. Is there some theory-neutral way to measure the relative complexity of the two approaches? As we have seen, the prospects are dim to nonexistent.

On the other hand, I have hinted at the importance of representations and rules that are perspicuous to the theorist, suggesting that simplicity may have more to do with properties of the theorist than properties of the natural world. To some, this may be a counterintuitive way of thinking about simplicity, but I would suggest that it is in fact the most reasonable way to think about simplicity and is in fact the notion of simplicity which is at play in the more established sciences.

The view certainly has a long pedigree in the philosophy of science, dating at least to Peirce (1931–1958), who held that we should "follow the rule that that one of all admissible hypotheses which seems simplest to the human mind ought to be taken up first" (vol. 6: 532). Peirce's idea here was that by first taking up hypotheses that are "simplest to the human mind," we achieve a kind of economy in the labor that we expend on our investigations. In Peirce's words "the simplest hypotheses are those of which the consequences are most readily deduced and compared with observation; so that, if they are wrong, they can be eliminated at less expense than any others" (532).

Moreover, Peirce was convinced that it was this notion of simplicity (and not the logical notion of extra machinery) which Galileo had in mind when he advised us to always choose the simpler hypothesis.

> That truly inspired prophet had said that, of two hypotheses, the *simpler* is to be preferred, but I was formerly one of those, who, in our dull self-conceit fancying ourselves more sly than he, twisted this maxim to mean the *logically* simpler, the one that adds least to what has been observed. . . . It was not until long experience forced me to realize that subsequent discoveries were every time showing I had been wrong, while those who had understood the maxim as Galileo had done early unlocked the secret, that the scales fell from my eyes and my mind awoke to the broad and flaming daylight that it is the simpler hypothesis in the sense of the more facile and *natural,* the one that instinct suggests, that must be preferred. . . . I do not mean that logical simplicity is of no value at all, but only that its value is badly secondary to that of simplicity in the other sense. (1931–1958, vol 6: 477)

Moving into this century, basically the same position is advanced by Ernst Mach, who argued that the notion of simplicity employed by Copernicus, Galileo, Adam Smith, and others involved a notion of simplicity as "mental economy"; the simplest theory is that which is the easiest for us to use:

> We must admit, therefore, that there is no result of science which in point of principle could not have been arrived at wholly without methods. But, as a matter of fact, within the short span of a human life and with man's limited powers of memory, any stock of knowledge worthy of the name is unattainable except by the *greatest* mental economy. Science itself, therefore, may be regarded as a minimal problem, consisting of the completest possible presentment of facts with the least possible expenditure of thought. (1960: 586)

Indeed, when we look at other sciences, in nearly every case, the best theory is arguably not the one that reduces the number of components from four to three, but rather the theory that allows for the simplest calculations and greatest ease of use. This flies in the face of the standard stories we are told about the history of science. For example, it is usually supposed that when we talk about the superiority of the Copernican model of the solar system over the Ptolemaic system it is because of the relative simplicity of the Copernican model, and it is further supposed that this is because of a deep assumption that simpler models are closer to the truth.[7] The fact of the matter is that by the time the Copernican model was fully fleshed out, it had enough technical resources (from minor epicycles to eccentrics) so that it may well have matched the Ptolemaic theory on the amount of technical machinery. One might suppose that the Copernican theory was nevertheless still the more aesthetically elegant of the theories, and that this might amount to a kind of simplicity. Indeed, Copernicus himself seems to have thought this. The only problem is that there is no accounting for aesthetic preference (particularly if religion plays a role in our aesthetic theories), and some of the chief arguments against Copernicus included arguments that could only be characterized as aesthetic in character. What appears to have saved the Copernican theory was not its aesthetic qualities, but rather the fact that it helped to simplify astronomical calculations. Notoriously, when *De Revolutionibus* was published in Leibzig, Osiander inserted a preface which characterized the theory as merely a convenient tool for calculating, and not to be taken seriously as a cosmological theory. Obviously, this move was designed to deflect religious criticism, but the fact remains that the overarching value of the theory to astronomers of the day was not its elegant cosmology, but its utility as a tool in carrying out what had previously been impossibly complex astronomical calculations.

This way of viewing simplicity requires a shift in our thinking—nothing so dramatic as a Copernican revolution, but a fairly radical one nonetheless. It requires that we see simplicity criteria as having not so much to do with the natural properties of the world, as they have to do with the limits of us as investigators, and with the kinds of theories that simplify the arduous task of scientific theorizing for us. This is not to say that we cannot be scientific realists; we may very well suppose that our scientific theories approximate the actual structure of reality.[8] It is to say, however, that barring some argument that "reality" is simple, or eschews machinery, etc., we cannot suppose that there is a genuine notion of simplicity apart from the notion of "simple for us to use."

In a certain sense, such a view is entirely natural. While we always seek the simplest theory, it is rare that we suppose that our theory closes the book on a particular domain of inquiry. To the contrary, we naturally suppose that complications will arise, and that the current theory shall have to be overthrown. Even if, for metaphysical reasons, we suppose that reality must be fundamentally simple, every science (with the possible exception of physics) is so far from closing the book on its domain that it would be silly to think that simplicity (in the absolute sense) must govern our theories on their way to completion. Whitehead underlined just such a point.

> Nature appears as a complex system whose factors are dimly discerned by us. But, as I ask you, Is not this the very truth? Should we not distrust the jaunty

assurance with which every age prides itself that it at last has hit upon the ultimate concepts in which all that happens can be formulated. The aim of science is to seek the simplest explanations of complex facts. We are apt to fall into the error of thinking that the facts are simple because simplicity is the goal of our quest. The guiding motto in the life of every natural philosopher should be, Seek simplicity and distrust it. (1955:163)

Let's suppose, however, that I am mistaken about most of the preceding discussion as it applies to the physical sciences. Let's suppose, that is, that there is a clear and serviceable notion of simplicity in some absolute sense (one independent of us as theorists). Does it follow that this notion of simplicity carries over to the other sciences (in particular linguistics)? Probably not.

Russell noted that little follows from the fact that in some sciences, "simple laws have hitherto been found to hold" (1917: 204). Not only are there no *a priori* grounds for supposing that the domains of other sciences are simple, but, he goes on, there are also no inductive grounds:

> . . . it would be fallacious to argue inductively from the state of the advanced sciences to the future state of the others, for it may well be that the advanced sciences are simple because, hitherto, their subject-matter has obeyed simple and easily ascertainable laws, while the subject-matter of other sciences has not done so. (205)

Indeed, as Chomsky and Lasnik (1993) have observed, simplicity as a rule does not seem to hold for biological systems, which "typically are 'messy,' intricate, the result of evolutionary 'tinkering,' and shaped by accidental circumstances and by physical conditions that hold of complex systems with varied functions and elements" (reprinted in Chomsky 1995: 29). One expects, therefore, that language, being a biological system, should be anything but simple. To Chomsky and Lasnik, therefore, while the Principles and Parameters framework[9] has advanced under a working hypothesis that Universal Grammar is simple, the fact that this hypothesis has been successful is "surprising."

This is a fairly sensible view to take in my view. If one has some general external view of simplicity (in the absolute sense),[10] and one finds that a linguistic theory obeys constraints of simplicity, this should not be trumpeted as evidence *for* the theory. Rather it is a surprising fact which in itself begs for some kind of explanation.

What we expect of a linguistic theory is that it be perspicuous enough for us to know what is predicted, and that its notation be easy for us to use.

In this sense, the simplicity criterion is not really an absolute criterion, but one that is relative to the investigators. For example, is it easier for linguists to posit a level of representation LF, or is it easier to utilize a device like Cooper's (1983) quantifier storage mechanism (where the set-theoretic resources of the model theory can do the work of quantifier raising)?[11] Neither is simpler absolutely, but there is an issue about which is easier for investigators to use, and which leads to further linguistic discoveries. For example, the question of relative simplicity of these theories might turn on the relative perspicuity of these theories when applied to the phenomenon of "inverse linking" described in May (1977), and accounted for within a quantifier storage framework by Larson (1985). The answer is not really one to be given by pronouncement, but one that emerges as the field as a whole, over time, gravitates to one framework or the other. Indeed, it may be that different subfields of linguistics, with different interests and training, may see the simplicity of these proposals quite differently.

We can summarize the above considerations in the following way.

I. Simplicity is in the eye of the theorist

By this I don't mean that simplicity is determined by individual theorists, but rather that it is determined by a community of theorists with a shared set of interests and a shared technical background. To such a community, given two proposals with roughly the same empirical coverage the simplest theory is that theory which they find the easiest to use for constructing and evaluating hypotheses.

Some provisos are necessary here. The point is not that the simpler theory will be recognized as such *immediately*. One has to allow time for the new theory to be understood. But the learning curve of the new theory should not be so steep as to swamp any advantages it might have once learned. Lindsay saw this point in the course of his discussion of the Machian "economy" notion of simplicity:

> If, for example, a person familiar with classical mechanics can become equally well acquainted with another physical theory in a time of the same order of magnitude as that which he took to learn mechanics, he should consider this new theory as simple as mechanics, no matter how complicated it may seem at first examination to one unfamiliar with it. Human life is short and time is fleeting. In endeavoring to understand the world around us we must make the most of the brief span allotted. We must therefore build our theories in such a way that, with given intellectual background, the manipulation of these theories leads in minimum time to success in physical prediction. (1937:166)

II. Simplicity may vary from research
community to research community

It may be that this sort of variation is temporary. Theorists utilizing different technical methods do communicate with one another after all, and after time research methods merge, or at least become more readily understood. But familiarity is not the only issue here. Different theorists have different interests and different philosophical assumptions resting at the base of their empirical theories.[12] Until those interests and philosophical differences are resolved, their views of simplicity may well fail to merge.

III. Simplicity will vary over time.

The quote from Lindsay suggested that some things may seem complex to us at first, and simple after a short while. This can happen for the field as a whole. So, theories that may seem complex at the outset may turn out to be viewed as utterly simple as the field progresses. As Lindsay notes, "we shall ultimately consider [theories] simple when we have grown sufficiently familiar with them to forget that they ever seemed difficult to understand" (1937: 167).

This is not just a point about technical machinery, however. It is also an important point about how certain basic concepts are viewed. The Kepplerian theory of planetary motion, for example, was considered aesthetically inferior by some commentators, who could not make the conceptual leap from the idea of circular orbits to that of less perfect ellipses. Sometimes it just takes time to "wrap your mind" around an unfamiliar concept or piece of machinery. On the other hand, sometimes it takes forever.

IV. Barring bad advice, theorists
will gravitate towards simplicity

This point is really the moral of the paper. I have argued that the simplest theory is that which allows us to simplify our calculations and theorizing (given our current interests). Assuming that theorists are sensible, simplicity will take care of itself, as investigators will naturally gravitate to the notation and theoretical resources that are the easiest to use and which therefore more naturally serve as discovery vehicles. Troubles only arise when, under the spell of bad philosophy of science, linguists suppose that they must adopt best theory criteria other than those which naturally guide their investigations.

Notes

1. Earlier versions of this paper were presented at the 3rd Central European Summer School in Generative Linguistics, Olomouc, the Czech Republic. I am grateful to course participants as well as to Jan-Wouter Zwart for helpful discussion.

2. Consider for example the simplicity measurement found in Chomsky and Halle (1968), which measures simplicity on the basis of the number of symbols contained in a phonological rule.

3. For example Reinhart (1983) and Häik (1984).

4. I don't mean to suggest that this mechanism is explicitly endorsed by Williams. In point of fact, he remains neutral between such a proposal and one in which the scope orders corresponding to such a representation are "arbitrary": "Is the order of quantifiers in such a case ordered or free? If determined, we will want to attach significance to the order of i and j in S:i,j; if not, we won't" (1986: 267).

5. The point here is that a compositional semantics presented with structures like (2) and (3) need look only at the immediate daughters of a node A in order to determine the semantic value of A. Interpreting structures like (2') and (3') present certain difficulties which would force us to abandon strict compositionality.

6. The many perplexities involved in trying to define a formal notion of simplicity are catalogued in, among other places, Goodman (1972: section VII), Barker (1961), and Rosenkrantz (1977: ch. 5). Perhaps Kyburg sums up the state of affairs best when he says:

> The whole discussion of simplicity has been curiously inconclusive. Not only has there been no growing body of agreement concerning the measurement of simplicity, but there has been no agreement concerning . . . the precise role that simplicity should play in the acceptance of scientific hypotheses. (1964: 267—268)

7. In point of fact, however, the Copernican model probably triumphed because it was able to account for certain facts (known in Copernicus' time) which the Ptolemaic system could not handle. See Rogers (1960: chs. 14, 16) for discussion of this point.

8. Of course this view is *consistent* with scientific antirealism like that articulated in van Fraassen (1980). The point is that we are not forced to antirealism. One way of knitting together a subjective notion of simplicity with a realist theory of the world has been offered up by Quine and Ullian, who propose that there are evolutionary reasons for our having the subjective preferences that we do:

> Innate subjective standards of simplicity that make people prefer some hypotheses to others will have survival value insofar as they favor successful prediction. Those who predict best are likeliest to survive and reproduce their kind . . . and so their innate standards of simplicity are handed down.(1970: 47)

I have to confess that I find this a pretty implausible thesis. As Nozick (1980) has observed, while our simplicity judgements concerning hypotheses about midsize earth-bound objects may have stood the test of time, the same can not be said for our simplicity judgements concerning theories of quantum mechanics and cosmology.

9. See Chomsky (1981), Chomsky and Lasnik (1993).

10. Chomsky (1995) appears to allow for the possibility of such a notion of simplicity, characterizing it as an "imprecise but not vacuous notion of simplicity that enters into rational inquiry generally" (p. 8). Again, this is not to be confused with the technical, theory internal, notion of simplicity found in Chomsky (1975) and elsewhere.

11. I should note that Cooper (1983) does not offer simplicity considerations on behalf of his theory—rather he appeals to processing considerations. There are, however, arguments in the oral tradition parallel to those raised in Postal (1972)—specifically arguments that a theory utilizing quantifier storage mechanisms is "simpler" because it avoids overt quantifier movement and the level of representation LF.

12. A not so distant point was stressed by Quine (1976), who argued that simplicity would vary with our conceptual schemes.

References

Barker, S. 1961. "On Simplicity in Empirical Hypotheses." *Philosophy of Science* 28: 162–171.

Chomsky, N. 1975. *The Logical Structure of Linguistic Theory.* New York: Plenum Press.

———. 1981. *Lectures on Government and Binding.* Dordrecht: Foris.

———. 1995. *The Minimalist Program.* Cambridge: MIT Press.

Chomsky, N. and M. Halle. 1968. *The Sound Pattern of English.* New York: Harper and Rowe.

Chomsky, N. and H. Lasnik. 1993. "The Theory of Principles and Parameters." In *Syntax: An International Handbook of Contemporary Research,* edited by J. Jacobs, A. von Stechow, W. Sternefeld, and T. Vennemann. Berlin: Walter de Gruyter. Reprinted as chapter 1 of Chomsky (1995).

Cooper, R. 1983. *Quantification and Syntactic Theory.* Dordrecht: D. Reidel.

Häik, I. 1984. "Indirect Binding." *Linguistic Inquiry* 15: 185–224.

Halle, M. 1961. "On the Role of Simplicity in Linguistic Description." *Proceedings of Symposia in Applied Mathematics* 12 *(Structure of Language and its Mathematical Aspects:* 89–94.

Hempel, C. 1966. *Philosophy of Natural Science.* Englewood Cliffs: Prentice Hall.

Goodman, N. 1972. *Problems and Projects.* Indianapolis: Bobbs-Merrill.

Katz, J. and J. A. Fodor. 1963. "The Structure of a Semantic Theory." *Language* 39: 170–210.

Kyburg, H. 1964. "Recent Work in Inductive Logic." *American Philosophical Quarterly* 1: 249–287.

Larson, R. K. 1985. "Quantifying Into NP." Unpublished manuscript, MIT Linguistics.

Lindsay, R. B. 1937. "The Meaning of Simplicity in Physics." *Philosophy of Science* 4: 151–167.

Mach, E. 1960. *The Science of Mechanics,* 6th edition. Chicago: Open Court.

May, R. 1977. *The Grammar of Quantification.* Unpublished PhD thesis, MIT Linguistics.

Nozick, R. 1983. "Simplicity as Fall-Out." In *How Many Questions: Essays in Honor of Sydney Morgenbesser,* edited by L. Cauman, I. Levi, and C. Parsons. Indianapolis: Hackett Publishing: 105–119.

Peirce, C. S. 1931–1958. *Collected Papers of Charles Sanders Peirce,* 8 vols. Edited by C. Hartshorne, P. Weiss, and A. Burks. Cambridge: Harvard University Press.

Postal, P. 1972. "The Best Theory." In *Goals of Linguistic Theory,* edited by S. Peters. Englewood Cliffs: Prentice-Hall: 131–179.

Quine, W. V. O. 1976. "On Simple Theories of a Complex World." In *The Ways of Paradox and Other Essays.* Cambridge: Harvard University Press: 155–258.

Quine, W. V. O. and J. Ullian. 1970. *The Web of Belief.* New York: Random House.

Reinhart, T. 1983. *Anaphora and Semantic Interpretation.* London: Croom Helm.

Rogers, E. 1960. *Physics for the Inquiring Mind.* Princeton: Princeton University Press.

Rosenkrantz, R. 1977. *Inference, Method and Decision: Towards a Bayesian Philosophy of Science.* Dordrecht: D. Reidel.

Russell, B. 1917. "On the Notion of Cause." In *Mysticism and Logic.* London: George Allen & Unwin.

Sober, E. 1975. *Simplicity.* Oxford: Oxford University Press.

van Fraassen, B. 1980. *The Scientific Image.* Oxford: Oxford University Press.

Whitehead, W. N. 1955. *The Concept of Nature.* Cambridge: Cambridge University Press.

Williams, E. 1986. "A Reassignment of the Function of LF." *Linguistic Inquiry* 17: 265–299.

PART FOUR

A Case Study in Philosophy and Linguistics: Mixed Quotation

7

Semantics for Quotation[1]

Herman Cappelen & Ernie Lepore

Our quotation practices are richly diverse. We can *directly* quote another, as in (1); *indirectly* him, as in (2); or we can *purely* quote an expression in order to talk about it, as in (3).

(1) Clinton said, 'I'll cut taxes'.
(2) Clinton said that he'd cut taxes.
(3) 'lobster' is a word.

These are all philosophically familiar. There is another sort of quotation, however, which, though rarely discussed in the philosophical literature, is probably the most utilized form of quotation in natural language. We will call this *mixed quotation,* as in (4).

(4) Clinton said that he'd 'cut taxes'.

The semantics of these four sorts of quotation cannot be entirely disunited. That utterances of (2) and (4) respectively agree in one sense about what was said all by itself indicates:

C1 Mixed and indirect quotation should receive overlapping semantic treatments.

Similarly, utterances of (1) and (4) partially agree in another sense about what was said, thus supporting:

C2 Direct and mixed quotation should receive overlapping semantic treatments.

However, utterances of (1) and (2) might not be in agreement about what was said in any sense, at least not unless we assume that (1) attributes (understanding of) an English utterance to Clinton. For all we know, (1) may be ascribing to him an utterance of some other language that merely happens to share certain lexical items with English; or Clinton may not know any English but merely have uttered 'I'll cut taxes' in an effort to clear his throat. All which leads us to conclude that:

C3 Direct and indirect quotation must receive distinct semantic treatments.

Finally, because (1) and (4) imply pure quotations (5) and (6) respectively,

(5) A token of 'I'll cut taxes' was uttered.
(6) A token of 'cut taxes' was uttered.

it is reasonable to conclude that:

C4 Quotation in pure, direct, and mixed quotation should receive overlapping semantic treatments.

Our chief aim here is to develop an account that satisfies constraints C1–C4. We will begin by raising doubts about whether leading semantic accounts for indirect and for pure (and direct) quotation do, or can easily be refined so as to, accommodate mixed cases.

Semantics for Indirect Quotation

(A) is a standard assumption among semanticists of attitudinal reports:

> **A** Any propositional attitude report is true only if the proposition (or proposition-like content) expressed by the report's complement clause matches the proposition (or proposition-like content) of the agent's attitude (or utterance).

(A) requires that (4) is true just in case Clinton uttered something matching the propositional content of its complement clause. Mixed cases, we believe, make it difficult for any theory incorporating (A) to be inadequate. So, for example, according to Soames, (4) is true iff Clinton uttered a sentence S in an associated context C such that for some S' that can be readily inferred from S, the content of S' in C = the content of 'I'll cut taxes' in the context of the report (Soames 1989: 411). Soames doesn't discuss mixed quotation. Should we try to extend his account, in the obvious way to mixed quotation, an utterance of (4) correctly reports Clinton's utterance *u,* say, of 'I'll cut taxes' just in case *'he'd 'cut taxes''* expresses the same proposition as (an utterance of) a sentence that can be readily inferred from 'I'll cut taxes'.

Even if (as we think unlikely) that 'I'll 'cut taxes'' expressed a proposition, how could it express anything readily inferable from 'I'll cut taxes'? (T1) and (T2) are obvious truths about (4) and *u.*

> **T1** Clinton was talking about taxes; he was not talking about words.
>
> **T2** (4)'s complement clause includes quotation marks and therefore, in some sense, says something about linguistic entities.

So, if (4) were an example of indirect quotation, we could indirectly quote another without using a complement clause matching the content of the reported utterance, contrary to what Soames's account tells us.

Here's another challenge mixed quotation presents for accounts of the semantics of indirect speech respecting (A). Suppose propositional attitude reports relate an agent to an Interpreted Logical Form (ILF).[2] An ILF is a logical form in the sense of Chomsky (1981) augmented by semantic values at each node in the phrase marker. So, an ILF effectively incorporates information about the proposition expressed by an utterance, the logical structure of that proposition, and the lexical means by which that proposition is expressed. Adapting an example from Larson and Segal (1995: 438–40), 'Peter said that Lori met Cary Grant' is true just in case Peter said

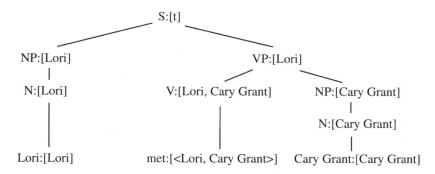

where semantic values appear in the square brackets to the right of each node.

Mixed, pure and direction quotation have not yet been discussed among ILF theorists. But were an ILF theorist to treat quotes as functioning in the same way and as having the same semantic value in whatever linguistic context in which they occur, a constraint, following Davidson, that Larson and Segal (1995: 436–7) and Larson and Ludlow (1993: 332) explicitly endorse, then, for mixed cases like (4), expressions quoted must be annotated as semantic values in the ILF of (4)'s complement clause (because the semantic value of a quotation is the quoted expression) and it must contain the quotation itself as a lexical element. This requires that there must be a node in which "cut" occurs as a lexical item and the semantic value of 'cut', whatever that may be, occurs as well. So, (4) would be claiming that Clinton stands in the saying-relation to such an ILF. However, Clinton does not bear this relation to any ILF as described above.

ILF theorists disagree among themselves about whether standing in the saying-relation to an ILF is to any extent pragmatically determined.[3] We ourselves support appeals to pragmatic considerations in an effort to characterize our practice of indirect quotation (and other propositional attitude attributional practices). But these appeals cannot solve the problem posed by mixed quotation. It is not a pragmatic issue whether a mixed report requires the reported speaker to stand in the saying-relation to an entity containing lexical elements as semantic values. Typically, a mixed quoted speaker said nothing about words and it is a straightforward semantic fact that he did not. Any theory that does not respect this fact, or tries to dodge it by deporting it to pragmatics, is inadequate.

So, to sum up, whatever its other merits, ILF theory establishes no advance over Soames's account with respect to mixed cases. Whatever content, if any, is expressed by the complement clause of a mixed case, it must be at least partially about words. But any person correctly reported by a mixed quote like (4) has not uttered anything about words. So, no theory requiring for the truth of an indirect quotation that the reported speaker stand in the saying-relation to the proposition expressed by the complement clause of the report can accommodate mixed cases.

One reaction to mixed cases would be, for example, applied to Soames's account, to give whatever contribution quotation marks make, so to speak, wide scope over 'says that'. This fits in well with the not implausible intuition that quotes in mixed quotation behave much like an after word, adding 'and, by the way, he used these words in saying it'. This intuition might lead one to modify theories satisfying (A) to treat cases like (4) along the lines of (7):

(7)   Clinton said that he'd cut taxes and he said it uttering, in part, the words 'cut taxes'.

First, what may be a minor point, (7) fails to account for the fact that mixed quotations contain a single component serving two functions concurrently; the quoted part is employed both to report what the speaker said and to say, at least partially, what he actually uttered. In (4), 'cut taxes' (together with other words) functions to report what Clinton said, namely, that he'd cut taxes, and it also functions to report that Clinton tokened 'cut taxes'. So, 'cut taxes' unambiguously serves two functions. In (7), no component serves these two functions; and so, it cannot explain how a single token can serve double duty.

Second, suppose Bob tells Ted 'Carol is an oenophile'. He can be correctly mixed quoted by (8):

(8) Bob said that Carol is an 'oenophile'.

Someone who utters (8) might be mixed quoting Bob's utterance of 'Carol is an oenophile' because he is uncertain about what 'oenophile' means. He might assume that Bob's vocabulary is larger than his own and mixed quotes him in order to indicate that 'oenophile' is an unknown word for him. Or he might be convinced that Bob is linguistically incompetent and wants to make this transparent to others without committing Bob's mistake himself. Either way, mixed quotation is used to report what another said when part of what was uttered is unintelligible or just plain odd to the reporter.

An account of mixed quotation along the lines of (7) does not adequately extend to (8), say, along the lines of (9):

*(9) Bob said that Carol is an oenophile and he said it using, in part, 'oenophile'.

In uttering the first conjunct of (9), normal English speakers fail to report anything at all. Since Ted can correctly report Bob with (8), the account adumbrated by (7) fails.

None of this proves that leading accounts of the semantics of indirect quotation cannot be extended to account for mixed quotation. But once C1-C4 are adopted as adequacy constraints on a unified semantic theory of quotation, these accounts face a so far unmet challenge.

Semantics of Pure Quotation

The two influential accounts of pure quotation are the proper-name account and the description account; both preempt C1-C4. According to the proper-name account (e.g., Quine 1961: 140 and Tarski 1956: 159), quotations are unstructured proper names of the quoted expressions and so there is no systematic correlation between what occurs inside quotes and the referent of the entire quotation. Applied to (4), the proper-name account issues in ungrammaticality. Since on this account quotations behave just like proper names, (4) semantically parallels (10):

*(10)   Clinton said that he'd Hillary.

According to the description account (e.g., Quine 1960: 202, Tarski 1956: 160, Geach 1957: 79, and Geach 1970), there is a set of basic units in the language, either the words (Geach) or the letters (Quine). At this basic level, we retain the proper-name account either by treating à la Quine the basic alphabetic units as names, e.g., 'a' is a name of one letter, 'b' a name of another, etc., or by treating à la Geach the morphemes as names 'red', 'un-', etc. Quotations with more than one basic unit are treated as descriptions of concatenations of whatever the basic units are. So, e.g., (4) (à la Quine) is construed as (11):

(*11)   Clinton said that he'd 'c' - 'u' - 't' - ' ' ' - 't' - 'a' - 'x' - 'e' - 's'

where '-' is the sign for concatenation. Since according to the description account when quotes surround basic units, the result is a name of the expression, (11) is analogous to saying that Clinton said that he'd Hillary-Chelsea-Al- etc. That's not anything like what Clinton said.

So, on the basis of this brief discussion of these two accounts we see that any account of quotation according to which the semantic function of word-tokens inside quotation marks is to refer to word-types (or some other type of linguistic entity) fails to assign the correct truth-conditions to (4).

In summary, our criticisms of accounts of indirect, direct, and pure quotation show that in order to account for mixed cases an account must do two things: it must account for how the complement clause of, e.g., (4) can be employed to effect simultaneously a report that Clinton uttered 'cut taxes' and one that Clinton said he'd cut taxes. We turn to proposals for how to execute these.

Davidson on Pure Quotation

Davidson's paper 'Quotation' is mostly about pure quotation. Davidson construes (3) as (12),

(12)   Lobster. The expression of which this is a token is a word.

where an utterance of the second sentence is accompanied by a demonstration of an utterance of the first. On his view, quotes are definite descriptions containing demonstratives. The demonstrative picks out the token within the quotation marks and the definite description denotes an expression, instantiated by the demonstrated token.

Extending Davidson's idea to direct quotation, (1) would be semantically construed as (13),

> (13) Clinton said (produced) a token of the expression instantiated by that. I'll cut taxes

where an utterance of the first sentence is accompanied by a demonstration of an utterance of the second.

Unifying Davidson's demonstrative account of pure and direct quotation incorporates four attractive features:

I. We can explain why learning to quote is learning a practice with *endless* application.

Understanding quotation is understanding 'the expression instantiated by that'. There is no mystery about how we acquire this capacity, nor about how to account for it in a finitely axiomatic semantic theory.

ii. We can do this while preserving *semantic innocence.*

A semantic account T for a language L is *semantically innocent* just in case what an expression of L means according to T does not vary systematically according to context [see, Davidson 1968:106; 1975:166]. Semantic innocence is preserved at two levels. First, the account does not assume words take on new semantic values when quoted. Secondly, it makes the device of quotation unambiguous; quotes in pure quotation are treated semantically in exactly the same way as quotes in direct quotation, thus, respecting C4.

Semantic innocence so construed, however, is compatible with there being contexts in which what an expression means is *not in active use*. So, even though 'Clinton' names Clinton, it is *semantically inert* in (14):

> (14) 'Clinton' has seven letters.

iii. We can explain why quotational contexts are *opaque.*

Sentences containing demonstratives need not preserve their truth value when different objects are demonstrated. If you substitute a word-token of one type for another of a different type as the demonstrated object, different objects are demonstrated and thus the truth-value of the original (utterance of that) sentence may change (see conclusion below).

iv. We can, thus, explain why *quantifying into* quotes in natural language produces absurd results.

'∃x('boxer' is a word)' cannot be inferred from "'boxer' is a word' nor can '∃x('x' is a word)'. The account explains why these inferences fail; since it makes no sense to quantify into a demonstrated object, it makes no sense to quantify into quotes on this account.[4]

Davidson's account can be modified so as to treat quotes as quantifying over tokens that stand in a certain relation, call it the *same-tokening* relation, to the demonstrated token. This suggests construing (3) as (15),

(15) ∀x((STx,that) → Wx). Lobster

where an utterance of the first sentence demonstrates the exhibited token of 'lobster', 'ST' means *same-tokens,* and 'W' means *is a word (token).* Whether two entities stand in a same-tokening relation to each other is not settled by the semantics.

This demonstrative account of pure quotation can be extended naturally to direct quotation. (1) should be construed as (16) (or, alternatively, as 17):

(16) ∃u(Says(c,u) & ∀y(ST(y,these) → ST(u,y))). I'll cut taxes.
(17) ∃u(Says(c,u) & ST(u,these)). I'll cut taxes.[5]

'Says' means *says.* So, Clinton said a token that same-tokens the demonstrated object.

Davidson on Indirect Quotation

In "On Saying That," Davidson paraphrases (2) as (18),

(18) He'd cut taxes. Clinton said that

where 'that' is accompanied by a demonstration of the first utterance and that second utterance is true just in case Clinton said something that same-says the demonstrated utterance. (18) is more perspicuously represented as (19),

(19) ∃u(Says(u,c) & SS(u,that)). He'd cut taxes

where an utterance of the first sentence demonstrates an utterance of the latter sentence, 'Says' still means says, and 'SS' means *samesays.*

We do not intend here to engage in an evaluation of Davidson's account of indirect quotation.[6] Our aim, instead, is to show how the accounts of direct and indirect quotation can be exploited and developed so as (at least) to satisfy C1–C4. Notice straight away that C3 is satisfied, i.e., indirect quotation is treated differently from direct quotation. The former invokes same-tokening; whereas the latter invokes samesaying.

Mixed Quotation

Earlier we argued that the available semantic accounts of pure (and direct) and indirect quotation do not integrate mixed quotation and therefore fail to satisfy C1–C4. The semantic theories of indirect speech canvassed earlier treat the complement clause as a semantic unit referring to (or in some other way determining) a proposition (or something proposition-like). The semantic theories of quotation canvassed earlier treat pure quotes as singular terms referring to abstract objects, expression types. For anyone receptive to either of these ideas mixed cases remain enigmatic. From these points of view mixed quoting seems to involve two entirely different activities taking place at the same time in the same place. How could the complement clause of (4) both determine a proposition not about words, and, concomitantly, refer to words Clinton used?

The merged demonstrative accounts offer an ingenious reply. Since the complement clause is in effect semantically excised from (4) and merely demonstrated, we can ascribe different properties to it. With one utterance we can say both that the demonstrated token samesays one of Clinton's utterances and say that it (or parts of it) same-tokens that utterance. Our suggestion, then, is to construe (4) as (19),

(19) $\exists u(\text{Says}(c,u)\ \&\ \text{SS}(u,\text{that})\ \&\ \text{ST}(u,\text{these}))$. He'd cut taxes

where an utterance of the first demonstrative demonstrates an entire utterance of 'He'd cut taxes' and an utterance of the second demonstrative demonstrates (only) the (sub)utterance of 'cut taxes'.[7] According to the unified account, mixed cases like (4) can be utilized both to attribute the same-tokening relationship between one of Clinton's utterances and the demonstrated (sub)utterance and to attribute a samesaying relationship between Clinton's utterance and the demonstrated utterance.[8]

In criticizing other accounts, we appealed to reports such as (8):

(8) Bob said that Carol is an 'oenophile'.

Our account treats (8) as (20)

(20) $\exists u(\text{Says}(b,u)\ \&\ \text{SS}(u,\text{that})\ \&\ \text{ST}(u,\text{these}))$. Carol is an oenophile

where 'that' is accompanied by a demonstration of the token of 'Carol is an oenophile' and 'these' by a demonstration of the token of 'oenophile'. Is our account better positioned to account for the truth of (8) than the account we criticized earlier? After all, an utterance t of (8), construed as (20), is true only if Bob's utterance samesays t's sub-utterance of 'Carol is an oenophile'. But can any such utterance by a normal English speaker express anything since 'oenophile' is not an English expression?

Anyone who has this concern has not understood how the extension of SS is determined. What samesays what is *determined* by the practice of indirect quotation; we place *no a priori constraints on what can samesay what.* Mixed reports containing meaningless or unknown words can be true.[9] It is simply part of the data that an utterance of an ill-formed sentence of English can samesay one of Bob's utterances. Maybe this is difficult to understand, but difficulty is no excuse for denial or dismissal.[10] So, what we actually do inside the complements of indirect reports *must* be reflected in the extension of samesay relation. Indeed, it constitutes this relation.

Conclusion

Adequate semantic accounts of pure, direct, mixed, and indirect quotation cannot disrespect C1–C4. A myopically developed account of either indirect or pure quotation is likely to do this. Our joint account, as far as we know, is the only one available satisfying all four constraints.

Also worth noticing is that this unified account satisfies C1–C4 with a simplicity and elegance not likely to be shared by any competing account. According to C4, quotes in pure, direct, and mixed quotation should be treated uniformly. It is hard to evaluate alternative accounts before they are supplemented with an account of direct and pure quotation. The joint modified Davidsonian account of pure and direct quotation is, for reasons discussed above, enormously attractive. If you share this view, it is certainly natural, *though not necessary,* to combine it with Davidson's account of indirect quotation.

What makes it almost irresistible to combine a demonstrative account of pure and direct quotation with a demonstrative account of indirect quotation is that this results in a unified account of opacity. Pure and indirect quotation are paradigms of opaque contexts. From a methodological point of view, it is both plausible and desirable that there be a common explanation of their opacity. This probably accounts for so many efforts in the history of this subject to assimilate indirect quotation to direct quotation (Carnap (1937: 248), (1947); Scheffler (1954); Quine (1956), (1960: secs. 30–32); Sellars (1955); and even Church (1954) given his metalinguistic solution to Mates's problem). Though the unified demonstrative account provides a uniform account of quotation, it does not do so by assimilating either form of quotation to the other and therefore, does not fall prey, as did its predecessors, to the standard Church arguments (Church 1950: 97).

Anyone who finds the account of quotation served in this paper unpalatable (perhaps because of the numerous objections to Davidson's account of indirect quotation) needs an alternative. But the situation here is unlike indirect quotation. There is no large number of more or less acceptable competing accounts to choose from. In other words, if C1–C4 are acceptable constraints on a general account of reported speech, then any account of indirect quotation is incomplete until supplemented with an account of pure and direct quotation.

Still, we'd like to end with a challenge for those philosophers unalterably convinced that Davidson's account of indirect quotation is wrong. (1) Take your favorite theory of indirect quotation and show that it can (be extended to) account for C1–C4. (2) *Either* develop a theory of pure quotation that combines with your favorite theory of indirect quotation to yield a unified account of opacity *or* explain why opacity doesn't admit of a unified account. When you've completed tasks (1) and (2), compare your results with the unified account with respect to simplicity and elegance.

Notes

1. This paper is an abridged version of our (1997) "Varieties of Quotation." *Mind* 106: 429–450.

2. Proponents include Higginbotham (1986), Segal (1989), Larson and Ludlow (1993), and Larson and Segal (1995).

3. See Higginbothgam (1986); Segal (1989); Ludlow and Larson (1993: 335–342); Larson and Segal (1995, Chapter 11) for pros and cons of this debate.

4. We are not claiming it's illegitimate to introduce a quotation-like device into English that allows quantification in. The point is rather that 'ordinary' quotation, which we are discussing, doesn't allow such quantification. Here we agree with Quine (1961) and Davidson (1979).

5. Given certain not implausible assumptions about ST, (21) and (22) are equivalent, since: $ST(u,these) \leftrightarrow \forall y(ST(y,these) \rightarrow ST(u,y))$.

6. See Higginbotham (1986); Lepore and Loewer (1989, 1990); Segal (1989).

7. Actually, there might be reasons for complicating this logical form by at least adding another quantifier ranging over a distinct (sub)utterance; and also, perhaps, adding another predicate in logical form indicating that whatever utterance this second quantifier ranges over must be a part of whatever utterances the first quantifier ranges over. We will ignore these technical niceties here.

8. Notice that 'cut taxes' is mentioned in (19) if 'mention' is defined as: an expression *e* is *mentioned* in an utterance *u* just in case the token of *e* occurring in *u* is produced in order to be demonstrated so as to talk about tokens that same-token it.

9. This, of course, doesn't mean that these utterances are utterances of grammatical sentences; that is something the account behind (10) *requires.* On the

demonstrative account we are demonstrating an utterance and not ourselves asserting it, but merely attributing a relational property to it.

10. See our "On an Alleged Connection between Semantic Theory and Indirect Quotation," for our views about what determines the extension of 'samesaying'.

Bibliography

Cappelen, H. and E. Lepore. 1998. "On an Alleged Connection between Semantic Theory and Indirect Quotation." *Mind and Language,* pp. 278–296.

Cappelen, H. and E. Lepore. 1997. "Varieties of Quotation." *Mind* 106: 429–450.

Carnap, R. 1937. *Logical Syntax of Language.* London: Routledge and Kegan Paul.

———. 1947. Meaning and Necessity. Chicago: University of Chicago Press.

Chomsky, N. 1981. *Lectures on Government and Binding.* Foris: Dordrecht.

Church, A. 1950. "On Carnap's Analysis of Statements of Assertion and Belief." *Analysis* X: 97–99.

———. 1954. "Intentional Isomorphism and Identity of Belief." *Philosophical Studies* V, 5: 65–73.

Davidson, D. 1968. "On Saying That." Reprinted *in Inquires Into Truth and Interpretation,* Oxford: Oxford University Press, pp. 93–108. First published in *Synthese* 19: 130–146.

———. 1975. "Thought and Talk." In *Inquiries Into Truth and Interpretation,* Oxford: Oxford University Press, pp. 155–170.

———. 1979. "Quotation." In *Inquiries Into Truth and Interpretation,* Oxford: Oxford University Press, pp. 79–92.

Geach, P. 1957. *Mental Acts.* London: Routledge Kegan Paul.

———. 1970. "Quotation and Quantification." In *Logic Matters,* Oxford: Basil Blackwell.

Higginbotham, J. 1986. "Linguistic Theory and Davidson's Semantic Program." In *Truth and Interpretation,* edited by E. Lepore, Oxford: Basil Blackwell, pp. 29–48.

Larson, R. and P. Ludlow. 1993. "Interpreted Logical Forms." *Synthese* 95: 305–356.

Larson, R. and G. Segal. 1995. *Knowledge of Meaning.* Cambridge, Mass: MIT Press.

Lepore, E., and B. Loewer. 1989. "You Can Say That Again." In *Midwest Studies in Philosophy,* edited by H. Wettstein, et al., Notre Dame University Press, pp. 338–356.

Lepore, E., and B. Loewer. 1990. "A Study in Comparative Semantics." In *Propositional Attitudes,* edited by C. Anderson and J. Owens, Stanford: CSLI.

Quine, W. V. O. 1956. "Quantifiers and Propositional Attitudes" *Journal of Philosophy.*

———. 1960. *Word And Object.* Cambridge, Mass: MIT Press.

———. 1961. "Reference and Modality." in *From a Logical Point of View,* Cambridge, Mass: Harvard University Press, pp. 139–159.

Scheffler, I. 1954. "An Inscriptional Approach to Indirect Quotation." *Analysis* X: 83–90.

Segal, G. 1989. "A Preference for Sense and Reference." *Journal of Philosophy* 86: 73–89.

Sellars, W. 1955. "Putnam on Synonymity and Belief." *Analysis* XV, 5: 117–120.

Soames, S. 1989. "Direct Reference and Propositional Attitudes." in *Themes From Kaplan,* edited by J. Almog, J. Perry, and H. Wettstein, New York: Oxford University Press, pp. 393–419.

Tarski, A. 1956. "Concept of Truth in Formalized Languages." in *Logic, Semantics and Metamathematics,* Indianapolis: Hackett.

8

Mixed Quotation

Reinaldo Elugardo

In an important and very provocative paper, "Varieties of Quotation," Herman Cappelen and Ernest Lepore present a rich array of data concerning mixed quotation, indirect quotation, direct quotation, and pure quotation.[1] They argue for the following two theses. First, certain well-known accounts of the semantics of indirect discourse and pure quotation cannot adequately explain the data they describe. Second, one can account for all the data by combining and modifying Donald Davidson's paratactic accounts of indirect quotation and pure quotation.[2]

In this paper, I shall comment only on their second thesis and only in regard to their analysis of mixed quotations. I will argue that their analysis fails to give the correct truth-conditions for mixed quotations.[3] The reason is that the reporter of a mixed quotation and the reported speaker can mean different things by the same quoted expression. Difference in intended meaning entails a difference in what the reported utterance and the reporting utterance mean in the pragmatic sense of "samesay." Still, the mixed quotation could very well be true. More generally, their paratactic analysis of the corresponding indirect quotation that is entailed by a mixed quotation is open to several counterexamples, regardless of whether samesaying is defined as a semantic relation or as a pragmatically determined relation between utterances.

This paper consists of three sections. In the first section, I present Cappelen and Lepore's analysis and their main argument for that analysis. In the second section, I argue that their analysis fails to express a necessary and sufficient condition for the truth of a mixed quotation if, as Davidson sometimes puts it, samesaying is a synonymy relation between utterances. In the third section, I argue for that same conclusion while granting Cappelen and Lepore's very plausible claim that samesaying is a pragmatically determined relation.

I. Cappelen and Lepore's Thesis

Let us use Cappelen and Lepore's main example (1997a: 429). Suppose that Alice assertively utters,

(1) Life is difficult to understand

which makes my mixed quotation of her remark true:

(2) Alice said that life "is difficult to understand."

On their modified Davidsonian paratactic analysis, (2) is to be understood as,

(3) There is an utterance *u* of Alice's such that *u* samesays *that* and some part of *u* same-tokens *these*. [Life is difficult to understand]

where an utterance of the first demonstrative demonstrates an entire utterance of the sentence, "Life is difficult to understand," and an utterance of the second demonstrative demonstrates only the sub-utterance of "difficult to understand" (pp. 443–444).[4]

On Cappelen and Lepore's analysis, quotation marks function as quantifiers that range over utterance-tokens, when they have a quotational role.[5] The mentioning and reporting roles they have at the surface level of a mixed quotation are transformed into the parts of the logical form that read, "Same-Tokens(u^*, x)" and "Samesays(u, y)," respectively. The first argument-place of each predicate represents a slot for a quantified variable ranging over utterance-tokens. The second argument-place represents a position for a demonstrative the utterance of which demonstrates an utterance of some expression or other.[6]

Which expression? In the case of "Samesays(u, y)," it must be the quoteless version of the entire sentence following the complementizer of the report. With respect to (2), that would be the sentence, "Life is difficult to understand," with its standard semantic properties in place. After all, mixed quotations are used to report the content of what the reported speaker said. Thus, it must be the whole complement sentence, *sans* quotes, whose utterance is demonstrated at the deep level of analysis since it functions to convey the content of the reported utterance. Otherwise, the reporting role of the quotation marks in a mixed quotation report will not be preserved at the level of logical form.

Similarly, in the case of "Same-Tokens(u^*, x)," the relevant expression must be the quoted material that appears in the complement of the report.

With respect to (2), that would be the expression, "is difficult to understand." For, mixed quotations are also used to report the expressions the reported speaker used in saying what he or she said. Hence, it must be the quoted material, *sans* quoted, whose sub-utterance is tokened at the deep level of analysis. Otherwise, the quoting role of the quotation marks of a mixed quotation will not be captured at the level of logical form. And so, at the level of logical form, the entire complement of a mixed quotation (minus the "that" and minus the quotation marks) is paratactically linked to a quantified sentence that contains demonstrative elements.[7] If Cappelen and Lepore's analysis of mixed quotations is correct, then quotations marks in mixed quotations are eliminable at the level of logical form.

Cappelen and Lepore's main argument for their analysis of mixed quotations is essentially an "inference to the best explanation" type of argument. First, they argue that no extant account of the semantics of pure quotations or of indirect quotation can adequately explain the fact that, in the mixed quotation,

(2) Alice said that life "is difficult to understand"

the quoted expression,

> "is difficult to understand" serves two functions. It (together with other words) functions to report that Alice said that life is difficult to understand; but it also functions minimally to report that Alice tokened the words "is difficult to understand." So, "is difficult to understand" serves two functions, without incurring ambiguity. (p. 436)[8]

Second, they argue that their modified paratactic account can explain and capture this particular feature of mixed quotations.[9] For, on their analysis, a mixed quotation is true just in case the reported utterance samesays a certain demonstrated sentential utterance and some part of the reported utterance same-tokens a certain demonstrated part of the larger demonstrated utterance. Both relations jointly echo the dual roles that the quoted material in a mixed quotation concurrently serves. For the sake of discussion, I will concede the first step of their argument and focus on the second step in the remainder of this paper.

II. Is The Paratactic Analysis True?

Cappelen and Lepore claim that their account gets the truth-conditions of mixed quotations right. Presumably, their analysis is correct only if it provides a necessary and sufficient condition for the truth of a mixed quotation. That in turn will depend on how the samesaying and same-tokening relations are understood. For purposes of this discussion, I will examine their analysis from the perspective of Davidson's line on the samesaying relation.

Consider the indirect quotation:

(4) Alice said that life is difficult to understand.

According to Davidson, an utterance of (4) has the logical form of two paratactically related sentential utterances,

(5) Alice said that. Life is difficult to understand

where an utterance of "that" in the first sentence demonstrates an utterance of the second sentence.[10] The second sentence in (5) occurs with its standard semantic properties in place. The properties are semantically inert because the sentence (or some utterance of it) is demonstratively displayed in an utterance of (5).

Since on Davidson's analysis the complementizer of an indirect quotation functions as a demonstrative, an utterance of the first sentence in (5) must be semantically evaluated relative to a context in which an utterance of the second sentence is demonstrated. In this case, an utterance of "Alice said that" is true or false relative to the context in which "Life is difficult to understand" is uttered. According to Davidson, the first utterance is true relative to that context if and only if the following condition holds:

(6) There is an utterance u such that Alice produced u and u
samesays that. [Life is difficult to understand]

where an utterance of the demonstrative demonstrates an utterance of the displayed sentence, "Life is difficult to understand."[11] The truth-conditions of an utterance of the second sentence in (5) are the standard ones: an utterance of "Life is difficult to understand" is true just in case life is difficult to understand. Thus, the two sentential utterances that make up an utterance of (5) are semantically independent given that their truth-conditions are logically independent.

According to Davidson, a reported utterance must samesay an utterance of the complement of an indirect quotation if the report is to be true. What is it for one sentential utterance to samesay another? He gives what others might regard as two different answers to that question. According to the first, samesaying is the relation of *synonymy* between utterances, e.g., the reported utterance and the reporter's own (demonstrated) utterance of the sentence complement of "said that." For example, in discussing his parat-

actic analysis of an utterance of "Galileo said that the earth moves," Davidson contends that:

> ... what an utterance of "Galileo said that" does is announce a further utter-
> ance. Like any utterance, this first may be serious or silly, assertive or playful;
> but if it is true, *it must be followed by an utterance synonymous with some
> other.* (1986a: 105–106, emphasis added)

Suppose that an utterance of "Galileo said that" is true relative to some
context in which the utterance of "that" demonstrates an utterance of "the
Earth moves." Then the demonstrated utterance of "the Earth moves,"
must in that context be "synonymous with some other" utterance, namely,
the reported utterance, which in this case is Galileo's utterance of "Eppur
si muove."

Some of Davidson's commentators think that he is committed to this interpretation of samesaying. The reason is that, since indirect quotation is a
species of indirect discourse, to indirectly quote what someone said one
must produce an utterance which is similar in meaning and in reference
with the reported utterance. For example, Tyler Burge writes:

> The notion of samesaying deserves comment. Davidson's idea is that the no-
> tion is an 'unanalyzed part' of the 'content' of 'said'. It is invoked, I think quite
> legitimately, to explicate the use of the predicate; and its complexity (saying
> the same thing) is not seen as complicating the predicate's logical form. To use
> indirect discourse, *one must be able to use utterances that are relevantly syn-
> onymous with utterances of the original speaker.* The utterance to which 'that'
> is held to refer is a performance whose point is to mimic the content (not nec-
> essarily the mode) of the speaker's utterance. (1986: 192, italics added)

Davidson's use of "synonymous" encourages this interpretation of samesaying.[12]

Davidson also gives a second, quite different, answer to our question
about the notion of samesaying. In discussing the report, "Galileo said that
the Earth moves," he says that,

> The second utterance, the introduced act, may also be true or false, done in the
> mode of assertion or of play. But if it is announced, it must serve at least the
> purpose of *conveying the content of what someone said.* (1986a: 106–107, em-
> phasis added)

So, if an utterance of "the Earth moves" is "announced" by an utterance of
"Galileo said that," then the former utterance must (in that context) serve
to convey the content of what Galileo had reportedly said. This idea is
sometimes put in terms of the notion of translation:

The paratactic semantic approach to indirect discourse tells us to view an utterance of 'Galileo said that the Earth moves' as consisting of the utterance of two sentences, 'Galileo said that' and 'the Earth moves'. The 'that' refers to the second utterance, and the first utterance is true if and only if an utterance of Galileo's was the *same in content* as ('*translates*') the utterance to which 'that' refers. (1986c: 176–177)[13]

There are important conceptual differences between synonymy and translation. Synonymous utterances must have the same referential truth-conditions and, of course, must be the same in meaning. Thus, if samesaying is the relation of synonymy, then it follows that two truth-evaluable utterances samesay each other only if they have the same meaning, and thus, have the same truth-conditions. By contrast, one utterance can adequately translate another without their being the same in meaning. For, in translating another person's speech, the reporter's job is to convey the content of what the speaker said. In some cases, that can be done by uttering a sentence that differs in meaning from the sentence-token produced by the reported speaker. Here is a simple example: I can convey what you said by your utterance of "I am sleepy" by pointing to you and saying "You are sleepy." I conveyed what you said about yourself by using a sentence that differs in meaning from the one you used. In some cases, the reporter can give a true indirect quotation even though the sentence complement she tokens differs in its truth-conditions from those of the sentence that the reported speaker actually uttered. (Some examples will be given later in the text.) Thus, if samesaying is a translation or an interpretation relation, then two utterances can samesay each other even though they differ in meaning and in their truth-conditions. It is therefore important that we distinguish these two different ways of understanding the samesay relation.

With this distinction in mind, we can now return to Cappelen and Lepore's analysis of mixed quotation. The question at hand is whether their analysis provides the correct truth-conditions if samesaying is a semantic relation as defined. I will try to show that it does not.

A. An Argument Against the Sufficiency of the Analysis

Let us assume, both in this subsection and in the next, that samesaying is the relation of synonymy. Now imagine that Alice never used the sentence, "Life is difficult to understand," to state that life is difficult to understand. She never made such a claim. She instead assertively uttered:

(7) Either life is difficult to understand or life stinks.

Since she assertively uttered a disjunction, she did not use the words, "Life is difficult to understand," to state anything about life in that context. Nor was that ever her intention.[14] Thus, my mixed quotation,

   (2) Alice said that life "is difficult to understand"

is false.[15]

But, on Cappelen and Lepore's analysis of (2), namely,

   (3) There is an utterance, u, of Alice's and an utterance-part, u^*, of u such that u samesays *that* and u^* same-tokens *this*. [Life is difficult to understand]

(2) should come out true. For, in uttering (7), Alice also produced a sentential utterance that satisfies the conditions expressed in their paratactic analysis given the Davidsonian interpretation of "samesaying." To see this, let $u\#$ be Alice's utterance of (7) and let u be that part of $u\#$ that is her utterance of its first disjunct, namely, her sub-utterance of sentence (1) ("Life is difficult to understand") which is also a sentential utterance. Relative to the context in which she uttered (7), u samesays the demonstrated utterance of "Life is difficult to understand," relative to the context in which I uttered (2). For, the two utterance-tokens have the same meaning and truth-conditions in their respective contexts. Now u also same-tokens the whole demonstrated utterance of the sentence, "Life is difficult to understand." Thus, u also contains a proper sub-utterance, u^*, that same-tokens the demonstrated sub-utterance of the expression, "is difficult to understand." And so, u and u^* meet the conditions expressed in (3), given the context in which Alice uttered (7) and the context in which I uttered (2). Thus, (3) is true.

But (2) is a false report. By hypothesis, Alice never predicatively used the words, "is difficult to understand," to say of life that it is difficult to understand. Also, by the same hypothesis, she never made such a general claim about life. In which case, (2) is false even though, in our story, (3) is true. Hence, (3) does not express a sufficient condition for the truth of (2) given a Davidsonian semantic reading of the logicosemantic predicate "Samesays(x, y)."

One might try to avoid this problem by requiring that the reported utterance not be a sub-utterance of any structurally complex assertive utterance that the reported speaker produced. One could then revise Cappelen and Lepore's paratactic analysis of mixed quotations to reflect this constraint. But that will not help. Imagine that Alice assertively utters:

   (8) Life is difficult to understand and it stinks too.

If she had uttered (8), then (2) would have been a true mixed quotation report. For, if a speaker assertively utters a conjunction of the form, "P and Q," where "P" and "Q" represent any pair of truth-evaluable English sentences, then she will have thereby assertively uttered P and assertively uttered Q. Hence, if Alice asserts (8), then she will have also assertively uttered (1). In so doing, she will have said something that makes (2) true. But the proposal just presented would be unable to explain why (2) is true since her sentential utterance of "Life is difficult to understand" is a sub-utterance of her structurally complex assertive utterance of (8).[16]

A more telling objection to my argument is the following. The verb, "to say," has a broad meaning in English. A speaker can be said to have said something if she produces an utterance that has some locutionary meaning. For instance, suppose that Smith utters, "I lost my wallet," but you did not quite hear what he said. Jones, who did hear, informs you what he said by his utterance of "Smith said that he lost his wallet." Given the right context, Jones's indirect quotation may have correctly described what Smith said even if Smith was not stating at the time that he lost his wallet. Smith may have instead been reciting a line from a play, telling a joke, etc. Still, there is a reading of "said that" according to which Jones's report is true in all of these cases, namely, the sense in which the verb construction has a broad locutionary meaning rather than a narrow illocutionary meaning.

As we noted earlier, in uttering the disjunction,

(7) Either life is difficult to understand or life stinks

Alice produced a sub-utterance that means *life is difficult to understand*. On a Davidsonian view, that just means that she produced an utterance that samesaid an utterance of "Life is difficult to understand." Moreover, in uttering (4), Alice also produced an utterance that same-tokens an utterance of the verb phrase "is difficult to understand." Now, on Cappelen and Lepore's analysis, both facts jointly form a sufficient condition on mixed quotation. Thus, if their analysis is correct, then it follows that the mixed quotation,

(2) Alice said that life "is difficult to understand"

is true after all in the context in which Alice uttered (7) given the broad locutionary sense of "to say" and given the Davidsonian semantic interpretation of "samesay."

Let us grant that "say" has a broad locutionary meaning. I will also assume that "said that" has that same meaning in mixed and indirect quotations in certain contexts. Still, several replies can be made. First, even if "say" has a broad locutionary meaning, it does not follow that an utterance of,

   (4) Alice said that life is difficult to understand

is true in my original example. The claim that (4) is true runs counter to linguistic practice. Given our linguistic practice of indirect quotation, (4) is false in my example (and thus, so is the mixed quotation (2)). If that is right, then the burden falls on those who think otherwise. They must provide a plausible reason for thinking that (4) is true on some other reading that is consistent with our linguistic practice, which would then warrant the rejection of the above linguistic intuition.

   Second, according to the objection, we can justifiably discount the intuition that (4) is false if (4) is interpreted to mean,

   (4a) Alice uttered something which means *life is difficult to understand*

since (4a) is a true in my example. It is also being claimed that (4a) is to be understood as,

   (5) There is an utterance *u* that Alice produced and *u* samesays *that:* [Life is difficult to understand]

which I have argued is also true in my example. And so, (4) is true after all. But now the move of stipulating a sense of "to say," which has the consequence that (4) is correct if and only if (5) is true, becomes questionable. For, it assumes that our linguistic practice of indirect quotation would rule (4a) as the correct interpretation of what (4) expresses in my example, and thus, would justify the view that (4) is true after all. However, that assumption is precisely what is at issue, and so the objection begs the question on a very crucial point. Besides, if the "said that" construction is to be understood in its broad sense, and if the paratactic analysis of (4) applies only in contexts in which the construction has that meaning, then the analysis will not capture the sense in which a speaker is reported to have stated something. However, proponents of the paratactic analysis take themselves to be giving the correct truth-conditions of just such a report. Thus, the objection under consideration runs contrary to some of the aims of the paratactic analysis.

   Third, even if my linguistic intuitions about my example should be discounted, the objection fails for another reason. A speaker, *A,* could say something that makes a report of the form, "*A* said that *P,*" true even though nothing that *A* uttered means the same as any utterance of the sentential complement of the report. If that is correct, then the paratactic analysis of such reports, given the synonymy reading of "samesay," fails to provide a necessary condition on indirect quotation and also, therefore, on mixed quotation. I will now argue this point in the next subsection.

B. An Argument Against The Necessity Of The Analysis

Consider the following example. While entertaining some guests at her cocktail party, Nika notices that Consuelo is standing alone at the corner of the room. She turns to one of her guests, Marc, nods in Consuelo's direction, and whispers to him:

(9) That woman is a spy.

Let us suppose that that was the only time that Nika ever uttered anything by virtue of which she asserted that Consuelo is a spy.

Years pass and Marc has since forgotten much about the event. He has forgotten who the person was that Nika was referring to at the time and even whether the individual in question was a woman or a man. But he still remembers a few things. When Consuelo asks him some years later about what Nika had told him on that particular evening, Marc answers:

(10) Nika said that someone was "a spy"—those were the words she
       used but I don't remember who she was referring to at the time.[17]

In spite of the fact that he does not remember, Marc's mixed quotation in (10) is true. In uttering (9), Nika referred to a certain person at the cocktail party and attributed to that person the property of being a spy. In which case, she said of someone who was at her party that that person was a spy. Furthermore, she did utter "a spy" in making her statement. Thus, in uttering (9), and given the context in which she made the remark, Nika said something that makes Marc's mixed quotation true.

On Cappelen and Lepore's analysis, Marc's utterance of the mixed quotation in (10) involves (at the level of logical form) a demonstrated utterance on his part of the sentence,

(11) Someone was a spy.

Suppose that is true. Let u be that utterance. Does Nika's utterance of (9) at the party samesay u? No. The reason is that they have different truth-conditions even if, unbeknownst to Marc, his use of "someone" is somehow referentially connected, via some causal-historical chain involving Nika's utterance of (9), to Consuelo. That is, the two utterances differ in their truth-conditions even if Consuelo is Marc's speaker referent if anyone is. And, while Consuelo's being the only spy at the party makes u true relative to the context in which Marc uttered (10), u is not about her.

Nika's utterance of "That woman is a spy" at the party is the only utterance by which she ever said of Consuelo that she is a spy. There is no utterance that she produced which samesaid Marc's demonstrated utterance of the complement of (10) *sans* quotes, namely, his utterance of "Someone was a spy," relative to the context in which he uttered (10). In that case, Cappelen and Lepore's analysis of Marc's mixed quotation, namely,

(12) There is an utterance u and a sub-utterance u^* of u such that Nika produced u (and u^*), u same-said *that,* and u^* same-token *these.* [Someone was a spy]

is false. And so, (12) fails to express a necessary condition for the truth of the mixed quotation contained in (10).

It might be objected that, relative to the context in which Marc uttered (10), u and Nika's actual utterance of (9) do samesay one another. The argument runs as follows. First, Marc used "someone" referentially to refer (unbeknownst to him) to Consuelo. Second, as a consequence, u expresses in that context an object-dependent proposition involving Consuelo. In fact, so goes the argument, u is true at any possible world exactly if, in the world in question, Consuelo was a spy (at the time she was at Nika's party). Hence, Nika's actual utterance of (9) and u samesay each other since they express the same object-dependent proposition involving Consuelo.

The second and third premises of the argument are questionable. The second premise is true only if the fact that an expression like "someone" is used referentially in u entails that it semantically fixes the speaker referent as its semantic contribution to the proposition expressed by u relative to the context in which Marc uttered (10). But, of course, "someone" is not a singular term but is instead a quantifier, and thus, its semantic contribution is not the speaker referent.[18] For the same reason, the third premise is false since it is wrong about the truth-conditions of u. But even if I am wrong about the premises, the argument is invalid. For, Nika's utterance of (9) entails that some *woman* is a spy whereas Marc's utterance of "someone was a spy," at the level of logical form, does not. Hence, they could not be samesaying the same object-dependent proposition in any case if samesaying is a semantic relation between synonymous utterances.

III. The Pragmatics of Samesaying

Both counterexamples to Cappelen and Lepore's paratactic analysis of mixed quotation and, for that matter, indirect quotation, exploit the view that utterance-tokens samesay one another if and only if they have the same meaning and reference.[19] However, it is not obvious that that is the best way to understand the samesay relation. In fact, Davidson does not understand it in that way. In a reply to an objection that John Foster raises against his paratactic analysis, he says this:

> But what is this relation between utterances, of stating the same fact or proposition, that Foster has in mind? . . . if both reference and meaning must be preserved, it is easy to see that very few pairs of utterances can state the same fact provided the utterances contain indexical expressions . . . I cannot twice state the same fact by saying 'I'm warm' twice. (Davidson 1986c: 177)

In Davidson's example, the same speaker (Davidson) produces two synonymous indexical utterances that do not samesay each other if samesaying is a matter of different utterances stating the same fact. Thus, synonymy is not sufficient for samesaying in that sense. I earlier gave an example ("You are sleepy" / "I am sleepy") to show that it is not necessary for samesaying either. Thus, the idea that samesaying is not a semantic relation is on the right track.

One can then reject the semantic view of samesaying and accept Cappelen and Lepore's paratactic analysis of mixed quotation, pure quotation, direct quotation, and indirect quotation.[20] Indeed, their strategy is exactly that. They hold that samesaying is a pragmatically determined relation and contend that a semantics of mixed and indirect quotation need not address the question of the nature of the samesaying relation. According to them, "it's the actual practice of making indirect reports of others that fixes that extension [of the samesaying relation]" (p. 446). They also note that "there are no *a priori* constraints on what can samesay what" (p. 445).

Lepore develops the pragmatic view of samesaying more fully in a series of papers that he co-authored with Barry Loewer. According to them, our linguistic practices of indirect quotation fix the extension of the samesaying relation:

> . . . it is clear that these [interpretive] practices, and in particular the practice of indirectly reporting others, is sufficiently robust to establish a distinction between correct and incorrect reporting and even degrees of correctness in reporting. The practice within a linguistic community of indirect discourse reporting, correcting, revising, and so on, fixes the extension of the samesay relation. (Lepore and Loewer 1990: 109–110, bracketed expression added)

This idea is expanded in the following passage:

> It is recognized by speakers of any language that no utterances are likely ever to carry exactly the same information to all audiences. Because of this speakers treat the samesay relation as flexible and pragmatic. Whether a claim that

two utterances samesay each other is counted as among speakers of a language depends on pragmatic matters, including the point of making the claim and its intended audience. Sometimes a great deal of leeway is allowed. Indeed, since speakers recognize that others may use somewhat different dialects and that over time the import of words change, they sometimes get into discussions and debates concerning whether two utterances samesay each other. But for most matters, there is sufficient agreement and speakers master the art of recognizing when two utterances do or do not stand in the samesay relation to each other. So, even if philosophers studying the speakers of a language cannot provide necessary and sufficient conditions for the relation in, say, physicalistic or even psychological or semantic terms, they and we can be confident that the practices of the speakers suffice to fix (with some margin of vagueness and indeterminacy) the predicate's extension. (Lepore and Loewer 1989a: 76, footnote 12)

Lepore and Loewer's proposal is attractive and not *ad hoc*. On the contrary, it is well-motivated, as the following examples will illustrate.

A. Some Examples In Defense of the Pragmatic View

If the pragmatic view of samesaying is correct, then it ought to be possible for a true indirect quotation to contain a complement whose tokens samesay the reported utterance but which do not have the same truth-conditions as the reported utterance. Indeed, it is possible. Consider, for example, this exchange:

> Miriam: David will be home in time for dinner.
> Ruth (to Miriam): Don't hold your breath!

It is arguable that, given the conversational context, at least one of the following is a correct report of what Ruth said:

(13) Ruth said that David will not be home for dinner
(14) Ruth said that David will be late for dinner
(15) Ruth said that Miriam should not expect David to be home for dinner at all
(16) Ruth said that Miriam should not expect David to on time for dinner

In which case, relative to the context in which Ruth sarcastically uttered, "Don't hold your breath," to Miriam, her utterance samesays a (demonstrated) utterance of at least one or more of the four complements. But no token of any of the complements will have the same conventional linguistic meaning as Ruth's utterance. Indeed, her sentential utterance lacks a truth-condition whereas any utterance of the complements of (13)–(16) will have one.

If the pragmatic view is right, then it ought to be possible for an indirect quotation to be false, that is, no token of its complement samesays the reported utterance, even though the tokens have the same truth-conditions as the reported utterance. Again, that is possible. For example, speaking to the multitude at Julius Caeser's funeral, Cassius mockingly said of Brutus:

(17) Brutus is an honorable man.

Once again, it is arguable that, in some sense of "said that," (18) is true but (19) is false:

(18) Cassius said that Brutus is a dishonorable man.
(19) Cassius said that Brutus is an honorable man.

The context is such that Cassius's utterance of (17) does not samesay a (demonstrated) utterance of (19)'s complement even though they have exactly the same referential truth-conditions, and even though an utterance of (19)'s complement has the same truth-conditions of Brutus's utterance of (17).

The objection to my earlier counterexamples is, then, that what samesays what is purely a pragmatic matter and is not fixed solely by the semantic properties of utterance-tokens that stand in that relation.[21] On this view of the samesaying relation, Cappelen and Lepore's general thesis is that the truth-conditions of assertion-ascriptions already build in the pragmatic elements of the reported utterance by way of the samesaying relation.[22] Their paratactic analysis of indirect and mixed quotations is intended to reflect that idea.[23]

B. Objections

Adopting the pragmatic view of the samesaying relation will not change the situation in any significant way, however. For, even if samesaying is a pragmatic relation between speakers, utterances, and contexts, Cappelen and Lepore's modified paratactic analysis still fails to deliver the correct truth-conditions for mixed quotations. In what follows, we shall assume that samesaying is a pragmatically determined relation.

To begin with, my first example involving Alice still stands. Given our linguistic practice, her sub-utterance of "Life is difficult to understand," relative to her context of her disjunctive utterance, samesays my utterance of the quoteless version of the complement of the mixed quotation, "Alice said that life 'is difficult to understand'," relative to my context of utterance. After all, she meant by her sub-utterance exactly what I meant by my utterance of the same sentence even though neither one of us stated, nor intended to state by our utterances of that sentence, that life is difficult to understand. Furthermore, Alice's utterance of the words, "is difficult to understand" same-tokens my utterance of those same words, which I mentioned in my report. In that case, Cappelen and Lepore's analysis of my mixed quotation is true. But my mixed quotation is false since it entails that she did make a specific (non-disjunctive) claim about life which, by hypothesis, she never did. Thus, even on the assumption that samesaying is a pragmatically fixed relation, Cappelen and Lepore's analysis fails to express a sufficient condition for the truth of a mixed quotation.

However, my "Nika and Marc Example" can be discounted. For, Cappelen and Lepore can argue that, pragmatically speaking, Nika's utterance of "That woman is a spy," and Marc's utterance of the complement sentence (*sans* quotes), "Someone was a spy," do samesay one another relative to their respective contexts. Nika meant to be referring to Consuelo by her utterance of "that woman," and she did refer to her then. Marc used "someone" referentially to refer to the person that Nika referred to by her utterance, namely, Consuelo. His utterance of "someone" is, in that context, causally connected to her by way of its causal connection to Nika's utterance. Thus, on pragmatic grounds, we may type-count Nika's utterance of "That woman is a spy" and Marc's utterance of "Someone was a spy" as instances of samesaying. In which case, Cappelen and Lepore's paratactic analysis of Marc's mixed quotation report is true rather than false. My second example, then, does not show that their analysis fails to express a necessary condition if samesaying is construed pragmatically.

But this next example does. Imagine that Shifty Sam tells Naïve Ned the following:

(20) I have a gold watch to sell you. But don't tell anyone because it is a hot piece.

Ned, who is unaware that Sam meant *stolen merchandise* by "hot piece," interprets him as literally meaning *popular merchandise.* In reporting what Sam said, Ned utters the mixed quotation:

(21) Sam said that he has a "hot" gold watch to sell me.

(21) is undoubtedly true.

On Cappelen and Lepore's analysis, Ned's report is true if and only if the following holds:

(22) There is an utterance u and a sub-utterance of u, u^*, such that
    Sam produced u and u^*, and u samesaid *that* and u^* same-to-
    kens *this:* [Sam has a *hot* gold watch to sell me]

where an utterance of "that" demonstrates an utterance of the displayed
sentence and an utterance of "this" demonstrates a sub-utterance of the
underlined displayed expression. However, relative to the context in which
Ned uttered (21), (22) is false even on a pragmatic reading of "samesaying." For, given their different interpretations of "hot piece," Sam did not
mean by his utterance of (20) what Ned meant by his utterance of the complement of (21) (*sans* quotes).[24] Ned's utterance of the complement of (21)
has this speaker meaning:

(23) Sam has a *popular* gold watch to sell me (= Ned).

Sam's utterance of (20) has, in part, this speaker meaning:

(24) I, Sam, have a *stolen* gold watch to sell you (= Ned).

Relative to the contexts in question, given the differences in speaker meaning, our linguistic practice type-counts what Sam said by his utterance of
(23) as being different in content from what Ned said by his utterance of
the complement of (24). In other words, pragmatically speaking, (23) and
(24) do not samesay one another. Moreover, we may stipulate in our example that Sam never produced an utterance that samesaid, in the pragmatic sense, an utterance of (20). Thus, even on the pragmatic view of
samesaying, Cappelen and Lepore's analysis of (21), namely, (22), is false
but (18) remains true. Their analysis, therefore, does not provide a necessary condition on mixed quotation.
    It might be objected that Ned's mixed report is correctly analyzed as (25)
rather than as (22) given what Sam, as oppose to Ned, meant by "hot piece"
in his utterance of (20):

(25) There is an utterance u and a sub-utterance of u, u^*, such that
    Sam produced u and u^*, and u samesaid *that* and u^* same-to-
    kens *this:* [Sam has a *stolen* gold watch to sell me]

The problem is that (25) is false but for a different reason: Sam never uttered "stolen" in his remarks to Ned. In fact, we may suppose that the word,
"stolen," is not even part of Shifty Sam's vocabulary, that is, he never uttered it or any other expression the utterance of which same-tokens it.
Hence, (25) is false since it entails that he once produced a sub-utterance
that same-tokens some demonstrated utterance of "stolen" (presumably,

Sam's utterance of "hot" does not same-token any utterance of "stolen" in English). Still, Ned's mixed quotation report is true.

That the above strategy fails to save Cappelen and Lepore's analysis should come as no surprise. For, as the "Sam and Ned Example" shows, the reporter of a mixed quotation may mean something different by the quoted material than what the reported speaker meant by it. On a pragmatic understanding of the samesaying relation, that means that in such cases the reported utterance does not samesay the reporter's utterance of the complement of the mixed quotation (*sans* quotes). And yet, the mixed quotation may still be true in spite of that fact. The reply to my objection essentially involved a charitable re-interpretation of the reporter's quoted material at the level of logical form, one that captures the reported speaker's intended meaning of the quoted expression. However, the interpretation will not guarantee that the reported speaker ever produced an utterance that same-tokens an utterance of the translating expression. In which case, the paratactic analysis fails once again.

Conclusion

I conclude, then, that Cappelen and Lepore's modified paratactic account of mixed quotation is unsuccessful, regardless of whether samesaying is a semantic relation or a pragmatic relation. The problem is that their analysis fails give the right truth-conditions for the corresponding indirect quotation that is entailed by a mixed quotation. The reason is that the reporter of a mixed quotation and the reported speaker may mean different things by the same quoted expression. Difference in intended meaning entails a difference in what the reported utterance and the reporting utterance mean in the pragmatic sense of "meaning." In which case, the two utterances will not samesay each other. Still, the mixed quotation could very well be true.

In spite of my reservations of their project, Cappelen and Lepore are on to something quite important and may, in spite of what I have argued here, be headed in the right direction. They have certainly advanced the discussion of the semantics of attitude ascriptions to a new level. Since it is unclear how mixed quotations actually work, Cappelen and Lepore have succeeded in making this an important and exciting topic for further investigation.[25]

Notes

1. Cappelen and Lepore (1997a). All page references in the text are to this paper. An earlier version of their paper was presented to the American Philosophical Association, Pacific Division, 1996. This paper is an expansion of the comments

I gave at their session. Also, for the record, an example of a mixed quotation is "Fodor said that meaning holism is 'patently absurd'," an example of an indirect quotation is "Fodor said that meaning holism is patently absurd," an example of direct quotation is "Fodor said, 'Meaning holism is patently absurd'," and an example of pure quotation is "'Fodor' is a surname."

2. See the following influential papers by Donald Davidson: Davidson (1986a), and Davidson (1986b). The modifications that Cappelen and Lepore make to Davidson's paratactic accounts of pure quotation and indirect quotation are as follows. First, quotation marks function as quantifiers that range over utterance-tokens. Second, the samesaying relation is a relation that holds between utterance-tokens rather than speakers (although Davidson himself flirts with this view, cf. Davidson (1986a), p.104, footnote 14). They combine the two Davidsonian analyses to account for the semantics of mixed quotations.

3. Actually, a more accurate way of putting my criticism is that their analysis fails to provide the right truth-conditions for mixed quotations under certain interpretations of the samesaying relation. My objections in this paper, even if sound, are compatible with the view that Cappelen and Lepore's analysis provides the correct *form* for specifying the truth-conditions of such reports. Also, nothing I say here undermines their main arguments in Cappelen and Lepore (1997a).

4. In their original analysis of mixed quotations, Cappelen and Lepore do not quantify over sub-utterances of utterances although they acknowledge in a footnote that they must (footnote 22, p. 444). The reason is that, e.g., an utterance that same-tokens an utterance of "difficult to understand" will not samesay an utterance of "Life is difficult to understand." Conversely, an utterance may samesay the latter without it, or any part of it, same-tokening the former, e.g., an utterance of a Chinese sentence that translates "Life is difficult to understand."

5. This claim follows from their analysis of pure quotations. On their analysis, the English sentence, "'Dog' is a noun" is to be understood as, "Any utterance-token that same-tokens that is a noun. [Dog]," where an utterance of the demonstrative demonstrates an utterance of "dog" (p. 441). As this example shows, the claim that quotation marks in pure quotation function as quantifiers presupposes that there are, at the level of logical form, demonstrative elements that supply the requisite demonstrata. Presumably, the domain of discourse of the paratactic analyzandum is contextually delimited by the language of which it is a sentence. Otherwise, with respect to this example, there could be languages in which what same-tokens, say, this token of "dog" is not a noun but a verb. If there were any, then Cappelen and Lepore's paratactic analysis of the English sentence, "'Dog' is a noun," is false but the sentence would still be true.

6. In an earlier version of this paper, I assumed that Cappelen and Lepore's analysis committed them to Davidson's controversial claim that complementizers semantically function at the surface level as demonstratives. I argued that their position is subject to all the same criticisms that other philosophers have raised against Davidson's claim. Lepore convinced me, however, that their analysis is logically independent of the linguistic thesis about complementizers. Still, it is hard to believe that, at the level of logical form, there is a *demonstrative act of reference* to an utterance of the complement of an indirect or mixed quotation. In uttering,

"Herman said that quotations function as quantifiers," I used the complement to say what it is that Herman said by some utterance he made. It is hard to see, though, why that should mean that, at some deep level of analysis of the truth-conditions of what I asserted, I demonstratively referred to my own utterance of the complement sentence just by my act of assertively uttering the indirect quotation. After all, I had no such referential intention to refer to any utterance of mine at the time of my assertion. For some criticisms of the view that the complementizer of a that-clause functions as a demonstrative, see: Burge (1986), Higginbotham (1986), and Segal (1989). Lepore and Loewer (1989b) is a response to some of these criticisms in his paper. Stainton (1997) offers a new set of criticisms to the Davidsonian view.

7. If by a "complement clause" one means a surface-level construction involving the complementizer, "that," followed by a sentence, then the mixed quotation (1) lacks a complement clause since what follows the "that" is not a sentence. Part of the expression that follows the "that" in (1) is used and the other part is mentioned. So, in a sense, there is no complement clause that I am uttering when I utter (1). I owe this point to Kent Bach.

8. Suppose that Cappelen and Lepore are correct in saying that the quoted material in a mixed quotation concurrently serves two different roles: it mentions an expression and is used to report what a speaker said. Then, the Identity Theory of Quotation cannot be true. On that view, the quoted expression *is* the quoting expression, and the quotation marks merely serve as punctuation marks to signal that the expression they enclosed is being used in a *nonstandard* way. If that is true, then the quoted expression in (2) is not reporting (along with the other words) what Alice said about life since that would be its *standard* use. See Washington (1992).

9. Cappelen and Lepore (1997a) offer other reasons as well. For instance, their paratactic account can explain the following facts. First, direct and indirect quotation do not semantically overlap but pure, direct, and mixed quotation do (pp. 430–432). Second, indirect, direct, and mixed quotations contain referentially opaque contexts (440). Third, quantifying into such contexts is not permissible (pp. 440–441). Fourth, learning to quote "is learning a practice with endless but non-iterable application" (p. 439). Their account, as does Davidson's, preserves semantic innocence (pp. 441–442). Furthermore, their account does not commit one to the existence of any dubious entities, e.g., Fregean senses, propositions, interpreted logical forms, etc.

10. Davidson (1986a, pp. 105–106)

11. Ibid.

12. Davidson does not hold a metaphysically robust view of synonymy. For one thing, on his extensionalist view of semantics, the semantic properties of a language are exhausted by the truth-conditions of the sentences (and the entailment relations) as characterized by a correct, finite, recursively axiomatizable, truth-theory for the language. On his view, such a theory will not postulate any meanings, propositions, abstracta, etc., or other intensional entities that can plausibly stand in the relation of synonymy. For another, the paratactic account is supposed to explain how a Tarskian truth theory for a language can be a theory of interpretation, and thus, a theory of meaning for the language. Thus, postulating a relation (samesaying) the concept of which presupposes the very notion to be explained, namely, sameness in

meaning, might pose a circularity problem for Davidson's program unless the concept of synonymy is reconstructed from other concepts central to his program,
namely, the concepts of truth and interpretation. (Davidson thinks that the notion
of synonymy can be so reconstructed in Davidson (1986c:178)). Thus, when he describes samesaying as a case of two utterances being synonymous, I take him simply to mean that one utterance is an interpretation of the other, i.e., one utterance
says in one language what the other says in its (possibly the same) language. As we
shall see, the idea that one utterance says in L what another utterance says in L^*
need not imply that the sentences produced in a pair of samesaying utterances are
the same in meaning. However, for purposes of our discussion, I will treat the semantic notion of samesaying as if it had this implication. For, that is how some
philosophers understand the notion, e.g., Burge. I owe these general points to
Ernest Lepore.

13. Again, in fairness to Davidson, one should not interpret him to mean by
"translation" here simply the correlation of sentences that have the same truth-conditions. For, as he has argued, one can know that a certain sentence translates (in
that sense) the sentence uttered by a speaker without knowing what the speaker
said or without knowing what the translating sentence means, cf. Davidson
(1986c:175). Davidson's idea is that to understand what a speaker said by an utterance it suffices for one to know that the speaker produced an utterance that samesaid an utterance that one already understands, i.e., one knows its truth-conditions.
The kind of knowledge that, for Davidson, suffices for understanding another
speaker's speech is interpretative. I propose that we understand his use of "translates" in the quotation given to mean what an interpreter already knows prior to
communication.

14. The main idea presented here was made long ago by Michael Dummett in
the classic Dummett (1959).

15. On Cappelen and Lepore's analysis, the mixed quotation, "Alice said life is
'difficult to understand'," entails the indirect quotation, "Alice said that life is difficult to understand." For, their paratactic analysis of the former entails their paratactic analysis of the latter. Thus, since in my example the indirect quotation, "Alice
said that life is difficult to understand," is false, so is the mixed quotation, "Alice
said that life is 'difficult to understand'."

16. Suppose I assertively utter, "Life is hard to comprehend," and Alice assertively utters, "Either life is difficult to understand or it stinks." Then there is at
least one thing we both said: she said it, in part, by way of her sub-utterance of the
first disjunct, "Life is difficult to understand," and I said it by way of my utterance,
with which her sub-utterance is synonymous. Hence, her sub-utterance samesaid
mine even though I was the one who stated (in one way) that life is difficult to understand whereas she did not.

17. I am ignoring the fact that the mixed quotation in (7) is subject to different
scope-readings. If anything, that indirectly supports my claim that Nika's utterance
of (6) does not samesay anything that Marc uttered in his utterance of (7) in the
synonymous sense of "samesay." I will focus on the narrow scope-reading of "someone" in (7) since Cappelen and Lepore's analysis applies on that interpretation.

18. For a defense of this line of reply, see Neale (1990).

19. On certain semantic views, e.g., Fregean ones, sameness of truth-conditions is insufficient for samesaying. For example, on this view, utterances of "Hesperus is Hesperus" and "Hesperus is Phosphorus," have exactly the same referential truth-conditions but do not say the same thing.

20. At our APA session, Cappelen and Lepore gave this reply. They develop their idea of the samesay relation as being a pragmatically determined relation more fully in Cappelen and Lepore (1997b).

21. This is not a wildly implausible hypothesis given that "what a speaker said" can have different meanings. As Kent Bach noted, it can be used to describe the case in which a speaker meant something she said (i.e., meant what the words she used mean) and meant something else as well. It can be used to cover the case in which a speaker did not mean what she said but meant something entirely different, as in the Cassius example. It can also be used to describe the case in which the speaker says something and not mean anything at all by it. For a nice discussion of these distinctions and other related topics, see Bach and Harnish (1979).

22. Cappelen and Lepore argue for this claim in Cappelen and Lepore (1997b).

23. Cappelen and Lepore argue that there is no conceptual or theoretical connection between a truth-conditional semantics for a natural language and the truth-conditions for indirect assertion-reports made in the language, cf. Cappelen and Lepore (1997c). If they are right, then that would undermine the Davidsonian project of explaining the role of a truth-theoretic semantics in an explanation of linguistic understanding.

24. It goes without saying that Sam did not mean, by his utterance, this bizarre reading of the complement of (21): Sam has an extremely warm (temperature-wise) gold watch to sell to Ned.

25. I am indebted to the following individuals for their very helpful comments on an earlier version of this paper and for discussions on this general topic: Kent Bach, Hugh Benson, Kirk Ludwig, William Lycan, Adam Morton, Greg Ray, and Chris Swoyer. And, I am especially grateful to Herman Cappelen and Ernie Lepore for their detailed and valuable comments on my paper and for their discussions of their view.

References

Bach, K. and R. M. Harnish. 1979. *Linguistic Communication and Speech Acts.* Cambridge: MIT Press.

Burge, T. 1986. "On Davidson's 'Saying That'." *In Truth and Interpretation,* edited by E. Lepore, Oxford: Basil Blackwell: 190–208.

Cappelen, H. and E. Lepore. 1997a. "Varieties of Quotation." *Mind* 106: 429–450.

———. 1997b. "Semantic Theory and Indirect Speech." *Protosociology.* 10: 4–18.

———. 1997c. "On An Alleged Relationship Between Indirect Speech and Semantic Theory." *Mind and Language.* 12: 278–296.

Davidson, D. 1986a. "On Saying That." Reprinted *in Inquires Into Truth and Interpretation,* edited by D. Davidson, (Oxford: Oxford University Press). First published in *Synthese* 19: 130–146.

————. 1986b. "Quotation." Reprinted *in Inquires Into Truth and Interpretation,* edited by D. Davidson, (Oxford: Oxford University Press). First published in Theory and Decision 11: 27–40.

————. 1986c. "Reply To Foster." Reprinted in *Inquires Into Truth and Interpretation,* edited by D. Davidson, Oxford: Oxford University Press. Originally published in *Truth and Meaning: Essays in Semantics,* edited by Gareth Evans and John McDowell, Oxford: Oxford University Press, 1976.

Dummett, Michael. 1959. "Truth." *Proceedings of the Aristotelian Society* 59. Higginbotham, James. 1986. "Linguistic Theory and Davidson's Semantic Program." In *Truth and Interpretation,* edited by E. Lepore, Oxford: Basil Blackwell, 29–48.

Lepore, E. and B. Loewer. 1989a. "You Can Say That Again." In *Midwest Studies in Philosophy,* edited by P. A. French, T. E. Uehling, Jr., and H. Wettstein, 338–356, Notre Dame: University of Notre Dame Press.

————. 1989b. "What Davidson Should Have Said." *Grazer Philosophische Studien* 36: 65–78.

————. 1990. "A Study In Comparative Semantics." In *Propositional Attitudes,* edited by C. Anderson and J. Owens, Stanford: CSLI Publications, pp. 91–112.

Neale, S. 1990. *Descriptions.* Cambridge: MIT Press.

Segal, G. 1989. "A Preference for Sense and Reference." *The Journal of Philosophy.* 86: 73–89.

Stainton, R. 1997. "Remarks On The Syntax And Semantics Of Mixed Quotation." Photocopy.

Washington, C. 1992. "The Identity Theory of Quotation." *The Journal of Philosophy.* 89: 582–605.

9

Compositional Quotation (without Parataxis)

Paul M. Pietroski

Cappelen and Lepore (henceforth, "C&L") draw attention to the under-discussed phenomenon of mixed quotation, and use this phenomenon as a touchstone for their unified account of opacity. This is a good strategy for achieving a desirable end. Building on Davidson's (1968, 1979) work, C&L offer a paratactic account of constructions like

(1) Nora said that Fido 'yelped'.

which exhibit features of both direct and indirect quotation. C&L's proposal concerning these mixed cases conjoins their treatments of direct and indirect quotation, as in

(2) Nora said 'Fido yelped'.
(3) Nora said that Fido yelped.

And while C&L do not extend their proposal to propositional attitude constructions like

(4) Nora believes that Fido yelped.

others (including Lepore and Loewer (1989)) have made useful suggestions on this front.

It is no small achievement to have offered a *common* explanation for why substitution of coreferential terms for 'Fido' in (1)–(3) affects the truth conditions of the matrix sentences. Moreover, C&L can explain why (1) entails (3)—and even why (1) follows from (2), on the assumption that Nora speaks our language. This reveals the strengths of paratactic approaches.

And fairly enough, C&L offer a challenge to those who reject paratactic theories: provide another unified treatment of opacity; or show why opacity is not a unified phenomenon.[1] C&L also ask that alternatives be compared for simplicity and elegance, respects in which their account rates highly. But there are other virtues. For example, a semantic theory should account for the facts concerning quantificational examples, like 'Every lawyer$_i$ admitted that he$_i$ lied'. And other things equal, a semantic theory should mesh with our best syntactic theory, in that the structural descriptions (of sentences) required by the semantics are provided *and independently motivated* by the syntax. Here, C&L's proposal fares less well. But I agree with their general point: those who reject paratactic theories have tended to focus on attitude ascriptions, thereby ignoring valuable data about quotation; and it would be a strong point in favor of paratactic theories, if they offered the *only* unified account of opacity. So I take up C&L's challenge. I contend that opacity arises because of a gap between compositionality and substitutivity; and Fregeans can exploit this gap to provide a unified theory of opacity. My proposal, developed more fully elsewhere (Pietroski 1996), is broadly Davidsonian. But *pace* C&L, I think appeals to interpreted logical forms can help in providing a non-paratactic semantics of quotation.

1.

For familiar reasons, I assume that natural languages are compositional in the following sense:

> the meaning of a word fixes its semantic value (perhaps relative to a context) in sentences; coreferential expressions have the same semantic value; and the truth conditions of a sentence S are determined, given S's logical form, by the semantic values of S's constituents.

I take it that C&L (as good Davidsonians) share this view; so I will not worry here about its defense. It can seem that any compositional language must respect a principle of substitutivity:

> if a sentence $S2$ of the language is the result of replacing some expression in sentence $S1$ with a coreferential expression, then $S1$ and $S2$ have the same truth conditions.

For if the semantic values of words fix the truth conditions of sentences (given logical form), it can seem that substituting terms with the same semantic value must preserve truth. But substitutivity apparently fails in cases like (1)–(4).

Suppose that every night, Nora hears her neighbor's dog yelping, where-upon the neighbor yells 'Fido, be quiet'; each morning, Nora sees a quiet dog walking in the park with someone who says, 'Good dog, Rex'; and un-beknownst to Nora, the morning dog *is* the evening dog. If Rex is Fido, then 'Rex' and 'Fido' are presumably coreferential (and thus have the same se-mantic value). Yet compare:

(1) Nora said that Fido 'yelped'.   (5) Nora said that Rex 'yelped'.
(2) Nora said 'Fido yelped'.   (6) Nora said 'Rex yelped'.
(3) Nora said that Fido yelped.   (7) Nora said that Rex yelped.
(4) Nora believes that Fido yelped.   (8) Nora believes that Rex
                                              yelped.

Each of (1)–(4) can be true, while (5)–(8) are false; substituting 'Rex' for the coreferential 'Fido' affects truth. Quine (1953) drew attention to other apparent failures of substitutivity:

(9) Slim is so-called because he is thin.
(10) Jim is so-called because he is thin.

Even if 'Jim' is coreferential with 'Slim', (10) can be false while (9) is true. And similarly for

(11) Slim is often called that by his wife.
(12) Jim is often called that by his wife.

Or consider:

(13) If the first name in this sentence rhymes with the second, then James is taller than Tim.
(14) If the first name in this sentence rhymes with the second, then Jim is taller than Tim.

Suppose that James (a.k.a. Jim) is *shorter* than Tim. The material condi-tional (13) is true, since its antecedent is false; but (14) is false, even though 'Jim' has been substituted for 'James'.

In (9)–(14), it is not hard to explain why substitutivity fails. An obvious suggestion for (9)–(10) is that 'so-' has a (context-dependent) semantic value, and this value is determined by the phonetic (or orthographic) prop-erties of the matrix subject. This suggestion seems unavoidable in (11)–(12), which involves overt demonstratives; here it seems clear that substituting 'Jim' for 'Slim' affects the semantic value of 'that'. And in (13)–(14), the description 'the first name in this sentence' is satisfied by different names. These cases involve a kind of self-reference: the semantic value of one expression depends on features of some other expression in the same sentence. But this does not threaten compositionality. The semantic value of the whole is still determined by the semantic values of the parts; though some parts get their semantic values in a nonstandard way. Thus, I am inclined to draw the following moral from (9)–(14):

> The effect of a term T on the truth of its matrix sentence may not be wholly determined by T's semantic value, since T might affect the truth of its matrix sentence in two ways: directly, by virtue of the fact that T has a certain semantic value; and indirectly, by virtue of the fact that the semantic value of some other expression in the sentence depends on properties (other than the semantic value) of T. But this does not touch the claim that the semantic value of a complex expression (relative to context C) is determined by the semantic values of its constituents (relative to C), given the expression's logical form.

And I think this moral applies, in an important way, to (1)–(8).

I have been using 'semantic value' where Frege (1892) would have used '*Bedeutung*'. Recall that Frege's notion of *Bedeutung* was rooted in his idea that every meaningful expression has a semantic power—*viz.*, the power to affect the truth of sentences in which the expression appears. But (9)–(14) suggest that if effects on truth include an expression's indirect effects—*i.e.*, the effects on truth an expression has because it affects the *Bedeutung* of another expression—then terms with the same *Bedeutung* will not always have the same semantic power. Alternatively, if a semantic power is the power to affect truth values directly, then substituting terms with the same semantic power will not always preserve truth. Either way, Frege's notion of substitutivity is sometimes violated. And this suggests a general strategy for dealing with opacity: find a way to exploit the idea that substitutivity can fail, since the semantic value of some expression in the sentence can (without violating compositionality) depend on features (other than the semantic value) of *another* expression in the sentence.[2]

It is worth noting the difference between (9)–(14) and similar examples like:

(15a) Fido yelped. Nora said so.   (16a) Fido yelped. Nora said that.
(15b) Rex yelped. Nora said so.   (16b) Rex yelped. Nora said that.

A natural claim about (15)–(16) is that the truth conditions of the second sentences are affected by substitutions made in the first sentence, because the second sentence has a term ('so'/ 'that') whose semantic value depends on a feature (affected by the substitution) of the first sentence. But here, there is no failure of substitutivity. No single sentence in (15)–(16) is such that replacing a term in *it* with a coreferential term affects the truth conditions of the whole: substitutions occur in the first sentences, where truth conditions are unchanged; and while the truth conditions of the second sentences differ, so do the semantic values of 'so'/'that'.

With such cases in mind, one might try to explain away all apparent failures of substitutivity with paratactic analyses, according to which the substitution does not occur in a sentence that includes the term whose semantic value is affected by the substitution. This is an initially attractive idea: *apparent failures of substitutivity are merely apparent; and a correct analysis of logical form removes the misleading appearance.* But as Stainton (this volume) noted, such hypotheses about logical form face serious difficulties. For example, it is hard to see how to capture the truth conditions of

(17)   Every lawyer$_i$ admitted that he$_i$ lied.

if 'he' is not a constituent of the same sentence as 'every lawyer'. But if 'he' and 'every lawyer' are constituents of the same sentence in (17), then similarly for 'Nora' and 'Fido' in

(3)   Nora said that Fido yelped.

And then replacing 'Fido' with 'Rex' in (3) provides a *genuine* counterexample to substitutivity.

Similarly, C&L will be hard pressed to extend their account of opacity to cover (9)–(14), without implausible hypotheses about the relevant logical forms. Moreover, we do not *need* paratactic hypotheses to preserve compositionality, if failures of substitutivity are compatible with compositionality. In that case, we may as well have a syntactically innocent logical form: 'that' is a *complementizer* in (3); and 'Fido' is a constituent of the same sentence as 'Nora'. My suggestion is that (1)–(8) all contain complementizers, and that this makes these sentences relevantly like (9)–(14), because complementizers allow for a kind of sentence-internal reference: the semantic value of a complementizer can depend on features of embedded expressions.

2.

A simple proposal would be that the semantic value of the complementizer in 'S said that p' is the Fregean sense of the embedded sentence 'p'; where the sense of a sentence is determined (given its logical form) by the senses of its component expressions. Then the sentences

(3)   Nora said that Fido yelped.

(7) Nora said that Rex yelped.

would have different truth conditions. For so long as 'Fido' and 'Rex' differ in sense, the complementizers in (3) and (7) would have different semantic values, even though 'Fido' and 'Rex' have the same semantic value. This proposal would be like Frege's treatment of attitude ascriptions, minus his (problematic) claim that the semantic value of an embedded term *is* its customary sense. But this is not a fully satisfactory account of 'that'-clauses, for reasons (having to do with Mates-type sentences) discussed in Pietroski (1996). And in any case, assigning senses as the semantic values of complemetizers provides no basis for an account of quotation. To provide a unified treatment of opacity, I need to introduce a bit of technical apparatus.

Let a *linguistic form* be a phrase marker whose terminal nodes are lexical items. A phrase marker is a suitably labeled *tree:* a partial ordering of points, such that the resulting structure has a unique root; where each point—*i.e.,* each node of the tree—is labeled as a token of some syntactic type in accordance with a correct theory of syntax for the language in question (see Higginbotham (1986)). Let a lexical item be an n-tuple of features, including a phonetic form and a point labeled as a terminal phrase marker node. How much information is lexicalized is an empirical question. But at a minimum, verbs have subcategorization features that constrain which phrase markers the verbs can appear in—*e.g.,* 'yelped' takes a noun-phrase subject and no object (NP [V]), while 'hit' takes noun-phrase subjects and objects (NP [V NP]). The linguistic forms of 'Fido yelped' and 'Rex yelped' can thus be represented in Figure 1.

We get an interpretation of a linguistic form, by replacing each terminal node with an interpretation of that lexical item, and each nonterminal node with the interpretation of the relevant expression (which will be determined by the interpretation of its constituents, given logical form). Those who have appealed to such entities have typically taken the interpretation of an expression to be its semantic value (*Bedeutung*). But this is not mandatory.[3] One can replace each terminal node with the *sense* of that lexical item, and each nonterminal node with the *sense* of the relevant expression. The result is the sense of a sentence, perhaps relative to a context of use. For 'Fido yelped' and 'Rex yelped', we get

Here the nodes are *ways of thinking about:* the common truth value of the two sentences, the dog Fido/Rex, and the semantic value of 'yelped'; where $WT_{fy} \neq WT_{ry}$, since $WT_f \neq WT_r$. On this view, an interpreted linguistic form (ILF) is the pairing of a linguistic form with its *sense*.

Now suppose that in 'that *p*': the semantic value of 'that' is the ILF of '*p*'; and the semantic value of 'that *p*' is the *second element of* the semantic value of 'that'. Then the semantic value of 'that' in 'that Fido yelped' is the ordered pair

and the semantic value of 'that Fido yelped' is the second element of this pair (*i.e.*, the sense of 'Fido yelped'). The semantic value of 'that' in 'that Rex yelped' is the ordered pair

and the semantic value of 'that Rex barks' is the second element of this pair (*i.e.,* the sense of 'Rex yelped'). This captures an attractive idea: a 'that'-clause abstracts away from specifically linguistic features of the embedded sentence, leaving the sense expressed. Hence, a German 'daß'-clause can share its semantic value with an English 'that'-clause. And since there is no shifting of semantic values inside 'that'-clauses, semantic innocence is preserved; 'Fido' and 'Rex' have the same value, even in 'that'-clauses. So there is no difficulty with sentences like

(18) Nora said that Fido$_i$ barks, and he$_i$ does bark.

Replacing 'Fido' with 'Rex' affects the semantic value of the *complementizer*.[4]

Suppose that quoted sentences are complementizer phrases, like 'that'-clauses. Indeed, I will speak of 'quote'-clauses. For the idea is to render (2) and (6) as (2Q) and (6Q):

(2) Nora said 'Fido yelped'.   (6) Nora said 'Rex yelped'.
(2Q) Nora said quote Fido yelped. (6Q) Nora said quote Rex yelped.

where 'quote' (like 'that') is a complementizer that introduces an embedded sentence. If the semantic value of a complementizer is the ILF of the sentence it introduces, then: in 'quote Fido yelped', the semantic value of 'quote' is the first of the two ordered pairs represented above; and in 'quote Rex yelped', the semantic value of 'quote' is the second of the two ordered pairs represented above. In general, the semantic value of 'quote' in 'quote *P*' is the ILF of '*P*'.

The simplest proposal about 'quote *P*' is that its semantic value just *is* the semantic value of the complementizer 'quote'.[5] Then the semantic values of 'quote Fido yelped' and 'quote Rex yelped' would be the (distinct) interpreted linguistic forms represented above. The idea is that the semantic value of a complementizer ('that' or 'quote') is the ILF of its complement. But the semantic value of a complementizer phrase is either the second element of the relevant ILF, or both elements, depending on which complementizer is used. So I must treat 'that' and 'quote' as different *kinds* of complementizers—*indirect* and *direct,* respectively. (This is independently plausible: 'that' must be followed by a complete sentence; while any part of speech can be quoted, as in 'Nora yelled "Fire!" when she saw smoke'.) This proposal can be formalized as follows, where 'Val($[_X$ ...$]$, Φ) = Z' means that Z is the value of expression $[_X$ ...$]$ in context Φ:

> Val($[_C$ ...$]$, Φ) = the ILF of the sentence introduced by the complementizer $[_C$ ...$]$ in Φ
> Val($[_{CP}$ $[_{C(i)}$ ...$][_S$ ...$]]$, Φ) = the second element of Val($[_{C(i)}$ ...$]$, Φ)
> Val($[_{CP}$ $[_{C(d)}$ ...$][_S$ ...$]]$, Φ) = Val($[_{C(d)}$ ...$]$, Φ)

This captures the intuition that 'quote'-clauses, unlike 'that'-clauses, do not abstract away from lexical/phonetic content. But substituting terms with the same semantic value can affect truth in quotational contexts for the same reason that such substitution can affect truth in attitude ascriptions: the semantic value of a complementizer depends on features (other than the semantic values) of the words in its scope. Substituting 'Rex' for 'Fido' in

(2Q) Nora said quote Fido yelped.

affects the semantic value of the complementizer 'quote', and hence the 'quote'-clause.

Initially, one might want to treat (2Q) on a par with an indirect discourse report like

(3) Nora said that Fido yelped.

where the complementizer phrase serves as direct object. But then 'said' would have to be true of: <agent, ILF> pairs, to accommodate (2Q); *and* <agent, sense> pairs to accommodate (3). Other things equal, one wants to avoid positing such diversity in the extension of verbs. Moreover, Munro (1982) offers several reasons for not treating direct discourse reports as transitive constructions. So one might treat (2Q) adverbially: Nora *said 'Fido yelped'-ly* (compare *ate quickly* or *muttered angrily*); where the 'quote'-clause is a complementizer phrase that is part of an adverbial phrase whose adverb is unvoiced. That is, the logical form of (2Q) might be:

(2Q-adv)   Nora said [quote Fido yelped]-(ly).

with the verb phrase depicted more perspicuously as follows:

$[_{VP} [_V \text{ said}] [_{AdvP} [_{CP} [_{C(d)} \text{ quote}]][_S \text{ Fido yelped}]] [_{Adv} \text{ (null)}]]]$

Treating adverbs along lines suggested by Davidson (1967), the idea would be that (2Q-adv) is true, if and only if: Nora was the agent of a saying, and the saying was done in a 'Fido barks' manner—*i.e.,* Nora said something by using (the interpreted linguistic form) 'Fido yelped'.[6]

Now consider a case where direct quotation occurs inside a 'that'-clause, as in:

(1) Nora said that Fido 'yelped'.

If (1) is true, Nora used the word 'yelped'. So perhaps (1) is a shortening of:

(1-adv) Nora said that Fido yelped 'yelped'(-ly).

where the direct object of 'said' is a 'that'-clause, and the basic verb phrase is modified adverbially by 'yelped'. The idea is that the verb phrase of (1-adv), which can be represented as

$$[_{VP} [_{V'}[_V \text{ said}][_{CP} [_{C(i)} \text{ that}][_S \text{ Fido yelped}]]]$$
$$[_{AdvP}[_{CP} [_{C(d)} \text{ quote}][_V \text{ yelped}]]][_{Adv} \text{ (null)}]]]$$

is true of those x, such that: x was the agent of a saying, the sense of 'Fido yelped' is what x said, *and* x did the saying in a 'yelped' manner.

C&L envision the possibility of such a treatment. Indeed, it is not far from the spirit of their own proposal. For they effectively treat (1) as follows:

(1-C&L)   Nora said that thusly: Fido *yelped.*

where 'that' refers to a sentential utterance and 'thus' refers to a subsentential utterance. So unless C&L are claiming (implausibly) that 'said' takes *three* arguments, it seems that they are appealing to some adverbial adjunct, in order to let the subsentential 'yelped' have a semantic effect on the matrix truth conditions. As C&L note, a virtue of their treatment is that they get 'yelped' to do double-duty; and they need not suppose that (1) is a *shortening* of anything. In this sense, C&L's account of mixed quotation is more elegant and simple than the one sketched here. But paratactic theories have other troubles. And it is not implausible to suppose that mixed quotation is a complicated use of language calling for a somewhat complicated analysis. I think C&L are right to ask for unified treatment of opacity; but a unified account may treat some examples of opacity as more complex than others.

3.

Let me end with a related point that C&L take up elsewhere (Cappelen and Lepore 1997). In

(19) Nicola said that Alice is a 'philtosopher'.

quotation is used to signal that 'philtosopher' is not a word of standard English, even though Nicola's report (of what Alice said) involved the phonetic form in question; and the utterer of (19) produces that phonetic form in the context of quotation. C&L say, and I agree, that an utterance of (19) could be true. An utterance that fails to express anything in English can samesay one of Nicola's utterances. (An utterance of 'der schee ist weiss' expresses nothing in English, but it can still samesay an utterance of 'snow is white'.) And I agree that a speaker of English can produce an utterance that expresses nothing in English yet samesays one of Nicola's utterances; for a speaker of English might *also* speak another language (like German). But in my view, an utterance of (19) cannot be an utterance of a sentence in standard English.

I think speakers *use* the words inside 'that'-causes. And one can *use* only words of standard English in standard English sentences. There may be a sense in which 'philtosopher' is used *and* mentioned in (19). But if it is not used, the 'that'-clause would be ill-formed, and so would (19). C&L will deny that a speaker of (19) must use 'philtosopher' in a sentence. For on a paratactic theory, a speaker of (19) utters the sentence 'Nicola said that' followed by a speech act *which need not be the uttering of a sentence in the speaker's language:* a speaker of (19) might, without uttering a sentence, do something that samesays with one of Nicola's utterances. But paratactic analyses are implausible and unnecessary. So if (19) is true, I conclude, it is not a sentence of standard English. And I think another aspect of Davidson's work is relevant here.

A speaker of standard English can understand Mrs. Malaprop, if she utters

(20) This is a nice derangement of epitaphs.

Mrs. Malaprop can be understood as saying that a certain object is a nice arrangement of epithets. And later on, the hearer might say to Mrs. Malaprop

(21) You said before that this is a nice derangement of epitaphs.

That is, a speaker of standard English can learn to converse in Mrs. Malaprop's nonstandard idiolect. In Davidson's (1986) terms, Mrs. Malaprop and her conversational partner can come to share a *passing theory* that is not a theory of standard English; and elsewhere (Pietroski 1994), I have defended Davidson's diagnosis of such communicative episodes. But here, let me just suggest that (19) is an interesting sentence in which *lots* of issues about interpretation converge. From a compositional semanticist's point of view, however, I think (19) should be glossed as

(19-adv)   Nicola said that Alice is a philtosopher 'philtosopher'-ly.

where 'Nicola said that Alice is a philtosopher' is *not* a sentence of standard English, but rather a sentence of Nicola's nonstandard idiolect (which is comprehensible to others besides Nicola).

C&L are likely to reply that this response to (19) trades on an inessential feature of the example—*viz.*, that 'philtosopher' can be interpreted in passing-theory fashion as the translation of an actual English word. But what if the term quoted within a 'that'-clause was nonsensical? One might imagine a speaker of standard English producing an utterance of:

(22) Nicola said that Alice was 'mimsy'.

Suppose that Nicola produced an utterance with a phonetic form that we might indicate with 'Alice was mimsy'. Here there seem to be two possibilities: in Nicola's idiolect, 'mimsy' has a meaning, though not one the speaker of (22) grasps; or Nicola's own utterance about Alice failed to have a meaning. In the second case, I think (22) is false: Nicola didn't *say* anything; she didn't express a proposition. How one responds to the first case will depend on whether one thinks a speaker can express a proposition with words whose meaning the speaker does not grasp. For the speaker of (22) seems like a person who knows no physics, but utters

(23) The physicist said that 'quarks' have 'charm'.

If a speaker can express propositions by "borrowing ungrasped meanings" from others, then perhaps (22) is like (19), with the added complication of meaning-borrowing. On the other hand, one might deny that (22) expresses any clear proposition at all; though of course, that would not preclude an utterance of (22) from achieving some pragmatic end—like conveying various things to the hearer about certain features (including semantic features) of Nicola's utterance.

My aim is not to provide a definitive diagnosis of these complicated cases. It is just to note that C&L cannot rely on such cases as support for their proposal. Cases of linguistic confusion are interesting; but I don't think we can use them to adjudicate between alternative accounts of opacity. (It seems better to use an independently motivated theory to describe such examples, than to suppose that we have reliable pretheoretic intuitions about them.) And I have tried to show that C&L's paratactic account is not the only unified account of opacity available.

While I have used a Fregean theory to make this point, I would not be surprised if other theorists could exploit the gap between compositionality and substitutivity in providing their own treatments of substitutivity failures. The issue, then, is how to compare the simplicity and elegance of C&L's proposal with the other virtues one can achieve by abandoning paratactic hypotheses about logical form. But once we see that parataxis is not the only unified game in town, the facts that Stainton (this volume) points to can and should receive considerable weight.

Notes

1. C&L say that an account of opacity must respect their theses C1-C4. But I have doubts about their claim that direct and indirect quotation must receive distinct semantic treatments. It is not clear that (2) would be true, if Nora knew no English—or if her "utterance" was made merely in an attempt to clear her throat. I suspect that C&L are operating with tendentious (nominalistic and/or behavioristic) assumptions about what counts as an utterance of a sentence. And while I cannot address this complex issue here, it will be in the background at several points below.

2. One might argue that (9–14) do not violate substitutivity. If (9) is uttered in a context where 'so-' is associated with a demonstration of 'Slim', one might insist on evaluating (10) relative to contexts with the same act of demonstration. In such contexts, (9) is true. (The semantic value of 'so-' need not depend on a term in its own sentence, as in, "Slim is a nice guy. He is so-called because he is thin.") Analogous replies will not be available for my proposal concerning 'that'-clauses: I treat 'that' as an indexical whose semantic value is always a feature of the embedded sentence; so one cannot hold context fixed while changing the embedded sentence. Thus, genuine counterexamples to substitutivity are at least possible; and I think 'that'-clauses provide actual counterexamples. In any case, (9–14) are counterexamples to the following principle: $E1$ (as uttered in context $\Phi1$) and $E2$ (as uttered in a context $\Phi2$, like $\Phi1$, except that $E2$ was uttered instead of $E1$) have the same semantic value, if they differ only in that some term T appears in $E1$ where T^* appears in $E2$, given that T^* has (in $\Phi2$) the same semantic value as T (in $\Phi1$).

3. And it leads to difficulties. For example, 'Nora believes that that is a ship' can be true in one context yet false in another, even if the same ship was demonstrated in both contexts. (Larson and Ludlow (1993) have a reply; but *cf.* Pietroski (1996).) For related reasons, I prefer to speak of interpreted *linguistic* forms, as opposed to interpreted *logical* forms.

4. If the semantic value of an embedded term is its customary sense, the coreferencing indicated in (18) cannot be as simple as it seems, else 'he' would refer to a sense. Earlier, I said that 'Every lawyer$_i$ admitted that he$_i$ lies' presents a difficulty for paratactic theories, since 'he$_i$' and 'Every lawyer$_i$' are constituents of the same

sentence. It is often thought that Fregeans also have a problem here—*viz.*, the sentence can be true, without there being any one way that each lawyer thinks of himself. But the sense of the variable 'he$_i$' can be (not a single sense, but) a function from possible ways of thinking about assignments to the variable to thoughts (determined in part by the senses of verb phrases with which the variable can combine). The idea is that 'Every lawyer$_i$ admitted that he$_i$ lies' is true, so long as each lawyer *x* believes admitted a thought determined by the sense of 'lies' and *some* way of thinking about *x*. (See Pietroski (1996)).

5. When talking *about* language, perhaps we use 'quote'-clauses purely syntactically: the semantic value of 'quote *p*' is the *first* element of the semantic value of 'quote'. But it is an *assumption* that, when quoting speech, we are just talking about language in this sense. I doubt that the sentence 'Nora screamed "Help!" when Nick fell' is *true*, if Nora's utterance sounded like 'Help,' but meant what 'Get up' means in English. (*Cf.* note 1 above.) One could, however, adjust what I say in the text to accommodate the tendentious assumption.

6. Pietroski (1998) offers an elaboration and defense of Davidson's event analysis, which turns out to have substantive consequences for the *sort* of event that can satisfy action predicates (including 'said') and be correctly described by adverbs of manner.

References

Cappelen, H. and E. Lepore. 1997. "Varieties of Quotation." *Mind* 106: 429–450.
Davidson, D. 1967. "The Logical Form of Action Sentences." In *The Logic of Decision and Action,* edited by N. Rescher. Pittsburgh: University of Pittsburgh Press.
———. 1968. "On Saying That." *Synthese* 19: 130–46.
———. 1979. "Quotation." *Theory and Decision* 11: 27–40.
———. 1986. "A Nice Derangement of Epitaphs." In *Truth and Interpretation,* edited by E. Lepore. Oxford: Basil Blackwell.
Frege, G. 1892. "Sense and Reference." In *Translations from the Philosophical Writings of Gottlob Frege,* translated by P. Geach and M. Black. Oxford: Blackwell, 1952.
Higginbotham, J. 1986. "Davidson's Program in Semantics." In *Truth and Interpretation,* edited by E. Lepore. Oxford: Basil Blackwell.
Larson, R. and P. Ludlow. 1993. "Interpreted Logical Forms." *Synthese* 95: 305–55.
Lepore, E. and B. Loewer. 1989. "You can Say *That* Again." In *Midwest Studies in Philosophy XIV: Contemporary Perspectives in the Philosophy of Language* II, edited by P. French *et al.* Notre Dame: University of Notre Dame Press.
Munro, P. 1982. "On the Transitivity of 'Say' Verbs." *Syntax and Semantics* 15: 301–18.
Pietroski, P. 1994. "A Defense of Derangment." *Canadian Journal of Philosophy* 24: 95–118.
———. 1996. Fregean Innocence. *Mind and Language* 11: 331–362.
———. 1998. "Actions, Adjuncts, and Agency." *Mind,* 107: 73–111.
Quine, W. V. O. 1953. "Reference and Modality." In *From a Logical Point of View.* Cambridge, MA: Harvard Univ. Press.

10

Remarks on the Syntax and Semantics of Mixed Quotation[1]

Robert J. Stainton

Cappelen and Lepore's "Varieties of Quotation" builds on Davidson (1968, 1979) to give an account of mixed quotation. The result is a rich paper, which introduces interesting data and raises many thought-provoking questions. Given this, I can't possibly discuss the paper in its entirety. Instead, I intend simply to paraphrase their position, develop it a little, and then raise a few concerns.

1. Paraphrase and Development

Let me begin with their example. Cappelen and Lepore give to sentence (1a) the neo-Davidsonian logical form in (1b).

(1)
(a) Alice said that life "is difficult to understand"
(b) $\exists u$[says (Alice, u) & samesays(u, that) & same-tokens(u, these)]. Life is difficult to understand

As a first pass: The logical form (1b) is true if and only if Alice said something which has both the same content and (at least in part) the same form as the demonstrated sentence 'Life is difficult to understand'. For Cappelen and Lepore, then, mixed quotation, like indirect quotation, gives the content of the reported utterance; and, like direct quotation, mixed quotation specifies (in part) the form of the reported utterance.

This is their proposal about what mixed quotation speech reports mean in English. But—a point which looms large in the following—the proposal isn't a *semantic theory* of mixed quotation reports . . . at least not yet. To get a semantics for mixed quotation Cappelen and Lepore need (at least) to specify some kind of *compositional mechanism* which, loosely speaking, takes mixed-quotation sentences as input and gives their meanings as output. (Less loosely speaking, the desired mechanism would take **surface structures** as input and give **logical forms** as output.) I want to begin by reflecting on what such a mechanism might look like. My reasons will emerge in due course.

Cappelen and Lepore aren't unaware of the need to provide a compositional mechanism for mixed quotations. They even provide a hint, in footnote 21, about what it would look like: 'says' in (1a), they maintain, takes as its grammatical object *both* the complement clause (2a) *and* the NP in (2b)—and this is why the sentence functions both as a direct and indirect speech report.

(2)
(a) $[_{CP}$ that $[_S$ life is difficult to understand]]
(b) $[_{NP}$ "life is difficult to understand"][2]

Putting aside the important question of how the verb 'says' can take two grammatical objects, this proposal demands an interpretive rule for 'say'— one which covers three possible cases: *nominal* object, *clausal* object, or both. Cappelen and Lepore don't provide an interpretive rule, but here's a simplified attempt. I intend it to be in the spirit of their view—so that, should there be problems with it, the problems will arise for their view as well.

(3) *Cappelen-Lepore Style Interpretive Rule for 'Says'*
(a) If the grammatical object of $\ulcorner\alpha$ says$\urcorner$ is of the form
$[_{CP}$ that $[_S$ β]] then generate the logical form
$\ulcorner\exists u[\text{says}(\alpha, u)$ & samesays $(u, \text{that})]$. β$\urcorner$[13]
(b) If the grammatical object of $\ulcorner\alpha$ says$\urcorner$ is of the form $[_{NP}$ "β"]
then generate the logical form $\ulcorner\exists u[\text{says}(\alpha, u)$ &
same-tokens $(u, \text{these})]$. β$\urcorner$
(c) If the grammatical object of $\ulcorner\alpha$ says$\urcorner$ is both of the form $[_{CP}$
that $[_S$ β]] and of the form $[_{NP}$ "β"] then generate the logical form $\ulcorner\exists u[\text{says }(\alpha, u)$ & samesays(u, that) &
same-tokens$(u, \text{these})]$. β$\urcorner$[14]

Returning to example (1a), rule (3) works as follows: Because, it's supposed, 'says' takes the clause (2a) as its grammatical object; and 'says' *also* takes the NP in (2b) as its grammatical object, both samesays and same-tokens enter into the logical form. By (3c).[5] (α in this case is 'Alice'; β is 'Life if difficult to understand'.) While 'samesays' deals with the content of the utterance, 'same-tokens' seizes on its form. Next step: 'that' demonstrates the whole of 'Life is difficult to understand', while 'these' demonstrates only 'is difficult to understand'. In which case, (1a) is predicted true iff Alice uttered something which (a) samesays 'Life is difficult to understand' and (b) same-tokens 'is difficult to understand'.

That, in a nutshell, is Cappelen and Lepore's proposal for the meaning of mixed quotation—fleshed out with a simplified compositional mechanism. I now want to consider some problems with the view. I'll begin with some difficulties it inherits directly from Davidson's paratactic view—in particular, his inclusion of a demonstrative in the logical form of speech reports.

2. Troubles with the "Demonstrative"

This section contains two arguments for the same conclusion: There is no demonstrative in the logical form of speech reports corresponding to the 'that' of 'says that'. If this is right, then there is no demonstrative, corresponding to 'that', in the logical form of *mixed quotation* speech reports. In which case, to put it bluntly, Cappelen and Lepore's proposal cannot work.

A Demonstrative in the Syntactic Structure?

As everybody knows, the English 'that' in speech reports corresponds to 'que' in French; and, of course, the word 'que' is not a demonstrative in French. This fact might suggest the following bad argument against Davidson's paratactic view:

(4) *The Bad Argument*
     Premise 1: The word 'que' in French belief reports isn't syntactically a demonstrative.
     Conclusion: Davidson's paratactic view is mistaken about French.

The argument in (4) is a glaring non-sequitur. As Lepore and Loewer say (1990: 98), "That a demonstrative does not appear, for example, in French and Italian propositional attitude sentences does not show that the paratactic account is wrong for these languages." One reason the premise doesn't entail the conclusion is this: There could be a demonstrative in the *logical form* of French speech reports, even if there is no demonstrative word in the surface structure.

Armed with this thought, consider the fact that, syntactically speaking, the *English* word 'that' which follows 'said' in (5a) is *not* the same word which precedes 'is a goof' in (5b).

(5)
(a) Alice said that Dole is a goof
(b) That is a goof

The former is a complementizer, not a demonstrative; the latter is a demonstrative, not a complementizer. In fact, these words are not in general pronounced the same: While the complementizer can be phonologically reduced to *th't,* or left out altogether, the demonstrative cannot. Given this, a different bad argument can be mounted—this time about English. And it too can be rebutted with ease.

(6) *The Bad Argument—English Version*
     Premise 1: The word 'that' in English belief reports isn't syntactically a demonstrative.
     Conclusion: Davidson's paratactic view is mistaken about English.
     Rebuttal: Even if there isn't a demonstrative word in the English surface structure, there could be one in the logical form of English belief reports.

I rehearse these bad arguments to distinguish them from my own quarrel with Davidson's paratactic account (and with Cappelen and Lepore). My argument is obviously different from the foregoing because, unlike them, mine is a pretty good argument. Here it is. (α and θ are variables over linguistic expressions.)

(7) *The Pretty Good Argument*
     Premise 1: The 'that' of 'says that' is not a demonstrative word in the surface structure of speech reports.
     Premise 2: If α is not a demonstrative word in the surface structure of θ, then *ceteris paribus* there is no demonstrative corresponding to α in the logical form of θ.
     Conclusion 2: Ceteris paribus there is no demonstrative, corresponding to the 'that' of 'says that', in the logical form of speech reports.

This argument is valid. Is it sound? In particular, is Premise 2 true?[6] I believe so—because it is supported by the following Interface Rule. And, as I'll now suggest, the Interface Rule itself is true—both in general, and in the case at hand.

(8) *Interface Rule: Ceteris paribus,* a hypothesis about logical form which respects syntax is preferable to a hypothesis which does not.

Given (8), the fact that English (and French) speech reports don't (generally) contain demonstrative terms in surface syntax suggests— doesn't entail, but suggests—that there's no demonstrative in their logical form. But why believe (8)? There is, first of all, a very good methodological reason: Downplaying syntax, when doing semantics, is a risky business. As I said above, semantics has two parts: On the one hand, the semanticist attempts to find the meaning of the various forms in the language; on the other hand, she looks for the compositional rules which map these forms onto their meanings. If you are interested in the mapping from structure to meaning, you obviously cannot ignore syntax: that would be to ignore one of the relata in the relation. (A familiar example: One solid motivation for assigning generalized quantifiers to English quantifier phrases, rather than treating them syncategorematically as Russell did, is that quantifier phrases are *syntactic constituents* of English sentences.) Indeed, even if your interest is restricted to finding out what expressions mean, you cannot ignore the combinatorial task—because *which* meaning ought to be assigned to an expression *E* will sometimes depend, in part, on what the simplest, most plausible, compositional mechanism assigns to *E*. So, semanticists ignore syntax at their peril.

A second reason for endorsing the Interface Rule: It is useful elsewhere. Consider the following case. Some wacky semanticist could, I suppose, convince himself that the Spanish (9a) has the logical form (9b):

(9)
(a) No sé si voy a ir [*trans.:* "I don't know whether I will go"]
(b) I don't know: Yes, I will go

Our eccentric semanticist might next conjecture that the logical form of the *English* 'I don't know whether I will go' is (9b) as well! This hypothesis is, I take it, quite absurd. How might we set this nutty semanticist straight? We might say: "But look, Spanish 'si' in (a) corresponds *not* to the English 'yes', but rather to the English 'whether'." To which he will undoubtedly reply: "That an affirmation marker does not appear in the corresponding English sentences does not show that my account is wrong." And he'll be right, because there could be an "affirmation marker" in the logical form of English sentences, even though there isn't one in surface structure. Nor need he be swayed by differences in intonation between affirmation-si and complementizer-si: He'll simply point out that, even if there isn't an affirmation word in the Spanish surface structure, there could be one at logical form.

Still, one need not give into the hypothesis that (9b) is the logical form of (9a)—and of its English translation. Here's one reason, among others:

Semantics should, *ceteris paribus,* respect syntax; and the syntax of English strongly suggests that (9b) isn't the logical form of the English sentence 'I don't know whether I will go'; similarly, comparative syntax suggests that 'I don't know: Yes, I will go' isn't the logical form of the Spanish (9a). Of course this response relies on (8), the Interface Rule. But surely the response, though not the only one possible, is among the reasonable rebuttals. And so is the Interface Rule on which it depends.

From here on, I'll assume that the Interface Rule in (8) is a sound principle. But does it apply to the case at hand? In particular, can it license the inference from Davidson's account not respecting syntax to its semantic inadequacy? The following example suggests that it can—and it provides more hints about *why* (8) is sound.

In discussing Davidson's paratactic account of propositional attitudes, Higginbotham (1986: 39) drew attention to sentences like 'Every boy believes that he is a nice fellow', in which a pronoun in the complement clause is bound by a quantifier in the matrix sentence. Mixed quotational sentences can be like this too. Witness (10).

(10) Every student says that she "is cool"

How would Cappelen and Lepore treat this sentence? The rough-and-ready rule I gave in (3) obviously will not work: If we take as α the quantifier phrase 'every student', the predicted logical form is:

(11) $\exists u$[says (every student, u) & samesays(u, that) & same-tokens(u, these)]. She is cool

The logical form (11) gives the existential quantifier widest scope, which (wrongly) predicts that there is a single utterance produced collectively by all the students. Rule (3) can be fixed however, to accommodate quantifier phrases in subject position, without doing violence to Cappelen and Lepore's proposal. Here's the result:

(12) *Quantifier-Friendly Interpretive Rule for 'Says':*
      If the grammatical object of 'says' is both of the form
      $[_{CP}$ that $[_S \beta]]$ and of the form $[_{NP}$ "β"] then generate
      $\ulcorner \lambda x.\{\exists u$[says (x, u) & samesays(u, that) & same-tokens(u, these)]\}. $\beta \urcorner$ and combine this with the grammatical subject α of 'says'.

The grammatical subject α can, of course, combine with the resulting logical form in two ways: Roughly speaking, where α is a singular term it becomes the argument to the clausal complement, as in (13a); where α is a quantifier phrase, α serves as the functor, and the clausal complement becomes the argument, as in (13b). (Read $[\![\alpha]\!]$ as "the semantic value of α.")

(13)
   (a) $\lambda x.\{\exists u[\text{says}\ (x, u)\ \&\ \text{samesays}(u, \text{that})\ \&\ \text{same-tokens}$
              $(u, \text{these})]\}.([\![\alpha]\!]).\ \beta$

   (b) $[\![\alpha]\!]\ (\lambda x.\{\exists u[\text{says}\ (x, u)\ \&\ \text{samesays}(u, \text{that})\ \&\ \text{same-tokens}$
              $(u, \text{these})]\}).\ \beta$

   (c)   [every student]$(\lambda x.\{\exists u[\text{says}\ (x, u)\ \&\ \text{samesays}(u, \text{that})\ \&$
         $\text{same-tokens}(u, \text{these})]\})$. She is cool.

Given this revised rule, sentence (10) gets cashed as (13c), in which the universal quantifier is correctly given wide scope.

But, even post-revision, there remains a problem for the paratactic account. Sentence (10) has a bound variable reading for 'she'—and this isn't captured by (13c), *because 'she', in that logical form, isn't in the scope of any quantifier.* 'She', not being bound, gets read as a free variable/indexical in (13c). So sentence (10) is predicted to have only the meaning that every student said that, e.g., *that girl there* is cool—'she' being said while demonstrating this particular girl. Clearly this is wrong: The salient reading of (10) has each student saying *of herself* that she is cool.

Consider now a different account of the semantics of speech reports, summarized in (14) below. Crucially, it uses the fact that 'that' in speech reports is a complementizer; and, respecting (8), it does not introduce a demonstrative into the logical form of such sentences. Lacking a name, let's introduce a perfectly arbitrary label: The Oxford-MIT Rule. (Note: There are many rules which would do the job here. The Oxford-MIT Rule is merely an illustration.)

(14)   *The Oxford-MIT Rule:*
      If the syntactic structure of θ is of the form $[_{VP}[_{V}\ \text{says}]$
      $[_{CP}[_{C}\ \text{that}]\ [_{S}...]]]$ then the logical form of θ is
      $\lambda x.\{(\exists y)\lambda z.[\text{similar}(z)([_{S}\ ...])](y)=1\ \&\ <x, y>\in [\![\text{says}]\!]\}$

The Oxford-MIT Rule, devised as it was with syntax in mind, can take advantage of the indices in the surface structure of sentence (10). That structure is given below:

(15)

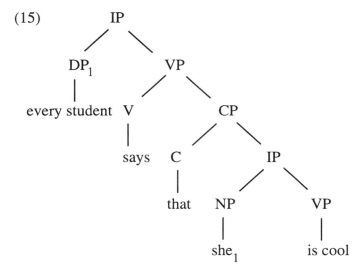

Taking this structure as input, the Oxford-MIT Rule (14) outputs the logical form (16a).

(16)
  (a) $[$every student$_1][\lambda x_2.\{(\exists y)\lambda z.[\text{similar}(z)([_S \text{ she}_1 \text{ is cool}])](y)=1$
          $\& <x_2,y>\in[\text{says}]\})$
  (b) $\forall x_1\{[\text{student}](x_1) \supset \lambda x_2.\{(\exists y)[\lambda z.[\text{similar}(z)([_S x_1 \text{ is cool}])](y)=1$
          $\& <x_2,y>\in[\text{says}](x_1)\}$

In essence, because 'she$_1$' in the embedded clause 'she$_1$ is cool' is co-indexed with the subject quantifier phrase in (16a), 'she$_1$' gets treated as a variable, bound by the universal quantifier. Applying the rule for a universal quantifier phrase, this gives rise to (16b). Applying lambda conversion—where, of course, x_2 gets changed to x_1—gives the salient reading for (10):

(17) $\forall x_1\{[\text{student}](x_1) \supset (\exists y)[\lambda z.[\text{similar}(z)([_S x_1 \text{ is cool}])](y)=1 \&$
         $<x_1,y>\in[\text{says}]\}$

The Davidsonian account—basically that in (12)—does not respect (8), and the fact that 'that' in speech reports is a complementizer; it *does* put a demonstrative into the logical form, and it thereby puts the complement clause outside the scope of any quantifier in the matrix sentence—which yields the wrong result. As Higginbotham (1986) puts the general point:

... indications of inscriptions are sealed off from any interaction with linguistic elements in main clauses. (p. 39)

The Oxford-MIT Rule, on the other hand, respects syntax. Doing so, it allows quantifiers (and other elements) in the matrix to bind items in the complement clause.[7] I think it's obvious that the Oxford-MIT Rule does better in this respect.

Could the neo-Davidsonian develop a compositional mechanism which handled this sort of sentence, while maintaining that there is a demonstrative in the logical form? I suppose so. Would the resulting compositional mechanism be as elegant and simple as that in (14)? I greatly doubt it. Ultimately, both accounts must provide a mapping from syntactic structure to the logical form each proposes for speech reports; but, and this is the crux of the matter, something like the Oxford-MIT Rule is likely to be simpler, more elegant and just plain better because it respects syntax. Syntactic structures are, after all, the *inputs* to semantic rules. So, semantic rules which profit from syntactic insights can't help but fare better. Generally speaking, anyway. That is why (8) is a sound inductive principle.

Another illustration of my contention that, in the case at hand, respecting syntax simplifies the semantics of speech reports. Some of our speech is declarative. But some of it isn't. And, when we speak in other moods, our speech can be reported; it can even be reported using mixed quotation. For instance, suppose Alice utters (18):

(18) Where did my brother buy all that beer?

Given that Alice's brother is John, I can truthfully report that:

(19) Alice asked where John "bought all that beer."

An account of mixed quotation must assign a meaning to (19); but neither the rough-and-ready rule in (3), nor the quantifier-friendly version in (12) will do the job. (For simplicity's sake, I'll discuss the former rule in what follows.) First, some obvious reasons: Sentence (19) doesn't contain the word 'says'; nor is the grammatical object of the speech-reporting verb of the form $[_{CP}$ that $[_S \beta]]$. Hence, strictly speaking, (3) does not apply. But this is easily taken care of: Just substitute 'speech-reporting verb' for 'says' in (3), and allow the grammatical object to be anything of the following form (taking γ to be a meta-linguistic variable over syntactic complementizers).

(20) $[_{CP} [_C \gamma] [_S \beta]]$

This yields the following generalized version of (3), where ψ is a speech reporting verb:

(21) *Generalized Cappelen-Lepore Interpretive Rule for Speech Reports:*
      If the grammatical object of ⌜α ψs⌝ is both of the form [$_{CP}$ [$_C$ γ]
      [$_S$ β]] and of the form [$_{NP}$ "β"] then generate the logical
      form ⌜∃u[ψs (α, u) & samesays(u, that) & same-tokens(u,
      these)]. β⌝.

This generalized version of (3) now applies to the syntactic structure of (19), 'Alice asked where John "bought all that beer"'.
     So much for obvious, and easily solved, difficulties with (3). Here's the harder case: What logical form does (21), the generalized version of (3), assign to (19)? If 'where' is treated as the syntactic complementizer in the surface structure—i.e., as [$_C$ γ]—then the predicted logical form is (22a); if, on the contrary, 'where' is treated as part of the embedded sentence—i.e., as part of [$_S$ β]—then the predicted logical form is (22b).

(22)
   (a) ∃u[asks (Alice, u) & samesays(u, that) & same-tokens(u,
          these)]. John bought all that beer
   (b) ∃u[asks (Alice, u) & samesays(u, that) & same-tokens(u,
          these)]. where John bought all that beer

Now, I'm not sure whether either of (22a–b) are well formed. But, even if they are, neither gives the right truth conditions for (19). Alice didn't ask *whether* John bought all that beer; she asked a where-question. Yet a whether-question would seem to be the only possible reading of (22a). As for (22b), it incorrectly says that Alice's utterance of 'Where did my brother buy all that beer?' samesays the *indirect question* 'where John bought all that beer'; but indirect questions and direct questions, though semantically related, are not samesayers: In the case at hand, the direct question denotes something propositional, while the indirect question denotes a location! Finally, of course, Alice didn't same-token 'bought all that beer'; she same-tokened 'buy all that beer'.
     One can react to this data about interrogative speech reports in two different ways. It certainly shows that Cappelen and Lepore's account is insufficiently general; so one could respond by trying to broaden the theory, while still refusing to respect syntax. I gather this is how the authors themselves will respond. I, on the other hand, take it as a sign that an account of speech reports which respects syntax is likely to be preferable. I won't burden you with such an account, but will simply note that the seeds of an account can be found in Higginbotham's (1993) recent work.

Okay then: The Interface Rule in (8), to prefer, *ceteris paribus*, a hypothesis about logical form which respects syntax, is reasonable (though defeasible); and, it appears to apply to the case at hand. Next point: The 'that' of 'says that' is not a demonstrative in the surface syntax of speech reports. This lends support to—though it does not entail—the conclusion that there is no demonstrative corresponding to 'that' in the logical form of speech reports. Hence Cappelen and Lepore's account is likely incorrect.[8]

Demonstrating "Rogue Utterances"

Here's a more direct argument: Whether or not there's a demonstrative in the surface structure of speech reports, positing a demonstrative in their logical form makes the wrong predictions about how speech reports get interpreted. Cappelen and Lepore cite with approval Davidson's (1979: 91) dictum that, "the device of pointing can be used on whatever is in range of the pointer . . ." I agree with the slogan. But I think it makes trouble for Davidson's paratactic account—and hence for Cappelen and Lepore. Notice: On Davidson's account, (23) is a perfect paraphrase of (5a):

(5a)   Alice said that Dole is a goof
(23)   Alice said that. Dole is a goof.

Now suppose I write on the board, 'Dole is a great patriot'. And suppose I say (23) while pointing to what is written on the board. I take it that, given these circumstances, I could assert that Alice said that Dole is a great patriot—following up my assertion by adding that, in my own opinion, Dole is a goof. Now compare an utterance of (5a), said while pointing at 'Dole is a great patriot'. Point how I may, in uttering (5a) I cannot report Alice as having said that Dole is a great patriot. There is, then, a striking contrast between (5a) and (23). What does the contrast amount to? The logical form of sentence (23) really does contain a demonstrative, and said demonstrative can be used to point to anything in the environment; the logical form of (5a), on the other hand, does not contain a demonstrative.[9]

This difficulty carries over to Cappelen and Lepore's account. According to them, sentence (1a) has the logical form (1b).

(1a)   Alice said that life "is difficult to understand"
(1b) $\exists u$[says (Alice, u) & samesays(u, that) & same-tokens(u, these)]. Life is difficult to understand

If that's right, one ought to be able to say (1a), point at a token of 'Dole is a great patriot', and thereby claim that some utterance of Alice's samesays

'Dole is a great patriot' and same-tokens 'is a great patriot'! In these circumstances an utterance of (1a) would mean, in effect:

(24) Alice said that Dole "is a great patriot." Life is difficult to
      understand

Obviously, no matter what is pointed at, (1a) cannot be used to say this.

In sum, because Cappelen and Lepore follow Davidson in positing a
demonstrative in the logical form of mixed quotations, they inherit two
problems: First, their theory does not respect syntax, which, given Interface
Rule (8) is a bad thing; second, their theory makes incorrect predictions
about how mixed quotation sentences can be used.

3. A Positive Alternative?

By now you'll be thinking: "Yes, there are difficulties with Cappelen and
Lepore's account of mixed quotation. But at least they *have* an account."
Fair enough, I owe a positive alternative. Here it is:

(25) *Rob's Mixed Quotation Rule:*
      Given a case of mixed quotation in a sentence θ, remove the
      relevant quotation marks. If the resulting syntactic struc-
      ture of θ is of the form $[_{VP}[_V$ says$][_{CP}[_C$ that$]$ $[_S...]]]$ then
      the logical form of this VP is $\lambda x.\{(\exists y)\lambda z.$
      $[\text{similar}(z)([_S ...])](y)=1$ & $<x,y>\in[\![\text{says}]\!]$.

Two observations about what (25) says, before I lay out some of its
virtues. Its first clause turns mixed quotations into indirect quotations; and
its second clause is just the Oxford-MIT Rule. In which case, (25) essentially treats mixed quotation as a variety of indirect quotation. Now for its
merits.

One thing that (25) has going for it is this: According to Cappelen and
Lepore, mixed quotation blends the devices of direct and indirect quotation. If that were right, there could be no mixed quotation device which was
not also a direct quotation device. Now, is it really so obvious that there
couldn't be a language which (a) had the translation of 'say' taking clausal
complements; (b) never has 'say' taking nominal complements—and yet
(c) exhibited mixed quotation? It would certainly *seem* possible. And this
would precisely be a language which had indirect and mixed quotation, but
no direct quotation. Travel to China might, I'm told, uncover such a language. But there are telling examples nearer to home. English has verbs
which can only be used in indirect speech reports; and yet they (margin-
ally?) allow *mixed* quotation with such verbs—even though direct quota-

tion is not an option. Sentence (26a) is reasonably well formed, for example; while (26b) is completely out.

(26)
   (a) Mary intimated that life "is difficult to understand"
   (b) *Mary intimated, "life is difficult to understand"

English has lots of verbs like this: 'communicate', 'assert', 'convey', 'suggest', 'state', 'deny', etc. In each case, mixed quotation using these verbs, if a bit awkward, is reasonably good; while direct quotation is grammatically quite bad.

Similarly, there are *constructions* for indirect quotation which do not accommodate direct quotation: e.g., $\ulcorner \alpha\ \phi\text{-ed}\ \beta\ \text{to}\ \theta \urcorner$. Yet these constructions permit mixed quotation. A case in point: (27a-b) are both fine; but which "device for direct quotation" combines with (27a) here, to yield (27b)?

(27)
   (a) Jim pleaded with the firefighter to save his dog
   (b) Jim pleaded with the firefighter to save "his precious doggy"

In contrast with Cappelen and Lepore's account, a rule like (25) allows for mixed quotation even where direct quotation would be awkward. That's a virtue.

Next virtue of (25). Cappelen and Lepore argue that mixed quotation poses a problem for what I will call "traditional propositional theories" of indirect quotation: theories which require the reported speaker to stand in the saying relation to the proposition expressed by the complement clause. Here is the problem: Assume $\ulcorner \alpha$ says $[_{CP}$ that $\theta] \urcorner$ entails $\ulcorner \text{says}([\![\theta]\!])(\alpha) \urcorner$. This assumption, an immediate consequence of traditional propositional theories, leads to one of two equally unhappy options, whenever θ contains mixed quotation—or so Cappelen and Lepore argue. If one supposes that $[\![\theta]\!]$ is nonsensical when θ contains mixed quotation, $\ulcorner \alpha$ says $[_{CP}$ that $\theta] \urcorner$ is falsely predicted to be nonsensical as well; if, on the other hand, one supposes that $[\![\theta]\!]$ has a coherent sense, it would seem that $[\![\theta]\!]$ would have to be about words—precisely because θ is (mixed) quotational. But then $\ulcorner \alpha$ says $[_{CP}$ that $\theta] \urcorner$ is wrongly predicted to relate α to a meta-linguistic proposition.

An example may make Cappelen and Lepore's objection to traditional propositional theories clearer. Take (1a), and suppose that $[\![$ 'Life "is difficult to understand"' $]\!]$ is nonsensical—because the sentence 'Life "is difficult to understand"' contains mixed quotation. On this assumption, there is no proposition to which Alice is related by (1a), since there is no proposition expressed by 'Life "is difficult to understand"'. Hence the entire sentence (1a) is falsely predicted to be nonsensical. Now the other horn of the dilemma. Suppose that ⟦'Life "is difficult to understand"'⟧ is a coherent proposition. What could it be about? It would seem that ⟦'Life "is difficult to understand"'⟧ would have to be a proposition about words—precisely because 'Life "is difficult to understand"' is (mixed) quotational. So, on this assumption, what (1a) expresses is a relationship between Alice *and a proposition about words.* But this just isn't right: In so far as (1a) relates Alice to any proposition, it relates her to a proposition about life, to the effect that life is difficult to understand. And this isn't a proposition about words.

Cappelen and Lepore take these false predictions to spell doom for any semantics that has speech reports relate the reported speaker to the proposition expressed by the complement clause. But I think the problem lies elsewhere. One gets into trouble by supposing that the complement clause *contains quotation marks* at the point of interpretation: This makes it appear that either there is no proposition expressed by the complement clause, or the proposition expressed is meta-linguistic. But, applying the rule in (25), this "problem" vanishes: The quotation marks are "erased" before the proposition expressed by the complement clause is determined. This allows there to be a perfectly coherent proposition, not about words, to which the reported speaker can be related: It's the proposition expressed by θ, absent the mixed-quotational marks.

So much for the virtues of my alternative. Now some worries. You may have noticed that the rule in (25) implements an essentially deflationary approach to mixed quotation—one which Cappelen and Lepore explicitly reject:

> ... where quotes appear in the complement clause of an indirect report, remove the contribution of the quotes to the content expressed, and the resulting content must be identical to that of ... the reported sentence (1997).[10]

The problem with the deflationary strategy is supposed to be that "it ignores the contribution quotes make in mixed cases." In particular, "the content expressed by the complement clause of a mixed case is about words"—and the deflationary strategy disregards this. (To clarify: Cappelen and Lepore argue that *the complement clause* isn't about words, as you just saw. But they maintain that *the matrix sentence*—the speech report, not the speech reported—is about words.) How, then, do I propose to defend (25)?

Here's my "defense": The deflationary strategy, as implemented in (25), does not "ignore" or "disregard" the fact that mixed quotations are (in part) about words, because mixed quotations *aren't* about words. It's just not true that mixed quotations say something both about the content *and* about the form of the reported utterance: Nothing about words/form is said. And, contrary to what Cappelen and Lepore (1997: 443) claim, no words/forms are *referred to* by the speaker. Returning to the original example: In uttering (1a) the speaker *asserts* nothing whatever about the words employed; he doesn't talk about words at all. What the speaker *asserts* is precisely what (25) predicts: that Alice said something similar to [$_S$ Life is difficult to understand]; in which case, rule (25) does not "ignore" the fact that (1a) is (in part) about words/form—because (1a) isn't about words/form. It's only "about" content.

That being said, it's obvious that a use of (1a) would be very misleading, and hence very infelicitous, in a situation where Alice *didn't* actually speak the words 'is difficult to understand'. This fact clouds intuitions about truth conditions: One is, for example, tempted to say that (1a) is *false* where Alice really uttered 'Life is tough to understand'. But this is a mistake, in my view. Here's a useful comparison, to highlight the nature of the error. Imagine Betty utters 'Alice said that life is difficult to understand', pronouncing 'is difficult to understand' in a drunken tone. Betty would assert only (28)—precisely what rule (25) predicts.

(28) $\lambda x.\{(\exists y)\lambda z.[\text{similar}(z)([_S \text{ Life is difficult to understand}])](y)=1$
    $\& <x,y>\in [\![\text{says}]\!](\text{Alice})$

And yet, at the same time, Betty would "show" (as one used to say) that Alice slurred the words 'is difficult to understand'—where the "showing" is so blatant that Betty's report would be fabulously out of line if Alice was not inebriated, and didn't sound it. Still, out of line or not, I don't think Betty would speak falsely—as long as Alice did, in fact, assert that life is difficult to understand.

If I'm right, mixed quotes aren't about words. So, how do they work their special magic? In a word, mimicry. Seen from this perspective, mixed quotation marks are—to borrow an idea from Corey Washington (1992)—punctuation marks: Putting these marks in allows the writer to highlight the echoic nature of the utterance; but, despite Cappelen and Lepore's repeated insistence to the contrary, a statement about words/form is no part of what the mixed-quote-user says. That is precisely why rule (25) does not err in erasing the quotes before computing the truth conditions of the mixed quotation speech report. Again: In mixed quotation, one "shows" the linguistic tools which were used by the reported speaker; and those "watching the show" acquire beliefs about the form of speech employed. But, to paraphrase Davidson's (1978: 261) thoughts on metaphor, it's an error to fasten on the contents of the thoughts a mixed quotation provokes, and to read these contents into the mixed quotation itself.

Other parallels are legion: A speaker could report parts of Alice's conversation in a squeaky voice, or with a French accent, or with a stutter, or using great volume. In none of these cases would the speech reporter say, assert, or state that Alice spoke in these various ways. Speaking thus, the audience will naturally take the speech reporter to be imitating Alice—why else speak in these peculiar ways? And, if the reporter wasn't accurately parroting Alice, the audience may rightly censure him. But this by no means establishes that anything false was *said* about Alice's voice, accent, tone, etc.: In these cases, the truth conditions of the speech report are exhausted by the meaning of the words, and how the words are put together; as far as truth conditions are concerned, the tone, volume, accent etc. add nothing whatever. Ditto, say I, for the quotation marks in mixed quotation. In which case (1a) isn't *false* where Alice actually speaks the words, 'is tough to understand'. It may, of course, be infelicitous and misleading. In spades. But this doesn't distinguish it from the infelicitous and misleading use of a drunken tone, when reporting the speech of a teetotaler. Given this, no special semantic rule is required to capture "the extra" truth conditions, the statement "about words," encoded in mixed quotations. There is none.[11]

The foregoing closely connects with another possible worry about (25). Cappelen and Lepore argue that a theory of quotation must satisfy four constraints:

(29) *Cappelen and Lepore's Constraints*
   C1: Mixed and indirect quotation should receive overlapping semantic treatments.
   C2: Direct and mixed quotation should receive overlapping semantic reatments.
   C3: Direct and indirect quotation should receive distinct semantic treatments.
   C4: Quotation in pure, direct, and mixed quotation should receive overlapping semantic treatments.

Now, rule (25) easily satisfies C1: If I'm right, mixed quotation is a *variety* of indirect quotation. And C3 poses no special problem either, since nothing in (25) conflicts with the idea that indirect quotation conveys the *content* of the reported speech, whereas direct quotation notes the *form*. It might seem that my account cannot satisfy C2; but, in fact, mixed quotation may *show* what direct quotation must *say*—so there is an overlap. The real problem is C4.

What pure and direct quotation have in common is that both are "about" form. And, if I'm right, this isn't true of mixed quotation: As far as truth conditions are concerned, mixed quotation is indirect quotation—hence mixed quotation *says* nothing about form. Therefore, in contrast with direct quotation, mixed quotation (as I see it, anyway) is not at all like pure quotation. Which violates C4.

Here I bite the bullet: My account, encapsulated in (25), fails with respect to C4. Happily, C4 may not be a valid constraint on theories of quotation. The principle argument which Cappelen and Lepore adduce in favour of C4 goes as follows: The arguments in (30) are valid; if C4 were false, these arguments would not be valid; therefore, C4 is true.

(30)
    (a) Alice said, "Life is difficult to understand." Therefore, a token of 'Life is difficult to understand' was uttered. [This inference indicates that direct and pure quotation are linked.]
    (b) Alice said that life "is difficult to understand." Therefore, a token of 'is difficult to understand' was uttered. [This inference indicates that mixed and pure quotation are linked.]

The problem with Cappelen and Lepore's argument for C4 is its first premise: (30b) is *not* a valid inference. As I said above, where a token of 'is difficult to understand' was *not* uttered, a use of 'Alice said that life "is difficult to understand"' would be extremely misleadingly and thoroughly unhappy. But it wouldn't be strictly speaking false—assuming Alice said something sufficiently similar to 'life is difficult to understand'. Just like the use of a drunken tone in indirect quotation doesn't automatically renders the report false, if the reported speaker was cold sober. Hence the premise of (30b) may be true while its conclusion is false. Given the *invalidity* of (30b), one cannot safely argue from its *validity* to the truth of C4! And, lacking a solid argument for C4, the latter cannot be used to discredit rule (25).[12]

Let me sum up. I noted two problems with Cappelen and Lepore's suggested account of mixed quotation. Both derive immediately from positing a demonstrative, corresponding to the 'that' of 'says that', in the logical form of these speech reports: First, inserting a demonstrative in logical form conflicts with the Interface Rule (8)—given the fact that there is not, in general, a demonstrative in the surface structure; second, positing a demonstrative in logical form leads to the (incorrect) prediction that "the demonstrative" can be used to pick out rogue utterances in the context.

Having noted these problems with Cappelen and Lepore's theory, I suggested a positive alternative: that mixed quotation is equivalent to indirect quotation—give or take some mimicry. If that's right, Cappelen and Lepore are likely mistaken when they claim that "the influential views on the semantics of indirect quotation cannot accommodate mixed quotation . . ." (p. 4). All these "influential views" require, to cover mixed quotation, is a story about verbal imitation consistent with their treatment of indirect speech.

Notes

1. This paper was written during Spring term 1996, while I was a visiting scholar at University of Massachusetts at Amherst. I am grateful to my hosts there—especially Edmund Gettier, Angelika Kratzer and Barbara Partee, who allowed me to sit in on their seminars. Thanks also to Carleton University for allowing the exchange, and to the Social Sciences and Humanities Research Council of Canada for a research grant.

2. As will emerge, that the whole sentence 'life is difficult to understand' is the nominal object of 'says' does *not* lead to the false prediction that Alice employed the word 'life'.

3. For those unfamiliar with the notation: $[_{CP} ...]$ denotes a Complementizer Phrase, a phrase marker composed of a complementizer $[_C ...]$ (e.g., 'whether' and 'if' in indirect questions, 'for,' 'that,' etc.) and a sentential complement, $[_S ...]$. *That*-clauses are paradigmatic Complementizer Phrases.

4. You might wonder why the third clause is required at all: Why can't *both* (3a) and (3b) apply, thus generating the desired logical form? The reason is: Sentence (1a)—and the logical form which Cappelen and Lepore give for it, namely (1b)—entail that there's a *single* utterance of Alice's which stands in *both* the samesaying *and* the same-tokening relation to 'Life is difficult to understand'. But (i), the result of applying both (3a) and (3b), has no such entailment.

   (i) $\exists u$[says (Alice, u) & samesays(u, that)]. Life is difficult to understand & $\exists u$[same-tokens(u, these)]. Life is difficult to understand

To see this, notice that (i) is true where Alice says (iia) and (iib), but nothing else.

   (ii)
   (a)   Life is tough to fathom
   (b)   Death is difficult to understand

Alice's saying (iia) makes the first conjunct of (i) true: She samesays 'life is difficult to understand', though she employed other words. Her saying (iib) makes the second conjunct of (i) true—where 'these' indicates just the Verb Phrase 'is difficult to understand'—because Alice thereby same-tokens 'is difficult to understand'.

5. Minor complication: The third clause, as its stands, won't quite work. Only 'is difficult to understand' is quoted in (1a), and (3c) copies *precisely the quoted material:* It takes $[_{NP}$ "β"] in surface structure and places β (as demonstratum) in the logical form. But what one wants "at the end of the logical form," so to speak, is the whole sentence 'life is difficult to understand', not just the quoted material 'is difficult to understand'. So the Interpretive Rule must be revised to allow the quotes to appear *within* β, or within parts of β, even while all of β is copied into the logical form. I leave this as an exercise.

6. One might put the point as: Do speech reports wear their logical form on their sleeve? Or again: Should speech reports be treated homophonically? Answering 'Yes' to these questions, I reject Davidson's paratactic treatment.

7. Though Higginbotham doesn't say so, very similar problems arise with (i) and (ii)—which clearly are not equivalent to (iii) and (iv) respectively:

(i)   Everybody who owns one says that their Saturn is reliable
(ii)   Maria doesn't eat liver, but she says that Olga does
(iii) Everybody who owns one says that. Their Saturn is reliable
(iv)   Maria doesn't eat liver, but she says that. Olga does.

8. I can just hear some hard core Davidsonians insisting: "But still, there could be a demonstrative in logical form anyway!" This is true, of course. But then again, it *could* be the case that every belief reporting sentence has the name 'Jehovah' in its logical form. The thing is, the syntax strongly suggests—does not prove, establish, or demonstrate, but suggests—otherwise.

9. One might say, with Lepore and Loewer (1990: 98): "It is a convention that [the referent of 'that'] is the portion of *u* following the occurrence of 'that'." But where does this convention come from, and why doesn't it apply to (23)? Worse, why should it be *impossible* to break the convention—a state of affairs the Davidson of "Communication and Convention" (1982) would never envisage—if the expression in question really is a demonstrative?

10. As they note, this approach presupposes "a systematic way for distinguishing mixed quotation from indirect quotation harbouring pure quotation." Lacking that, the sentence (i) would have its quotes erased—yielding incorrect results.

(i)   Alice said that "life is difficult to understand" is a sentence

I agree that this is presupposed. I don't agree that it's a problem.

11. Someone might say: Surely there's a difference between indirect-quotation-plus-a-drunken-tone on the one hand, and mixed quotation on the other—namely the explicit use of quotation marks; the quotation marks strongly suggests that direct quotation is in play. To which I might reply: Quotation marks are artificial; belonging, in the first instance, to the written form of a small sub-class of languages. One should not, then, pay too close attention to them when doing the semantics of *natural languages.*

12. As far as I can see, rule (25) also allows Cappelen and Lepore's sentence (11), from p. 436, to sometimes come out true:

(11) Nicola said that Alice is a "phil*t*osopher"

Here's the general idea. Assume Nicola stands in the says-relation to the proposition that Alice is a philosopher. This seems plausible: Surely Nicola could truly be reported as having said that. Assume further that the proposition ALICE IS A PHILOSOPHER is relevantly similar to the illformed, though interpretable, sentence 'Alice is a philtosopher'. (Whatever the independent merits of assuming similarity to ill-formed linguistic entities, Cappelen and Lepore really cannot object to it: In order to make their own view accommodate (11), they insist that it is simply part of the basic data that an utterance that doesn't express anything in English can samesay [another person's] utterances.) Given these two assumptions, there will be something similar to the complement clause of (11), to which Nicola stands in the says-relation. So, by rule (25), (11) comes out true. What then distinguishes (11) from the sentence 'Nicola said that Alice is a philosopher'? Mimicry. Again.

References

Cappelen, H. and E. Lepore. 1997. "Varieties of Quotation." *Mind* 106: 429–450.

Davidson, D. 1984. *Inquiries into Truth and Interpretation.* Oxford: Clarendon Press.

———. 1982. "Communication and Convention." In *Dialogue: An Interdisciplinary Approach,* edited by M. Dascal. Reprinted in Davidson (1984).

———. 1979. "Quotation." *Theory and Decision* 11: 27–40. Reprinted in Davidson (1984).

———. 1978. "What Metaphors Mean." *Critical Inquiry* 5: 31–47. Reprinted in Davidson (1984).

———. 1968. "On Saying That." *Synthese* 19: 130–146. Reprinted in Davidson (1984).

Higginbotham, J. 1993. "Interrogatives." In *The View from Building 20: Essays in Linguistics in Honor of Sylvain Bromberger,* edited by K. Hale and S. Keyser. Cambridge: The MIT Press.

Higginbotham, J. 1986. "Linguistic Theory and Davidson's Program in Semantics." In *Truth and Interpretation,* edited by E. Lepore. Oxford: Basil Blackwell.

Lepore, E. and B. Loewer. 1990. "A Study in Comparative Semantics." In *Propositional Attitudes,* edited by C. Anderson and J. Owens. Stanford: CSLI Publications.

Washington, C. 1992. "The Identity Theory of Quotation." *Journal of Philosophy* 89: 582–605.

11

Replies to the Commentaries

Herman Cappelen & Ernie Lepore

Before we begin our replies, we want to press a non-philosophical consideration we think dictates how any serious criticism of our unified account of quotation must go. Davidson's paratactic account of indirect quotation is not the sort of account a student of natural language semantics would conjure up on a first go around. (Are there any?) Rather it's the sort of account a semanticist is led to only after having canvassed one hundred years of reasonable (and unreasonable) failed alternatives. That's at least how we came to it. Surprisingly, though, it was not that account that inclined us towards our unified account for mixed quotation. It was, rather, Davidson's comparatively little-discussed theory of pure quotation. We find this account not only a plausible start (much like we do his account of indirect quotation), but compelling. (One of us thinks he has an argument for the conclusion that the demonstrative account of pure quotation must be correct.) Our reason for indulging in autobiography is that if you see where we're coming from, it will be easier to see how our commentators stumble.

Reply to Stainton

Stainton is exercised by our account of what we call mixed quotation. He aims to refute our account by refuting Davidson's account of indirect quotation, which he sees our account as presupposing. He starts with some meta-philosophical reflections. He says our account fails to respect the methodological principle that *ceteris paribus* a hypothesis about logical form which respects syntax is preferable to a hypothesis which does not. We find the principle (and therefore objections based on it) difficult to evaluate for two reasons.

First, Stainton doesn't say anything about what he means by "respect syntax." If this just means that a semantic theory should be compatible with a correct syntactic theory, we agree. We leave open the question how a se-

mantic theory should be merged with a syntactic theory (in part, because
we don't want to take a stand on the issue of what a correct syntactic theory looks like). Unless presented with an argument to the effect that it is
impossible to reconcile our theory with a correct syntactic theory, we don't
see even the beginning of an objection here.

A second and closely related worry is that Stainton doesn't say anything
about how we are to explain the *ceteris paribus* clause. This clause, in effect, says that there are cases where semantics doesn't need to "respect
syntax." We are surprised by his claim (and it makes us suspect we don't
know what he means by "respect syntax.") In order to evaluate Stainton's
principle we would like to know when and why disrespect of syntax would
be acceptable.

We turn now to Stainton's less meta-theoretical complaints against our
account. He cites a familiar alleged counter-example against the paratactic account of indirect quotation from Higginbotham. Consider sentence
(H):

(H) Every student says that she is cool.

Stainton asks: What logical form does the paratactic account ascribe to
(H)? He then goes through a number of friendly revisions to see whether
some extension of our account can accommodate what he (and Higginbotham) take to be two ambiguous readings of (H). In particular, they are
interested in the *de re* quantified-in reading, which we might frame in
quasi-English as (H?):

(H?) Every student said of herself that she is cool.

Both critics conclude that under the most generous revision of the paratactic account it can do no better than assign a reading to (H) to the effect
that "every student said that that girl is cool." Why can't we get reading
(H?) for (H) on a paratactic account? Samesaying is sufficiently broad (it
must be; as we say in the text, how people employ the variety of quotations
is constitutive of the extension of the samesay relation) so as to accommodate examples like (H). According to us, (H) asserts that every student asserted an utterance which samesays that: She is cool.

Stainton and Higginbotham can hold that this doesn't assign the correct
truth conditions to (H) only if they assume that samesaying is a transitive,
symmetric relation, something along the lines of: if some student A asserts
something which samesays an utterance of 'she is cool' and another student
B asserts something which samesays that same utterance of 'she is cool',
then A's and B's utterances must samesay each other. Indeed, even these
assumptions are insufficient to underwrite their complaint against the

paratactic account. They must add that if two utterances samesay each other and one makes reference, say, to Sally, then both must make reference to Sally. We reject all these assumptions (see Cappelen & Lepore 1998), and so we are still without a good reason to even pause vis-à-vis the paratactic account of indirect quotation.

Stainton presents another familiar worry about what he calls "rogue utterances." What's a paratactician to do about utterances of indirect reports where his concomitant demonstrative intentions are to demonstrate something other than the complement clause of his indirect report? Suppose, for example, someone utters "Galileo said that the earth moves" pointing at, and really wanting to demonstrate nothing but, his uncle. Hasn't he demonstrated his uncle and not his utterance of "The earth moves"? We find questions like this unhelpful in adjudicating between competitive semantic accounts.

Here's an analogy. Suppose someone utters "he" with a corresponding demonstrative intention and gesture aimed at a woman or a tree. What accrues to a semantic theory according to which the demonstration in this case fails? What accrues to the theory according to which in this case the utterance is without truth-value? What accrues to the theory according to which there is nothing semantically wrong with the said utterance and yet it indeed picks out the individual demonstrated and is true or false contingent on whether that demonstrated individual has the property predicated of it? Are these good questions? We are not sure. What we are sure of is that no worthwhile semantic theory should be refutable by these sorts of considerations alone.

For those still looking for a substantive, less rhetorical, less meta-philsophical reply, try this: any demonstrative element required by the semantics of indirect discourse (according to the paratactic account) cannot be overridden by a wayward intention or gesture. Perhaps it's built into the "character" of a complement "that" that an utterance of it must demonstrate the utterance which succeeds it (not unlike it's built into the character of "I" that an utterance of it must denote the speaker). How do we know any such convention exists? Because the paratactic account is the best overall theory around; for example, it better coheres with accounts of a variety of quotation than any competitor we are aware of; and so adopting some such convention protects the best overall theory from the sorts of "counter-examples" Stainton is advancing. Is there anything *ad hoc* about positing such a "convention"? No, since we have no pre-theoretic intuitions about the nature of the demonstrative posited for indirect quotation by the paratactic account. This we know since we have no pre-theoretic intuitions about whether quotation, in any of its diverse forms, harbors a demonstrative element.

We place a lot of weight on the broad explanatory power of our theory. This feature of our theory gives it an advantage over any theory of indirect quotation that doesn't also offer an account of pure quotation and a recommendation for how to put the two together. What then is Stainton's recommendation for mixed quotation? Woefully, it's no more than to ignore the semantic contribution of the quotes in a mixed quotation. We take it to be obvious that any theory that needs to underplay important linguistic aspects of the practice of indirect reporting, especially one that does so without arguing for it, is at a significant disadvantage.

Reply to Elugardo

Elugardo asks us to imagine Alice asserting (4):

(4) Life is difficult to understand or life stinks.

He wonders whether our account doesn't commit us to saying an utterance of (2) is true in these circumstances, even though most English speakers would agree that Alice never said that life is difficult to understand.

(2) Alice said that life is difficult to understand.

Our intuitions coincide with Elugardo, though we recognize that speaker intuitions on indirect reports are often murky. The key question of course is whether our account commits us to the report being true. Elugardo thinks it does. He writes: "after all, she meant by her sub-utterance exactly what I meant by my utterance of the same sentence even though neither one of us stated, nor intended to state by our utterances of that sentence, that life is difficult to understand." And, he says, "in that case, Cappelen and Lepore's analysis of my mixed quotation is true."

Our theory is committed to Elugardo's (2) being a correct report of his (4) only if samesaying is understood in a way we don't think it should be. We place no *a priori* constraints on the relation. The practice of indirect reporting provides the basic evidence for what is in the extension of "samesaying." Elugardo's example elicits interesting features of this practice. In Cappelen & Lepore (1998) we argue that samesaying is context sensitive in a number of ways. Elugardo's case shows that it is also sensitive to linguistic context. That observation is no doubt important, but does not provide the basis for a counter-example to our account.

Elugardo's second alleged counter-example involves equivocation. Suppose by "hot piece" one speaker intends to mean "stolen merchandise" and the other "popular merchandise." In mixed quoting Sam, Ned utters:

(19) Sam said that he has a "hot" gold watch to sell me.

Elugardo says that if by "hot piece" Ned meant popular merchandise and Sam meant stolen merchandise, we would have to say that (19) is false, even though, according to Elugardo "(19) is undoubtedly true."

We don't share Elugardo's intuitions in this case. If Ned genuinely misunderstands what Sam said, that prevents him from correctly indirectly reporting him (and hence from mixed quoting him). If, on the other hand, Ned mixquotes Sam because he is uncertain or wants to remain neutral about what Sam meant by "hot," the case is similar to the mixed quote we discussed in our paper involving "oenophile" and what we say about that case there applies here as well.

Reply to Pietroski

Pietroski starts out with the assumption that well-known objections (such as those presented by Stainton) make the paratactic theory sufficiently suspect to justify the search for an alternative. Since we don't see the current exchange as a platform to straighten out what's right or wrong about the paratactic account of indirect quotation, we'll silently (and skeptically) pass over this part of his paper.

Pietroski's alternative account to our approach provides an elegant and ingenious solution to some of the problems often raised in connection with the semantics for indirect reports, but if we are right that any account of the semantics for indirect discourse should satisfy our constraints/conditions C1–C4, then Pietroski's suggestion is unacceptable for fairly obvious reasons.

Direct reports, according to Pietrotski, have as their semantic values an ILF, i.e., an ordered pair consisting of a logical form and its sense (discussed further in both our papers). The semantic value of 'Quote p' is the ILF of p. So, on his account the semantic value of both indirect and direct reports is a function of the semantic values of their "complement" clauses. The way in which their semantics differ is that a direct report (and not an indirect report) is sensitive to its syntactic LF, and not just to the interpretation of the complement clause.

To see how implausible an account of direct quotation this is consider (1) and (2).

(1) Nora said, "Fido barks," but she didn't mean that Fido barks. You see, Nora is a CIA agent and she was speaking a secret code.

(2) Nora said, "Fido bjeffet," and I think this means something in Norwegian, but I'm not certain.

It's clearly preposterous to say that the semantic values of "Quote Fido barks" and "Quote Fido bjeffet" include their interpretations. You can interpret (1) without breaking the CIA's secret codes; and you can understand (2) without understanding Norwegian.

We have objected to his claim that interpretation should be a component of the semantic value. But that's not all that's wrong with Pietroski's suggestion. Putting the LF into the semantic value is equally misguided. Consider (3).

> (3) Nora said "axemy y awrow," and this might be a meaningful sentence in a secret CIA code, but I don't think so; it's probably just some nonsense she uttered in order to mislead us.

(3) illustrates three distinct points:

> (a) A direct report can be of an utterance that is not a well-formed formula (one that doesn't even include meaningful words), and hence of something that does not have an LF. So Pietroski's claim that direct reports always have the LFs of the reported utterance as part of their semantic values is mistaken.
>
> (b) One can understand a direct report of an utterance of something that is a sentence while knowing nothing about the LF of that sentence. If understanding an utterance requires knowledge of the objects referred to by that utterance, the fact that we can understand (3), but have no knowledge of the LF that Nora's has (if it has one), shows Pietroski's theory to be mistaken.
>
> (c) Even in reports of utterance that do have LFs, one need not know what that LF is in order to make the report. Pietroski says nothing about the mechanism through which direct reports pick out the LFs they denote, but we don't see any plausible such mechanism for sentences such as (3).

This objection goes further and connects to our insistence on a unified theory. In the main part of the text, Pietroski says nothing about pure quotation. This is surprising given his agreement with us that an account of opacity should be unified. For the same reasons as those given above, we don't see how an ILF account can give the semantic values of sentences containing pure quotation. Think about sentences such as (4).

> (4) "scruffles" and "..("07>>" aren't words in any language.

We don't see how ILFs can play a role in interpreting (4).

We stand by the conjecture we made in our paper, namely, that someone who accepts C1–C4 will find that both the LF and the I component of an ILF is irrelevant to the semantics of indirect, direct, mixed and pure quotation.